¡Listos! 2 Rojo

Clive Bell • Tracy Traynor

Teacher's Guide

heinemann.co.uk

✓ Free online support
✓ Useful weblinks
✓ 24-hour online ordering

01865 888058

Inspiring generations

Heinemann Educational Publishers,
Halley Court, Jordan Hill, Oxford OX2 8EJ.

Part of Harcourt Education Limited.

Heinemann is the registered trademark of
Harcourt Education Limited.

© Clive Bell and Tracy Traynor

First published 2003

07 06 05 04 03
10 9 8 7 6 5 4 3 2 1

A catalogue record is available for this book from the
British Library on request.

ISBN 0 435 42962 0

Produced by Ken Vail Graphic Design.

Original illustrations © Heinemann Educational Publishers 2003

Cover photograph by Eye Ubiquitous/Paul Thompson

Printed in the UK by Athenaeum Press Ltd

Tel: 01865 888058 www.heinemann.co.uk

Contents

Introduction

¡Listos! is a lively and easy-to-use Spanish course for pupils aged 11–16 of a wide ability range, which supports Foundation Subjects MFL, including the Framework for Teaching MFL. The materials are fully differentiated with parallel Pupil's Books from stage 2.

Teaching Foundation Subjects MFL and the MFL Framework using *¡Listos!*

Framework objectives

¡Listos! ensures that there is comprehensive coverage of all five strands of the framework:

✓ **Words** – teaching pupils to practise the meaning, spelling and sound of Spanish words together.
✓ **Sentences** – teaching pupils how to write simple, grammatically correct sentences.
✓ **Texts: reading and writing** – teaching pupils how to understand and write more complex text using connectives, pronouns and verbs.
✓ **Listening and speaking** – linking listening and speaking to help pupils speak more accurately and authentically.
✓ **Cultural knowledge and contact** – giving pupils the opportunity to learn about Spain and other Spanish-speaking countries.

All the **framework objectives** for Year 7 are **launched** and **reinforced** in *¡Listos! 1*. The reinforcement of an objective often takes place in a number of units.

Details of where the objectives are launched and reinforced are given:

a) in the Framework Overview grid on pages 12–13 of this Teacher's Guide to help you with your **long-term planning**;
b) in the Teacher's Guide in the overview grids at the beginning of each module (e.g. page 14) to help you with your **medium-term planning**:
c) in the Teacher's Guide in the overview boxes at the start of each teaching unit to help with your **short-term (i.e. lesson) planning**.

In addition, all activities in the Pupil's Book are cross-referenced to the MFL Framework to allow you to launch or reinforce the teaching objectives at different points in the course if you wish. The references are given in the Teacher's Guide at the start of each activity.

Lesson starters

Every unit in the Pupil's Book contains two lesson starters: the first at the beginning of every unit, the second approximately halfway through the unit at the point when a second lesson is likely to begin. All of the starters are described in the Teacher's Guide. Most of them are simple ideas that allow you to recap on previous knowledge or prepare the pupils for new language to be learnt in the unit. They are designed to get the lesson off to a brisk start, focusing the pupils' attention and promoting engagement and challenge. Some of the activities have an accompanying copymaster in the Resource and Assessment File. These copymasters include worksheets, games cards and material which can be photocopied onto overhead transparencies.

Plenaries

Every unit in the Pupil's Book ends with a plenary session. Again, these are simple ideas described in the Teacher's Guide. They aim to draw out the key learning points. Pupils are actively involved and are expected to demonstrate and explain what they have learnt in the unit. They identify links with what the pupils have learnt so far and what they will learn later in the course.

Thinking skills

Thinking skills are integrated into many of the Starters as well as into some of the Pupil's Book activities themselves. Many of the Skills Sheets in the Resource and Assessment File also involve thinking skills.

The components

¡Listos! 2 rojo consists of:
Pupil's Book
Cassettes/CDs
Workbooks
Resource and Assessment File
Teacher's Guide
Flashcards
Colour OHT File

Pupil's Book

The Pupil's Book consists of six theme-based modules which are subdivided into seven double-page units (six in *Módulo* 7). The seventh unit (*¡Extra!*) is an extension unit and can be left out if you are short of time or if it is not suitable for your pupils. It contains activities in all four skill areas and is to be used with whole classes in the same way as the other units. The activities tend to be slightly more difficult than in the core units, with longer reading and listening passages, which bring together the language of the module. No new core language is introduced.

¡Extra! is followed by two pages of module word lists (*Palabras*) organised by topic to help with vocabulary learning and revision.

At the end of each module there is a checklist of key functions and structures (*Resumen*) and revision activities that can be used as a practice test (*Prepárate*).

At the back of the Pupil's Book there are three sections of further practice and reference. The *Te toca a ti* section contains self-access differentiated reading and writing activities. *Te toca a ti A* is for lower-ability and *Te toca a ti B* for higher-ability pupils. There is a grammar reference and practice section where all the grammar points introduced in the core units are explained fully and accompanied by practice activities. Finally, there is a comprehensive Spanish–English word list, a shorter English–Spanish word list and a list of instructions covered in the Pupil's Book.

Cassettes/CDs

There are three cassettes/CDs for *¡Listos! 2 rojo*. These contain listening material for both presentation and practice. The material includes dialogues, interviews and songs recorded by native speakers. The listening material for all the *Pruebas* (the formal assessment tests in the Resource and Assessment File) can be found on the final CD/cassette.

Workbooks

For *¡Listos! 2 rojo* there is an accompanying workbook (Workbook B). This provides self-access reading and writing tasks which are designed to be fun. The workbook is ideal for homework. There is a page of activities for each double-page core unit in the Pupil's Book. There are also one or two pages of revision material (*Repaso*), one or two pages of grammar practice and a self-assessment page at the end of each module (*Resumen*).

Resource and Assessment File

The Resource and Assessment File is organised into modules for ease of use and contains the following photocopiable material:

- Worksheets/OHT masters to support starter activities.
- Sheets consisting of pictures with the matching Spanish words/phrases on a corresponding sheet.
- Skills Sheets, practising language learning skills (e.g. dictionary work) introduced in the Pupil's Book. Many involve thinking skills.
- Module word lists (*Vocabulario*): photocopiable versions of the word lists from the Pupil's Book.
- *Resumen*. A pupil checklist of language covered.

And for assessment:

- *Pruebas*: end-of-module (and end-of-year) tests for formal assessment, together with the teaching notes and the answers for the tests.
- Target-setting sheet for pupils and pupil-friendly descriptors of the NC Attainment Target Levels.

Teacher's Guide

The Teacher's Guide contains:

- Overview grids for each module.
- Clear teaching notes and full recording transcript.
- Suggestions for starters and plenaries.
- Mapping of activities to the Framework, the National Curriculum and 5–14 Guidelines.
- Guidance on using the materials with pupils of varying abilities.
- Suggestions for additional differentiated practice.
- Suggestions for ICT activities.
- Suggestions for numeracy and literacy activities.
- Help with using Spanish in the classroom.

Flashcards

There are 48 full-colour, single-sided flashcards with the name of the object in Spanish on the reverse for presentation or practice of language. A complete list of flashcards is given on page 8.

OHT File

There are 16 full-colour transparencies and 16 overlays for presentation or practice of language. The file contains detailed teaching notes on how and where in the course to use the OHTs.

Using *¡Listos! 2 rojo* with the full ability range

After initial teacher-led presentation work with the whole class, pupils move on to a range of individual pair and group activities, which allow them to work at different levels. There is a lot of scope in the core material for differentiation by pace and outcome. Suggestions are provided in the Teacher's Guide. The seventh unit (*¡Extra!*) is an optional extension unit. The activities in the Pupil's Book are supplemented by those in the *Te toca a ti* section at the back of the book. For each module there is a double page of activities: the *A* page activities are at reinforcement level and the *B* page activities are at extension level. For ease of use these activities are clearly flagged in the Teacher's Guide. Further differentiation is provided by means of the two parallel workbooks.

For those pupils who are ready to focus on the underlying structure of the language the grammar boxes in the teaching units are backed up by full explanations and practice in the grammar section at the back of the Pupil's Book as well as in the grammar worksheets. These activities can be done at any appropriate point. Although these tasks might be more suitable for higher-ability learners, it is assumed that most pupils will be able to attempt them at some point during the year.

Grammar

The key structures used in a unit are often presented in a grid on the Pupil's Book page, providing support for speaking and writing activities. A summary of the key structures of each whole module is given in the

Resumen at the end of each module. Key grammar points are highlighted in *Gramática* boxes on the page and there is a reference and practice section at the back of the Pupil's Book. In addition, there are worksheets which specifically focus on grammar in the Resource and Assessment File.

Progression

There is a clear progression within each module of the Pupil's Book and language is systematically revised and extended throughout the book. Clear objectives are given in the Teacher's Guide at the beginning of each unit to help teachers plan the programme of work which is appropriate for different ability groups.

Assessment for Learning

Revision and self-assessment

¡Listos! 2 rojo encourages learners to revise and check their own progress regularly. At the end of each module there is a *Resumen*, a checklist of key language covered. There is also a version of the *Resumen* in the workbooks, in the form of a page of open-ended writing.

Some Starters and Plenaries encourage pupils to reflect on their performance and how to improve it. In addition, the target-setting sheet in the Resource and Assessment File Framework Edition allows pupils to record their NC level in each Attainment Target and set themselves improvement targets for the next module. The File also contains the NC level descriptors in pupil-friendly language, to help with their target-setting.

Teacher assessment

The assessment scheme consists of ongoing assessment as well as more formal periodic assessment. The scheme in *¡Listos! 2 Rojo* focuses on Levels 3–7 in the four National Curriculum Attainment Targets (Levels C to E for the 5–14 Guidelines).

All activities have been matched against National Curriculum levels and the 5–14 Guidelines to assist teachers in carrying out continuous assessment. It must be stressed that performance in an individual activity can only contribute towards evidence that a pupil is achieving that level. Pupils must successfully carry out a range of activities at a particular level in order for the level to be awarded.

The end-of-module (and end-of-year) tests or *Pruebas* in the Resource and Assessment File provide a more formal means of assessment. The *Prepárate* in the Pupil's Book provides activities that will help pupils to prepare for the tests. The tests cover all four skills and can be used with pupils of all abilities. Again, the tasks are matched against NC levels.

The teaching sequence

Lesson starter (see page 4)

Presentation

New language can be presented using the cassettes or CDs, ensuring that pupils have authentic pronunciation models. However, the range of resources in the scheme enables the teacher to vary the way new language is presented.

Flashcards: These can be used in a variety of ways. Ideas for using the flashcards are included in the teaching notes. A list of the flashcards is given on page 8.

Visuals or picture sheets: The Resource and Assessment File contains picture sheets for each module. These can be photocopied and cut up for games or copied onto an overhead transparency and used for presentation work.

Colour overhead transparencies: These can be used for presentation or revision. The Colour OHT File contains detailed teaching notes with suggestions for additional practice.

Practice

Pupils move on to a variety of activities in which they practise the new language, usually in pairs or groups. Many of the practice activities are open-ended, allowing them to work at their own pace and level.

Reinforcement and extension

The units often end with a more extended activity of an open-ended nature. Pupils of all abilities can work on the same basic task and the teacher has an opportunity to work with individuals or small groups.

To cope with the range of ability in a class, additional reinforcement and extension activities are provided in the Pupil's Book (*Te toca a ti*) as well as the differentiated workbooks, already described.

Plenary (see page 4)

Using the target language

Instructions in the first two modules of the Pupil's Book are in Spanish and English. Thereafter they are translated into English the first time they appear. They have been kept as simple and as uniform as possible.

Integrating ICT

Suggestions for ICT activities have been included in the Teacher's Guide. These activities use the following types of software which are likely to be already available in schools.

Word-processing software

The essential difference between word processing and writing with pen and paper is that a word-processed text need never be a final product. Since errors can be corrected and texts can be developed and improved without spoiling the appearance of the work, writers gain the confidence to experiment as well as the motivation to take a more active interest in the language they are using.

Graphics software

Graphics software could take the form of word-processing programs that can import images, desktop publishing programs or graphics programs.

Learners can use this software to produce posters, booklets and leaflets in which they display newly acquired language in an attractive and original way. They can experiment with layout and select from a range of type styles and sizes as well as graphics.

Each module of *¡Listos! 2* contains suggestions for ICT activities.

There are also links to relevant websites in this book. In order to ensure that they are up to date, that the links work and that the sites are not inadvertently linked to sites that could be considered offensive, we have made them available on the Heinemann website at www.heinemann.co.uk/hotlinks
When you access the site, the express code is 9620T.

Games

Card games

The word/picture sheets in the Resource and Assessment File can be used for:

1 Matching pictures and labels.

2 Matching pictures and labels: Set a time limit and see which pair finishes first.

3 Pelmanism or pairs: A series of pairs of cards are laid face-down in random order. Pupils match the pictures with the labels. The winner is the person who manages to make the most pairs.

4 Guessing: Each pupil has four or more cards positioned so they can see the cards but their partner can't. Pupils take it in turns to guess their partner's cards using the structures and vocabulary from the unit. First one to guess all correctly is the winner.

Vocabulary games

1 Pupils make their own cards to play Pelmanism (drawing pictures and writing their own labels from the unit).

2 Spelling bees: Do these at the end of each unit.

3 Noughts and crosses (in a pair or whole-class team-game played on the board): Almost all vocabulary and structures linked to a unit can be practised playing this game.

Practising vocabulary: as in the Pupil's Book. The vocabulary being introduced is numbered. You/pupils write these numbers on a grid. Pupils guess what the word is for each number to get a nought or a cross (with or without looking in the Pupil's Book, depending on how difficult you want to make it).

4 Wordsearches: These are used throughout the book; however as an extension activity you could ask pupils to make up their own wordsearches.

5 'I went to market and I bought ...' Each pupil repeats the previous word and adds their own. This can be adapted for different topics.

6 Cracking codes: Get pupils to write their own code for partners to crack. Use the symbol function on a computer to make up a code.

7 Telephones: Write a variety of made-up telephone numbers on pieces of paper (keep a list of these numbers). Hand them out to pupils. The first pupil reads out a number and carries out a conversation with the person whose number it is, e.g. *¡Hola! ¿Cómo te llamas?* etc. Keep the pace fast. To make it more difficult pupils could ask how the name is spelt and write it down.

Number games

Once pupils have learnt numbers 1–20 there are lots of number games for them to practise.

1 Mexican wave: Pupils stand up as they say their number and then sit down.

2 Lotto/bingo:

   a quick lotto (use as a lesson starter): Ask pupils to choose seven numbers from, for example, 1 to 20. Pupils tick off their numbers as they are called out. First one to tick all numbers shouts out 'lotto'.

   b bingo: Same as lotto, except pupils draw a grid of, for example, 12 boxes and write the numbers in the boxes.

3 Buzz: Pupils all stand up and count from, for example, 1 to 20, and leave out multiples of, for example, five. Instead of saying this they must say 'buzz' or *'vaya'*. If they forget and say the multiple of five they are out and must sit down.

4 Counting with a soft toy: Count round the class throwing a soft toy.

5 Rub out the number on the board: Divide the board in half. Write the same numbers but in a different place on each half of the board. One member from each team stands in front of the board with chalk or a boardmarker and tries to be the first to cross out the number called out. Keep a tally showing which team has scored the most points.

Answers to *Gramática* activities (Pupil's Book pages 124–137)

1 Nouns (p.125)

1 regalos
2 cartas
3 viajes
4 invitaciones
5 peces
6 regiones
7 lugares

4.1 Cardinal numbers (p.127)

1 99   **d** noventa y nueve
2 107   **e** ciento siete
3 111   **g** ciento once
4 120   **h** ciento veinte
5 550   **b** quinientos cincuenta
6 1999   **c** mil novecientos noventa y nueve
7 2002   **a** dos mil dos
8 2003   **f** dos mil tres

5 Dates (p.127)

6.5 Talking about frequency

Pupils' own responses.

7.1 Agreement of adjectives (p.128)

1 Tengo los ojos   **d** marrones
2 Mi gato es   **c** blanco y negro
3 Las paredes de mi dormitorio son   **b** amarillas
4 La alfombra es   **a** blanca

7.1 Agreement of adjectives (p.128)

Pupils' own list.

7.2 Comparatives (p.129)

Pupils' own opinions.

7.3 Superlatives (p.129)

Pupils' own details.

8 Adverbs (p.130)

Pupils' own details.

12 Questions (p.132)

Examples:
1 ¿Cómo te llamas?
2 ¿Dónde vives?
3 ¿Qué tipo de comida te gusta?
4 ¿Cuándo es tu cumpleaños?
5 ¿Cuál es tu nombre? (¿Cuáles son tus pasatiempos favoritos?)
6 ¿Cuánto es? (¿Cuántos años tienes?/¿Cuántas zapatillas tienes?)
7 ¿Quién es? (¿Quiénes son?)
8 ¿Por qué te gustan las películas románticas?

¿Quieres salir conmigo esta noche?
¿Te hacen falta toallas?
¿Hablas español?

20 Verbs (7): *gustar* and expressing likes and dislikes (p. 135)

1 Me encantan   **d** los dibujos animados.
2 Me interesa   **b** la ciencia-ficción.
3 Me hace falta   **e** una secadora.
4 Me hacen falta   **f** champú y pasta de dientes.
5 Me duele   **c** la garganta.
6 Me duelen   **a** los pies.

List of flashcards

1   los huevos
2   las verduras
3   la carne
4   la sopa
5   un helado
6   el pescado
7   el pollo
8   los perritos calientes
9   las chuletas
10 el flan
11 las gambas
12 los plátanos
13 las peras
14 las uvas
15 las lechugas
16 las cebollas
17 las aceitunas
18 una botella de limonada
19 200 gramos de queso
20 500 gramos de jamón
21 una barra de pan
22 un cartón de leche
23 un paquete de galletas
24 una caja de pasteles
25 una lata de sardinas
26 un parque temático
27 un espectáculo de flamenco
28 un campo de golf
29 una fiesta de caballos
30 una pista de tenis
31 descansar
32 nadar en el mar
33 tomar el sol
34 ir de paseo
35 ir a discotecas
36 montar en bicicleta
37 sacar fotos
38 hacer surfing
39 el club de jóvenes
40 el parque de atracciones
41 la bolera
42 la pista de hielo
43 tener fiebre
44 tener insolación
45 tener tos
46 tener diarrea
47 tener una picadura
48 tener catarro

Covering the Programmes of Study

The table below indicates where in *¡Listos! 2 rojo* pupils have the opportunity to develop the skills and understanding prescribed in the National Curriculum Programmes of Study. For each area we have indicated where these appear in the core units of the Pupil's Book. There are further opportunities both in the Pupil's Book and the supplementary components. More detail is provided in the grids at the beginning of each module in this Teacher's Guide. Some skills are more appropriate or are practised more easily at later stages of language learning. Where this is the case we have indicated at what stage of *¡Listos!* pupils will encounter these. Some opportunities, especially in section four, are beyond the scope of a coursebook. We have used the symbol *** to denote these.

1 Acquiring knowledge and understanding of the target language – pupils should be taught:						
a the principles and relationships of sounds and writing in the target language	1.1;	2.1,3,4,5;	3.2;	4.1,3;	5.1;	6.3
b the grammar of the target language and how to apply it	Throughout					
c how to express themselves using a range of vocabulary and structures	Throughout					

2 Developing language skills – pupils should be taught:						
a how to listen carefully for gist and detail	1.5,7;	2.1,2,3;	3.3,4;	4.2,3;	5.1,3;	6.2,3
b correct pronunciation and intonation	1.1;	2.1,3,4,5;	3.2;	4.1,3;	5.1;	6.3
c how to ask and answer questions	1.1,4;	2.2,3,5;	3.5;	4.2,5;	5.1,2,4,5;	6.3
d how to initiate and develop conversations	1.3;			4.2;	5.1,4,5	
e how to vary the target language to suit context, audience and purpose	1.6,7;			4.1;	5.3	
f how to adapt language they already know for different contexts	1.4,7;	2.1,2,5;	3.4,5;	4.1;	5.4,5;	6.2,5
g strategies for dealing with the unpredictable		2.1;	3.1,3;	4.1,7;	5.1,4;	6.6
h techniques for skimming and for scanning written texts for information, including those from ICT-based sources	1.7;	2.2;	3.7;	4.1,7		
i how to summarise and report the main points of spoken or written texts, using notes where appropriate	1.4,7;	2.1,2;			5.1,2,3,4;	6.3
j how to redraft their writing to improve its accuracy and presentation, including the use of ICT			3.6;	4.5;	5.6,7	

3 Developing language-learning skills – pupils should be taught:						
a techniques for memorising words, phrases and short extracts		2.5;		4.5		
b how to use context and other clues to interpret meaning	1.7;	2.7;	3.1,7;	4.1,3,7;	5.3	
c to use their knowledge of English or another language when learning the target language			3.1,6,7;	4.2,3;	5.1,2,7	
d how to use dictionaries and other reference materials appropriately and effectively	1.6;	2.2,6;		4.3,7		
e how to develop their independence in learning and using the target language	Throughout					

Note: 2.1 = Module 2, Unit 1

4 Developing cultural awareness – pupils should be taught about different countries and cultures by:					
a working with authentic materials in the target language, including some from ICT-based sources	1.7;	2.5,6;	3.1,7;	5,3;	6.6
b communicating with native speakers	1.6;	2.1;	4.3;	5.4	
c considering their own culture and comparing it with the cultures of the countries and communities where the target language is spoken	1.3;	2.1,2,5,7; 3.5;	4.1,2;	5.2,3,4	
d considering the experiences and perspectives of people in these countries and communities	1.7;	2.7;		5.3,4;	6.4

5 Breadth of study – during key stages 3 and 4, pupils should be taught the knowledge, skills and understanding through:					
a communicating in the target language in pairs and groups, and with their teacher	Throughout				
b using everyday classroom events as an opportunity for spontaneous speech	Throughout				
c expressing and discussing personal feelings and opinions		2.2;	3.2,3,5;	5.2	
d producing and responding to different types of spoken and written language, including texts produced using ICT		2.7;	3.7;	4.3,6;	5.7;	6.4
e how to use a range of resources, including ICT, for accessing and communicating information	1.1;	2.2,5,6;	4.1;	5.2,3,7	
f using the target language creatively and imaginatively	1.7;		4.1;	5.3	
g listening, reading or viewing for personal interest and enjoyment, as well as for information		2.7;			6.1
h using the target language for real purposes		2.1,6;	4.1;	5.3,7	
i working in a variety of contexts, including everyday activities, personal and social life, the world around us, the world of work and the international world	Throughout				

Note: 2.1 = Module 2, Unit 1

¡Listos! 2 for Scotland (rojo)

All the activities in the *¡Listos! 2* Pupil's Book are matched to the 5–14 Guidelines. The following table shows where the different Strands feature in *¡Listos! 2 verde*. The table does not list every occurrence of a strand. It is designed to illustrate the range of coverage in the course. There are additional opportunities throughout the course which are clearly marked in this Teacher's Guide.

Information regarding the level(s) of an activity is given in the teaching notes in this Guide.

Strand	Module 1	Module 2	Module 3	Module 4	Module 5	Module 6
Listening for information and instructions	Unit 3, ex. 2	Unit 6, ex. 2	Unit 2, ex. 1	Unit 7, ex. 1b	Unit 6, ex. 1a	Unit 1, ex. 3a
Listening and reacting to others*						
Listening for enjoyment						Unit 1, ex. 2a
Speaking to convey information		Unit 4, ex. 1c	Unit 4, ex. 2			Resumen, ex.2
Speaking and interacting with others	Unit 2, ex. 4b	Unit 3, ex. 2b	Unit 1, ex. 1b	Unit 3, ex. 2	Unit 3, ex. 1c	Unit 4, ex. 3
Speaking about experiences, feelings and opinions	Unit 6, ex. 1b	Unit 1, ex. 1b	Unit 5, ex. 3b	Unit 5, ex. 3	Unit 2, ex. 2c	Unit 5, ex. 2
Reading for information and instructions	Unit 1, ex. 1a	Unit 5, ex. 3	Unit 3, ex. 3	Unit 6, ex. 1a	Unit 4, ex. 1	Unit 2, ex. 2
Reading aloud						
Reading for enjoyment			Unit 7, ex. 1a			
Writing to exchange information and ideas	Unit 5, ex. 3	Unit 2, ex. 3c	Unit 6, ex. 2b	Unit 4, ex. 1c	Unit 1, ex. 3a	Unit 3, ex. 2b
Writing to establish and maintain personal contact	Unit 6, ex. 2c	Unit 1, ex. 3c		Unit 2, ex. 3b	Unit 5, ex. 2 (Cuaderno B)	Unit 2, ex. 2 (Cuaderno B)
Writing imaginatively/ to entertain		Unit 3, ex. 4	Unit 3, ex. 3 (Cuaderno B)	Unit 1, ex. 2c	Unit 3, ex. 4	Unit 6, ex. 3b

* Since this strand is so closely linked to 'Speaking and interacting with others' it is not listed separately.

Coverage of the MFL Framework Objectives in ¡Listos! 1 and 2

The following charts show coverage of the Framework Objectives in ¡Listos! 1 and 2.

The charts indicate where an objective is launched and reinforced. The reinforcement of an objective often takes place in a number of units and the reference here is just an example.

Year 7 Objectives

Objective	Launch	Reinforcement	Objective	Launch	Reinforcement	Objective	Launch	Reinforcement	Objective	Launch	Reinforcement	Objective	Launch	Reinforcement
7W1	1.1	4.4	7S1	1.8	5.3	7T1	2.6	5.3	7L1	1.1	4.5	7C1	2.7	5.5
7W2	1.5	5.2	7S2	1.5	6.3	7T2	1.6	4.2	7L2	2.3	5.3	7C2	3.7	5.7
7W3	1.2	1.7	7S3	1.3	2.5	7T3	2.6	4.6	7L3	2.3	3.1	7C3	3.3	5.5
7W4	1.2	2.1	7S4	1.1	2.3	7T4	3.3	4.6	7L4	2.1	6.4	7C4	2.4	5.5
7W5	1.3 (present) 4.3 (preterite)	5.1	7S5	1.2	1.8	7T5	2.6	3.5	7L5	3.6	4.3	7C5	1.1	5.3
7W6	1.6	3.5	7S6	3.1	5.5	7T6	3.3	3.4	7L6	1.5	4.6			
7W7	4.3	5.2	7S7	3.4 (present) 5.6 (preterite) 6.5 (imm. future)	3.7	7T7	3.2	5.6						
7W8	1.4	5.7	7S8	1.2	2.3									
			7S9	1.6	5.1									

References are to ¡Listos! 1
1.2 = Módulo 1, Unit 2

Year 8 Objectives

Objective	Launch	Reinforcement	Objective	Launch	Reinforcement	Objective	Launch	Reinforcement	Objective	Launch	Reinforcement	Objective	Launch	Reinforcement
8W1	2.1r 2.2v	5.2	8S1	3.1	4.3r 6.4v	8T1	2.5r 4.1v	6.4r 4.3v	8L1	1.4r 2.4v	2.5r 3.3v	8C1	*	*
8W2	2.1r 2.2v	5.2	8S2	3.6r 3.5v	5S.r 4.3v	8T2	4.3r 4.4v	4.5r 5.4v	8L2	6.4	6.6	8C2	1.1	1 *Te toca a ti*
8W3	*	*	8S3	4.1r 3.6v	6.5r 6.3v	8T3	1.6	5.7r 2.7v	8L3	1.5r 2.3v	4.2	8C3	1.7	3.5
8W4	1.1	3.2r 1.3v	8S4	1.1	6.6r 5.1v	8T4	1.6	4.7r 2.1v	8L4	2.2	5.2r 4.4v	8C4	6.1r 2.7v	6.1v
8W5	1.2r 2.5r 4.3r 1.5v 3.4v 4.4v	2.6r 3.4r 4.4r 2.6v 3.6v 4.5v	8S5	1.4	2.6	8T5	5.6r 4.1v	6.2r 4.3v	8L5	5.2	*	8C5	2.5	5.4r 5.1v
8W6	4.5		8S6	1.1	5.2r 6.2v	8T6	1.6	4.3r 3.5v	8L6	5.1	5.4			
8W7	2.7r 3.7v	4.7r 4.6v	8S7	1.1r 3.4r 4.3r 1.1v 3.4v 4.4v	4.5r 5.5v	8T7	all	all						
8W8	3.6r 4.1v	6.4	8S8	3.6r 4.6v	4.1r 6.6v									

References are to ¡Listos! 2

r = *rojo*

v = *verde*

References without r or v apply to both books.

S = skills Sheet

Year 9 Objectives

Objective	Launch	Reinforcement	Objective	Launch	Reinforcement	Objective	Launch	Reinforcement	Objective	Launch	Reinforcement	Objective	Launch	Reinforcement
9W1	5.2		9S1	*		9T1	1.7	All 'Extra' 2.7	9L1	3.3r	5.1r	9C1	*	*
9W2	5.6r	5.7r	9S2	3.6r	'Extra' 3.7r	9T2	1.7	4.3r	9L2	3.4r	6.6r	9C2	1 *Te toca a ti*	
9W3	*		9S3	4.3r	4.7r	9T3	1.7	All 'Extra'	9L3	4.7r	5.4r	9C3	3.7	5.2
9W4	3.4r	4.4r	9S4	5.4	6.6r	9T4	All 'Extra' 1.6	All 'Extra' 6.1r	9L4	2.7r	6.6r	9C4	2 *Te toca a ti* r 4.6v	4.1r
9W5	1.7	4.5r	9S5	*	*	9T5	5.3	6.6r	9L5	5.2r		9C5	4.1	5.4
9W6	1.2r		9S6	5.6r	5.7r	9T6	6.5r		9L6	6.1r 6.3v	6.3r			
9W7	4.5		9S7	5.6r	6.6r	9T7	Through-out	Through-out						
9W8	All 'Extra' 1.7	All 'Extra' 2.7	9S8	4.7r										

References are to ¡Listos! 2

r = *rojo*

v = *verde*

References without r or v apply to both books.

'Extra' = Extension spreads at end of each Módulo.

Prep. = *Prepárate* (practice test)

Te toca a ti = self-access reading and writing section

Unit	Key Framework objectives	PoS	Key language and Grammar
1 Son muy famosos (pp. 6–7) Talking about yourself and other people Making comparisons	8W4 Word endings [L] 8S4 Question types [L] 8S6 Substituting and adding [L] 8S7 Present, past, future [L] 8C2 Famous people [L]	**1a** sounds and writing **2b** correct pronunciation/ intonation **2c** ask and answer questions **5e** range of resources	Review of language for talking about yourself: name, age, where from, physical description, etc. Comparatives and superlatives *Venus es más alta que Serena. Serena pesa menos que Venus.*
2 Juego bien al fútbol (pp. 8–9) Saying how you do something Talking about what you are going to do	8W5 Verbs (present) [L] 9W6 Meanings of syllables [L]		Adverbs: *rápidamente*, etc. The immediate future: *Voy a hacer mis deberes …* *Juego (muy) bien al fútbol. Juego (muy) mal al golf. Toco la guitarra bastante bien.*
3 Mucho gusto (pp. 10–11) Making introductions	8W4 Word endings [R] 8S4 Question types [R]	**2d** initiate/develop conversations **4c** compare cultures	Family members Demonstrative pronouns *Te presento a mi familia. Éste es (mi padre). Ésta es (mi madre). Éstos son (mis hermanos). Éstas son (mis primas). encantado/a mucho gusto*
4 Estás en tu casa (pp. 12–13) Asking for what you need Saying what you need	8S5 Negative forms and words [L] 8L1 Listening for subtleties [L]	**2c** ask and answer questions **2f** adapt language for different contexts **2i** report main points	*Me hace(n) falta una aspirina (toallas). ¿Te hace(n) falta … ? Le hace(n) falta … ¿Quieres ducharte? Si, quiero./No, no quiero. ¿Necesitas tomar algo? Necesito champú.*
5 Unos regalos (pp. 14–15) Buying gifts Describing someone's personality	8L3 Relaying gist and detail [L] 8W4 Word endings [R] 8S6 Substituting and adding [R]	**2a** listen for gist and detail	Direct object pronouns *Le compro una caja de chocolates. Les compro caramelos. Es deportista.*
6 Muchas gracias por el regalo (pp. 16–17) Writing a thank-you letter	8T3 Language and text types [L] 8T4 Dictionary use [L] 8T6 Text as a model and source [L] 9T4 Using support materials [L]	**2e** adapt language **3d** use reference materials	*Querido/a(s) … ¡Hola! Estimado/a(s) (Muchas) gracias por el regalo. Es muy/bastante (interesante). Me encanta. Me gusta (mucho). Eres muy amable/Sois muy amables. Quiero aceptar su invitación. Escríbeme pronto. Hasta pronto. Recuerdos a todos. Un saludo (cordial) Saludos Besos y abrazos Adiós*

Unit	Key Framework objectives	PoS	Key language and Grammar
Resumen y Prepárate (pp. 18–19) Pupils' checklist and practice test			
7 ¡Extra! ¡Escríbeme pronto! (pp. 20–21) Optional unit: a bulletin board on a website	8C3 Daily life and young people [L] 9W5 Verbs (conditional) [L] 9W8 Using grammar to understand words [L] 9T1 Understanding complex language [L] 9T2 Features for effect [L] 9T3 Authentic texts as sources [L]	2e adapt language 2f adapt language for different contexts 2h scanning texts 2i report main points 3b use context to interpret meaning 4a working with authentic materials 4d considering experiences in other countries 5f using the target language creatively	
Te toca a ti (pp. 112–113) Self-access reading and writing at two levels	9C2 Work of famous artists [L]		

1 Son muy famosos

(Pupil's Book pages 6–7)

Main topics

- Talking about yourself and other people
- Making comparisons

Key Framework objectives

- Word endings 8W4 (Launch)
- Question types 8S4 (Launch)
- Substituting and adding 8S6 (Launch)
- *Present*, past, future 8S7 (Launch)
- Famous people 8C2 (Launch)

Other aims

- Intonation with questions

Grammar

- Comparatives and superlatives

Key language

Me llamo …
Soy (español/a).

Soy de …
Tengo … años.
Mi cumpleaños es el …
Tengo un hermano y una hermana.
Soy (bastante) alto/a, bajo/a.
Tengo los ojos marrones.
Tengo el pelo castaño.

Serena es más baja que Venus.
Venus es más alta que Serena.
Serena pesa menos que Venus.
Soy más/menos … que mis hermanos.
Es el cantante español más famoso de los años 70.
Everest es la montaña más alta del mundo.

Resources

Cassette A, side 1
CD1, tracks 2 and 3
Cuaderno B, page 3
OHTs 1 and 2

Starter 1

Aim: to revise the three personal questions *¿Cómo te llamas? ¿Cuántos años tienes? ¿Dónde vives?*, including correct intonation.

Use a bean bag, plastic ball or fluffy toy. Throw it to a pupil and ask one of the questions, such as *¿Cómo te llamas?*. The pupil answers the question and throws it back: *Me llamo (Karen)*. Continue with another question and another pupil and increase the pace. You could add other personal questions from *¡Listos! 1* such as: *¿Cuál es tu nacionalidad? ¿Cómo eres? ¿Cómo es tu pelo? ¿Cuándo es tu cumpleaños?* Get pupils to work on appropriate intonation for questions.

1a Lee y escucha la información sobre Enrique y Shakira. Escribe una respuesta para cada pregunta. (AT1/3, AT3/3) [8S4; 8C2]

✖ Reading for information/instructions, Level D

Listening and reading. Pupils read and listen to two texts about Enrique Iglesias and Shakira, then answer questions in Spanish. Teachers may wish to precede this with a quick revision of personal information language, such as saying when your birthday is, describing your height, hair and eyes (covered in *¡Listos! 1*, Module 2). The texts contain examples of comparatives and superlatives. Once pupils have completed the exercise teachers may wish to ask them what they think the phrases containing the comparatives and superlatives mean, then refer them to the *Gramática* box, at the top of page 7, in which these points are explained.

Tapescript

Me llamo Enrique Iglesias Preysler. Soy español. Soy de Madrid pero ahora vivo en Miami. Mi cumpleaños es el 8 de mayo y tengo 28 años. Mi padre es el cantante español más famoso de los años 70. Se llama Julio Iglesias. Pero ahora soy más famoso que él. Tengo una hermana y un hermano. Mi hermana se llama Chabelí y mi hermano se llama Julio. Soy bastante alto. Soy más alto que mis hermanos. Tengo los ojos marrones y el pelo castaño.

Me llamo Shakira. Soy de Colombia en Sudamérica. Soy colombiana. Soy más famosa en los Estados Unidos que en el Reino Unido. Canto en español y en inglés. Mi cumpleaños es el 2 de febrero y tengo 21 años. Soy bastante alta. ¡Soy más alta que Kylie Minogue! Tengo el pelo ondulado y bastante largo.

Answers

1 Me llamo Enrique.
2 Soy español.
3 Vivo en Miami.
4 Tengo una hermana y un hermano. Mi hermana se llama Chabelí y mi hermano se llama Julio.
5 Soy de Colombia.
6 Mi cumpleaños es el 2 de febrero.
7 Tengo 21 años.
8 Tengo el pelo ondulado y bastante largo.

■■■■■■■■■■■■■■■■■■■■■■■■■■■■■■■■■■■■■■■

✚ As an extension, teachers could ask pupils to close their books, then play the recording again, pausing it at key points and asking them to complete the phrase, or to predict the next word/sentence.

1b Con tu compañero/a, haz una entrevista. Utiliza las preguntas de 1a (1–8). (AT2/3) [8S4]

✖ Speaking and interacting with others, Level D

Speaking. In pairs, pupils take it in turns to ask and answer the questions in 1a. They could do this twice, first answering as Enrique Iglesias or Shakira, then answering as themselves.

✚ More able students could be encouraged to use the comparative, as part of describing their hair, in question 8.

2a Lee la información de 1a otra vez. ¿Verdad (✓) o mentira (✗)? (AT3/3) [8W4]

✖ Reading for information/instructions, Level D

Reading. Pupils re-read the texts in 1a and do the true/false exercise, based on comparatives.

Answers

1 ✓   2 ✗   3 ✗   4 ✓

2b Corrige las frases falsas. (AT3/3)

✖ Reading for information/instructions, Level D

Reading and writing. Pupils correct the false statements from 2a.

Answers

2 Enrique es más alto que sus hermanos.
3 Shakira es más famosa en los Estados Unidos que en el Reino Unido.

Starter 2 [8W4]

Aim: to recap comparatives; to revise short vowel sounds.

Ask a couple of pupils to stand up and compare heights using *más* and *menos*. Mix boys and girls so pupils have to make the adjective agree with the subject of the sentence if they are using *alto, bajo* or *pequeño*. For example: *John es más alto que Ben. Ana es más alta que Tim.* Do several examples until you are happy that the class has got the idea. Draw attention to short vowel sounds in Spanish.

3a Lee la información sobre Venus y Serena Williams. Luego copia y completa las frases. (AT3/2)

✖ Knowing about language

Reading. Students read two sets of information about Venus and Serena Williams and complete sentences, using the comparative. This item introduces *menos … que* in addition to *más … que* and teachers may wish to point this out to pupils, to check their understanding, before they tackle the sentence-completion task.

Answers

Answers as tapescript in 3b

3b Escucha y comprueba tus respuestas. (AT1/2)

Listening. Students listen and check their answers to 3a.

Tapescript

1 *Venus es más alta que Serena.*
2 *Serena es más baja que Venus.*
3 *Venus es la más alta.*
4 *Serena pesa menos que Venus.*
5 *Venus pesa más que Serena.*

4a Completa las frases con *más* o *menos* según tus opiniones. (AT4/3) [8S6]

✖ Knowing about language

Reading. Pupils complete a series of sentences, giving their own opinions, using comparatives and superlatives.

Possible answers

1 menos   2 más   3 más   4 menos
5 más   6 más

4b Escribe cinco frases similares para dar tus propias opiniones. (AT3/2) [8S6]

✖ Exchange information/ideas, Level C

Writing. Pupils make up five similar phrases, giving their opinions, using comparatives and superlatives.

⬤ As project work, pupils could be encouraged to use the Internet to research information about other famous people and write profiles about them in Spanish, incorporating comparatives and superlatives where appropriate. [8C2]

módulo 1 1 Son muy famosos

Plenary

Ask someone to explain to the class the difference between comparatives and superlatives. Ask the rest of the class to contribute with examples. You might want to model some first.

Cuaderno B, page 3

1a Elige tres dibujos para cada descripción. (AT 3/1)

✕ Reading for information/instructions, Level D

Reading. Pupils read two sets of personal information and choose the correct three pictures for each description.

Answers

1 b, d, e	**2** a, c, f

1b Lee las descripciones de **1a** otra vez y contesta a las preguntas. (AT3/1, AT4/4) [8W4; 8S4]

✕ Reading for information/instructions, Level D

Reading and writing. After reading the texts in **1a** again, pupils answer questions in Spanish.

Answers

1 Tiene un hermano.
2 Su hermano es más bajo.
3 Clara vive en Ávila.
4 El pelo de Clara es rubio, corto y rizado.
5 El cumpleaños de Clara es el 7 de enero.
6 El padre de Francisco es mecánico.

1c Escribe una descripción similar sobre ti. (AT4/4)

✕ Exchange information/ideas, Level D

Writing. Using the descriptions on the page as a model, pupils write a similar text about themselves.

2 Juego bien al fútbol

(Pupil's Book pages 8–9)

Main topics

- Saying how you do something
- Talking about your routine

Key Framework objectives

- Verb tenses (present) 8W5 (Launch)
- Meanings of syllables 9W6 (Launch)

Grammar

- Adverbs
- Present tense
- Immediate future (mainly receptive)

Key language

Juego (muy) bien al fútbol.
Juego (muy) mal al golf.
Toco la guitarra bastante bien.

desafortunadamente   *bien/bueno*
normalmente   *mal/malo*
rápidamente
tranquilamente

Me levanto a la(s) …
Tomo (cereales).
Voy al instituto (a pie).
Las clases terminán a la(s) …
Como (en casa).
Después de comer (hago los deberes).
Juego (al baloncesto).
Me gusta (ir al cine).

Resources

Cassette A, side 1
CD1, tracks 4 and 5
Cuaderno B, page 4

Starter 1 [8W5]

Aim: revision of language for daily routine and other activities. This will include reflexives, regular and irregular -*ar*, -*er*, -*ir* verbs.

Write a few daily routine verbs on the board, e.g. *me levanto, desayuno, salgo* (or write in the infinitive if you prefer). Ask pupils to write down five things they do during the day. Ask pupils for some of their sentences and write these on the board. Reward pupils for using verbs other than those you wrote up at the start.

1 Escucha y escribe los dibujos en el orden correcto. (1–6) (AT1/2)

✂ Listening for information/instructions, Level B

Listening. Pupils listen and match up phrases (some of which use adverbs) with a series of drawings.

Tapescript

1 *Mi hermana toca la guitarra muy bien.*
2 *Mi hermano toca el violín bastante mal.*
3 *Juego bien al fútbol.*
4 *Juego muy mal al golf.*
5 *Me ducho y me visto rápidamente.*
6 *Desafortunadamente hoy tenemos un examen.*

Answers

1 *e*	**2** d	**3** c	**4** b	**5** a	**6** f

2 Copia y completa las frases con los adverbios correctos. (AT4/3) [9W6]

✂ Knowing about language

Writing. Pupils complete a series of sentences in which they must change adjectives into adverbs. Teachers should first refer pupils to the *Gramática* box on page 8, in which the formation of regular and irregular adverbs is explained. They may wish to demonstrate the formation of adverbs on a whiteboard or OHT. If using an OHT, the -*mente* adverb ending could be added via an overlay.

Answers

a *bien, mal*   **b** rápidamente   **c** Desafortunadamente   **d** Normalmente   **e** mal   **f** bien

Starter 2 [9W6]

Aim: to recap adverbs.

Write the following adjectives on the board and then ask pupils to convert them to adverbs: *desafortunado, rápido, normal, bueno, malo.*

When pupils have done this task ask them to tell you what each of them means in English.

3 Escucha y lee la carta. ¿Verdad (✓) o mentira (✗)? (AT3/5)

✂ Reading for information/instructions, Level D

Reading. Pupils read a letter in which a Spanish boy describes his weekday routine to a British boy who is going to visit him, then do a true/false exercise. The letter revises daily routine phrases (introduced in *¡Listos! 1*, Module 4) and the immediate future (introduced in *¡Listos! 1*, Module 5.) The *Gramática* box on page 9 reminds pupils about the formation of the immediate future tense.

2 Juego bien al fútbol

20 de septiembre
Querido Oscar
Gracias por tu carta. Vas a venir a Madrid en octubre. ¡Qué bien! Y vas a venir a clase al instituto. Pues, aquí tienes mi rutina diaria:
De lunes a viernes, me levanto a las siete. Desayuno.
Normalmente tomo cereales con leche y zumo de fruta.
Luego voy al instituto. Voy a pie porque está bastante cerca.
Las clases empiezan a las ocho y terminan a la una y media.
Voy a casa a comer y después hago los deberes.
Desafortunadamente tenemos muchos deberes.
Soy muy activo. Me gustan mucho los deportes. Juego al fútbol y al baloncesto. También me gusta ir al cine.
¿Qué te gusta a ti?
Saludos
Gerardo

Answers

1 ✓	2 ✓	3 ✓	4 ✗	5 ✓	6 ✗	7 ✗	8 ✗
9 ✓	10 ✓						

➕ As an extension, pupils could correct the false sentences in **3**.

4a Eres Gerardo. Escribe las frases de la carta para contestar a las preguntas. (AT3/4) [8S4]

✕ Reading for information/instructions, Level D

Reading and writing. Pupils write answers to questions in Spanish, as though they are Gerardo in **3**.

Answers

1 Me levanto a las siete.
2 Para el desayuno tomo cereales con leche y zumo de fruta.
3 Voy al instituto a pie.
4 Las clases terminan a la una y media.
5 Como en casa.
6 Después de comer hago los deberes.
7 Juego al fútbol y al baloncesto.
8 También me gusta ir al cine.

4b Con tu compañero/a, haz y contesta a las preguntas de **4a**. (AT2/4) [8S4]

✕ Speaking and interacting with others, Level D/E

Speaking. Pupils work in pairs to ask and answer the questions in **4a** for themselves.

ℝ Teachers may wish to precede the pairwork task with a demonstration of how pupils can adapt their answers to **4a** to talk about themselves. For further support, pupils could be given a sentence-building grid on an OHT or worksheet, if necessary.

4c Imagina que Gerardo va a venir a tu casa y escríbele una carta similar. (AT4/5) [8S6]

✕ Writing to establish/maintain contact, Level D/E

Writing. Pupils write a similar letter to the one in **3** about their own weekday routine. If they wish, teachers could present a version of the letter on an OHT to demonstrate how it could be adapted to refer to pupils' own routines. For example, a gapped version of the letter could be used and pupils could write their own version of the information on an overlay to fill the gaps. Pupils should be encouraged to use as many adverbs as possible in their letter.

Plenary [9W6]

Ask for a volunteer to explain how you form adverbs in Spanish. What is the general rule? What are some common exceptions? You could discuss with the class what are likely to be the five or six most useful adverbs. This could lead to some glossary/dictionary work if suggestions go beyond those introduced in the unit. What ideas do pupils have for memorising these useful words?

Cuaderno B, page 4

1a Empareja los dibujos con las frases. (AT3/2) [8W4]

✕ Reading for information/instructions, Level C

Reading. Pupils match sentences in the comparative with pictures.

Answers

1 c	2 d	3 e	4 a	5 g	6 f	7 b

1b Lee las frases de **1a** otra vez. Identifica las personas en cada dibujo y escribe sus nombres. (AT3/2)

✕ Reading for information/instructions, Level C

Reading. After a second reading, pupils must write down the name of the people in each picture.

Answers

a Hugo, Pepi
b Marta, Paz
c Javier, Alejandro
d Juana, María
e Rafael, Miguel
f Daniel, Mauricio
g Saturnina, Bernadina

2a Lee la carta. ¿Verdad (✓) o mentira (✗)? (AT3/3)

✉ Reading for information/instructions, Level D

Reading. Pupils do a true/false exercise after reading the letter.

Answers

1 ✓   2 ✗   3 ✓   4 ✗   5 ✗   6 ✓

2b Lee la carta otra vez y contesta a las preguntas. (AT3/3)

✉ Reading for information/instructions, Level D

Reading. Pupils re-read the letter and answer questions in English.

Answers

> **1** La Paz, Bolivia
> **2** a student
> **3** English and French
> **4a** David is the tallest.
> **4b** Nicolás is the best looking.
> **4c** Rebeca is the smallest – she's only 3.

3 Mucho gusto

(Pupil's Book pages 10–11)

Main topics

- Making introductions

Key Framework objectives

- Word endings 8W4 (Reinforcement)
- Question types 8S4 (Reinforcement)

Grammar

- Demonstrative pronouns

Key language

Te presento a mi familia.
Éste/Ésta es mi …
Éstos/Éstas son …

madre	*abuelo/a*
padre	*tío/a*
padres	*primo/a*
hermano/a	*hermanos*

encantado/a
mucho gusto
¿Qué tal el viaje?

Resources

Cassette A, side 1
CD1, tracks 6, 7 and 8
Cuaderno B, page 5
Grammar, Resource and Assessment File, page 7
OHTs 3 and 4

Starter 1 [8W4; 9W6]

Aim: to revise family members; to use word endings to help determine meaning.

Write the anagrams below on the board and see who can work them out first. What do the words mean in English? When going through the answers, focus on the endings of the words with '*a*', '*o*' or plural endings – how do the endings help you to work out the meaning of the word?

rdema (*madre*), orhemna (*hermano*), aeluab (*abuela*), otí (*tío*), smiorp (*primos*), mirap (*prima*), olbaue (*abuelo*), srdepa (*padres*), darep (*padre*), rmaehan (*hermana*)

1a Lee y escucha. (AT1/4; AT3/3) [8W4]

✖ Reading for information/instructions, Level D

Listening and reading. Pupils listen to a recording in which a Spanish boy introduces his family to a British visitor. At the same time, they follow the text on the page. As well as presenting demonstrative pronouns, this item revises and extends some of the family vocabulary that pupils came across in *¡Listos! 1*. The key nouns are listed in a vocabulary box on page 10. After listening, teachers may wish to discuss some of the social conventions used in the conversation, such as the expressions *mucho gusto* and *encantado/a*, as well as asking pupils when and why the speaker uses *éste, ésta, éstos* and *éstas*, before directing pupils to the *Gramática* box on page 10 in which these demonstrative pronouns are explained.

Tapescript

Gerardo	*Te presento a mi familia.*
	Ésta es mi madre, Claudia.
Madre	*Hola, Oscar. ¿Qué tal el viaje?*
Oscar	*Muy bien, gracias.*
Gerardo	*Éste es mi padre, Ignacio.*
Padre	*Hola, Oscar. Mucho gusto.*

Oscar	*Encantado.*
Gerardo	*Ésta es mi hermana, Lucía.*
Lucía	*Mucho gusto.*
Gerardo	*Ésta es mi abuela, doña Mercedes.*
Abuela	*Hola, Oscar. ¡Bienvenido!*
Gerardo	*Éstos son mis tíos y mi primo.*
	Mi tío se llama Jorge.
	Mi tía se llama Ana María.
	Y mi primo se llama Héctor.
	Éstas son mis primas. Se llaman Pilar, Paloma y Esme.

1b Dibuja un árbol genealógico para representar la familia de Gerardo. (AT3/3)

✖ Reading for information/instructions, Level D

Reading and writing. Pupils use the information in **1a** to draw Gerardo's family tree. Teachers may wish to ensure pupils are familiar with the conventions of family trees by presenting their own on the board or OHP. As a follow-up to exercise **1b**, teachers may also wish to ask pupils to draw and write or speak about their own family tree.

Answers

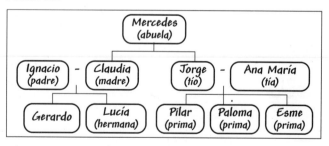

1c Copia y completa las frases sobre Gerardo. (AT3/3) [8W4]

✖ Reading for information/instructions, Level D

Reading and writing. Pupils copy a series of sentences about Gerardo's family and complete them with the correct form of the demonstrative pronoun.

Answers

a Éstos	**b** Ésta	**c** Ésta	**d** Ésta	**e** Éste	**f** Éstas

Starter 2 [8W4]

Aim: to recap demonstrative pronouns.

Using mini-whiteboards (or pen and paper), ask pupils to write down the Spanish for the following and hold them up for you to see: this (masculine), this (feminine), these (masculine), these (feminine). Not necessarily in this order, depending on the ability of your class. Insist on accurate use of accents.

2 Escucha y escribe 'a' o 'b'. (1–10) (AT1/3)

✖ Listening for information/instructions, Level B

Listening. Pupils look at two pictures of Isabel's family and pets, listen to them being introduced and note down whether each member referred to appears in picture **a** or picture **b**.

Tapescript

1 Éste es mi abuelo. Se llama Carlos.
2 Ésta es mi madre. Se llama Mayra.
3 Éste es mi padre. Se llama Luis.
4 Ésta es mi abuela. Se llama Carmen.
5 Éste es mi hámster. Se llama Savi.
6 Éste es mi ratón. Se llama Figo.
7 Éstos son mis tíos. Mi tío se llama Juan y mi tía se llama Nieves.
8 Éste es mi gato. Se llama Trufa.
9 Éste es mi hermano. Se llama Martín.
10 Ésta es mi prima. Se llama Susana.

Answers

1 *b*	**2** a	**3** a	**4** b	**5** a	**6** a	**7** b	**8** a	**9** a	**10** b

3 Con tu compañero/a, elige un dibujo, 'a' o 'b' y presenta a las personas. (AT2/3)

✖ Speaking and interacting with others, Level D

Speaking. Working in pairs, pupils choose either picture **a** or picture **b** from exercise **2** and create dialogues, introducing the family members and pets to their partner, who must respond using some of the social niceties listed in a box on page 10. Pupils should swap roles to ensure they each do the presenting.

4a Lee la carta de Oscar y contesta a las preguntas. (AT3/3) [8W5; 8S4]

✖ Reading for information/instructions, Level D

Reading. Pupils read a letter from Oscar and answer questions in Spanish. The letter revises key personal information topics, covered in *¡Listos! 1*, including:

saying where you live, what you have in the way of brothers, sisters and pets, and your nationality. The letter and questions also provide an opportunity to remind pupils of a range of different verb endings in the present tense.

➕ If teachers wish to provide further practice of present tense verb endings, pupils could be given a version of the letter on a worksheet or OHT, with the verbs (or verb endings) gapped. Depending on pupils' ability, either a 'menu' of the missing verbs could be provided for them to choose from, or they could be expected to work out/look up the verbs themselves. As a further extension, pupils could be asked to write a similar letter about their own home and family using a range of verb endings.

Answers

a Oscar vive en Birmingham.
b Vive en las afueras de la ciudad.
c Tiene dos hermanos.
d Su hermana tiene 9 años.
e Su hermano se llama James.
f Tiene un perro, unos peces y un conejo.
g Su padre es de Escocia.

4b Lee la carta de Oscar otra vez. Escucha y anota cinco diferencias entre lo que escribe Oscar y lo que dice su prima Sophie. (AT1/4, AT3/3)

✖ Listening for information/instructions, Level D

Listening. Pupils listen to Oscar's cousin Sophie describing her family, and spot five differences between Oscar and Sophie's descriptions.

Tapescript

Hola. Me llamo Sophie. Oscar es mi primo. Vivo con mis padres en las afueras de Glasgow. Tengo dos hermanos. Mi hermano James tiene 20 años y mi hermana Alice tiene 9 años. Tenemos muchos animales en casa: un perro, unos peces y una rata. Mi familia no es muy grande. Tengo tres primos.

Answers

1 *Glasgow/Birmingham*	**2** brother 20 years old/18 years old
3 Alice/Gemma	**4** mouse/rabbit	**5** 3 cousins/11 cousins

5 Eres Martín del dibujo **2a**. Escribe sobre tu familia. (AT4/4)

✖ Exchange information/ideas, Level D/E

Writing. Pupils imagine they are Martín in picture **2a** and write about their family.

🅡 ➕ Some pupils could simply write as though they were introducing the family, using demonstrative pronouns. Others could be encouraged to write more

fully, making up details about age, nationality, etc., and presenting the information in the form of a letter, similar to the one in exercise **3**.

Cuaderno B, page 5

1 Escribe las frases en los globos apropiados. (AT4/2) [8W4]

✕ Reading for information/instructions, Level C

Reading. Pupils match the sentences with the correct speech bubbles.

Answers

1 Éste es mi perro.
2 Éste es mi abuelo. Encantado.
3 Éstos son mis padres. Encantados.
4 Éstas son mis hermanas.
5 Te presento a mi familia. Encantados.

2a Mira el árbol genealógico y completa las frases. (AT3/2, AT4/2) [8W4]

✕ Reading for information/instructions, Level C

Reading and writing. A gap-filling exercise, based on a Spanish family tree.

Answers

1 tío   2 hermana   3 abuelo   4 tía   5 prima
6 tíos   7 abuela   8 madre

2b Escribe unas frases describiendo qué relación tiene Paco con cada persona. (AT4/3)

✕ Exchange information/ideas, Level C

Reading and writing. Pupils describe each person's relationship with Paco.

Answers

1 el padre de Paco   4 son los tíos de Paco
2 las primas de Paco   5 es la madre de Paco
3 es el primo de Paco   6 son los abuelos de Paco

2c Dibuja el árbol genealógico de tu familia y describe qué relación tienes con cada persona. (AT4/3)

✕ Exchange information/ideas, Level C

Writing. After drawing their own family tree, pupils write about how they are related to each person.

Grammar, Resource and Assessment File, page 7

Some key verbs

1 Pupils fill in a grid with 1st person singular, 3rd person singular and 3rd person plural verb forms in the present tense.

Answers

	Tener	Ser	Vivir
	To have	To be	To live
I	*tengo*	soy	vivo
He	tiene	*es*	vive
She	tiene	es	vive
They	tienen	son	*viven*

Making comparisons

2 Pupils look at the artwork prompts and make appropriate sentences using the comparatives *más* and *menos*.

Answers

a *Juan es más alto que Pedro.*
b Ana es más pequeña que Conchi.
c Neli es más grande que Lala.
d Miguel es menos joven que Chus.
e Isabel es más inteligente que María.

Demonstrative adjectives

3 Pupils choose the correct demonstrative adjective to complete each sentence.

Answers

a *Éste* es mi tío.
b Ésta es mi amiga Begoña.
c Éstos son mis animales.
d Éstos son mis padres.
e Ésta es mi hermana mayor.
f Éste es mi abuelo.

4 Estás en tu casa

(Pupil's Book pages 12–13)

Main topics

- Asking for what you need
- Saying what you need

Key Framework objectives

- Negative forms and words 8S5 (Launch)
- Listening for subtleties 8L1 (Launch)

Grammar

- Pronouns: *me hace(n) falta*, etc.

Key language

una aspirina	*jabón*
un cepillo (de dientes)	*gel de ducha*
champú	*pasta de dientes*
colonia	*desodorante*
un peine	*un secador*
una toalla	

¿Quieres ducharte/bañarte?
Sí, quiero lavarme el pelo.
No, no quiero acostarme.

¿Te hace(n) falta …?
Me hace(n) falta …
Te hace(n) falta …
una aspirina	*champú*
un cepillo (de dientes)	*colonia*

¿Necesitas (tomar algo)?
Necesito champú.

Resources

Cassette A, side 1
CD1, tracks 9, 10 and 11
Cuaderno B, page 6
Starter 2, Resource and Assessment File, page 4
Hojas de trabajo, Resource and Assessment File,
pages 5 and 6 (*colonia, un cepillo de dientes, pasta
de dientes, una toalla, champú, gel de ducha, jabón,
desodorante*)
OHTs 5 and 6

Starter 1 [8W4; 8S4, 5]

Aim: to talk about likes and dislikes.

Recap pronouns: *me, te, le* with *gustar* and
encantar before going on to use pronouns with a
different verb. Write a list of things on the board or
prepare an OHT beforehand. For example: *el
chocolate, los ratones, el deporte, la historia, jugar
al fútbol, jugar al baloncesto, la música …* . Ask
pupils to work with a partner and take it in turns to
ask each other about the list of things on the
board: *¿Te gusta(n) el/los …? Sí/No me gusta(n).*
Afterwards report back to the class. Ask pupils to
reveal one thing their partner likes or dislikes: *Le
gusta el chocolate (porque es delicioso).* (If you want
to extend this activity you could ask pupils to give
reasons for their answers: *Porque es/son
delicioso(s), aburrido(s).*)

1 Escribe el orden en que se mencionan las
cosas. (1–11) (AT1/1)

✖ Listening for information/instructions, Level A

Listening. Pupils hear a list of household items and
must note them down in the order in which they are
mentioned.

Tapescript

1 *un cepillo*
2 *un cepillo de dientes*
3 *una toalla*
4 *un secador*
5 *champú*
6 *un peine*

7 *pasta de dientes*
8 *desodorante*
9 *gel de ducha*
10 *jabón*
11 *colonia*

Answers

1 g	**2** i	**3** a	**4** d	**5** c	**6** f	**7** h	**8** b	**9** k	
10 j	**11** e								

This is an opportunity to revise the sounds 'j', 'g' and
'll'. You could play the recording again and ask pupils
to simply focus on these sounds. When they hear one
of them they should put up their hand and tell you
which of the three sounds they have identified. [8L1]

2 Escucha. Copia y rellena el cuadro. (AT1/4)
[8W4; 8S5]

✖ Listening for information/instructions, Level D/E

Listening. Pupils now hear a dialogue in which a host
asks a visitor whether they need certain items,
introducing the key structure *me/te* (etc.) *hace(n)
falta*, which is explained in the *Gramática* box at the
bottom of page 12. *Necesito* and *No necesito* are also
used. Pupils must copy and complete a grid, in
Spanish, of what the visitor needs or already has. As
completing the task successfully is dependent on
understanding the new structure, it is suggested that
teachers direct pupils to the *Gramática* box before
undertaking the listening task, as well as checking
understanding of *(No) necesito …* . To prepare pupils
for the listening exercise, teachers could also make
up sentences using *Me hace(n) falta …* and *(No)*

Necesito … combined with the items from exercise 1, then ask pupils to say what item is mentioned and whether the teacher has it already or needs it.

Tapescript

Aquí está tu dormitorio …
Y aquí está el cuarto de baño. ¿Te quieres duchar?
¡Ay, sí, necesito ducharme!
¿Te hace falta gel de ducha o jabón?
Sí, me hace falta gel de ducha. No necesito jabón.
El gel está aquí. ¿Necesitas algo más?¿Una toalla, colonia, un peine o un cepillo?
Necesito una toalla.
Toma, una toalla. ¿Te hace falta champú o desodorante?
No gracias, tengo champú y desodorante, pero me hace falta pasta de dientes.
Toma, pasta de dientes. ¿Te hace falta un cepillo de dientes?
No, gracias, tengo un cepillo de dientes pero necesito un secador.
El secador está aquí.

Answers

Le hace falta …	No le hace falta …
gel de ducha	jabón
una toalla	champú
pasta de dientes	desodorante
un secador	un cepillo de dientes

3a Mira la foto. ¿Qué necesitan estas personas? (1–5) (AT1/4) [8S4]

Listening for information/instructions, Level D

Listening. A further listening task, in which pupils show understanding of which items each speaker needs by noting down the letters of the items in the photograph.

Tapescript

1 *– ¿Te hace falta una toalla?*
– No, gracias, tengo una toalla pero necesito jabón.
– Toma, jabón.
– Gracias.
2 *– ¿Necesitas algo? ¿Gel de ducha, desodorante, champú?*
– Me hace falta gel de ducha.
– El gel de ducha está aquí en la estantería.
3 *– Quiero ducharme pero necesito una toalla, por favor.*
– Las toallas están en el armario. Toma las que quieras.
– Gracias
4 *– Me quiero lavar el pelo.*
– ¿Te hace falta champú?
– Sí, sí, necesito champú.
– Hay champú en el cuarto de baño.
– Vale.
5 *– ¿Necesitas algo?*
– Pues, me hacen falta el desodorante y la pasta de dientes.
– Toma, desodorante. Y la pasta de dientes está aquí.
– Muchas gracias.

Answers

1 j	2 k	3 a	4 c	5 b,h

3b Con tu compañero/a, pregunta y contesta. (AT2/4) [8S4,5]

Speaking and interacting with others. Level C/D

Speaking. Pairwork practice on asking whether your partner needs certain items. Pupils could be asked to each note down in secret three items they need, and then see which of them can find out the three items using the smallest number of questions. Pupils should be encouraged to use both *Me/Te hace(n) falta …* and *Necesito/Necesitas …*

Starter 2

Aim: to recap pronouns with *hacer falta*, including word order.

Using *Resource and Assessment File*, page 4, give each pupil a card with a word on it. Tell them to arrange themselves in groups of three in the correct order to make a sentence. Ask a pupil from each group to tell you what their sentence says in Spanish and then what it means in English. Clap your hands and get everyone to move round again. Do this several times.

4a Empareja los dibujos con las frases. (AT3/2) [8W5; 8S4]

Reading for information/instructions, Level C

Reading. Pupils match up a series of statements and questions about wanting or needing something/to do something, with the relevant pictures. A third structure, *Quiero/¿Te quieres* + infinitive has been added to *Me/Te hace(n) falta …* and *Necesito/ Necesitas …* . Teachers may wish to check pupils' understanding of this structure before pupils tackle the exercise. Teachers may also wish to draw pupils' attention to the position of the reflexive pronoun in infinitives such as *bañarme, ducharme, lavarme el pelo* and *acostarme*, contrasting this with the first person singular of these reflexive verbs, which were introduced in *¡Listos! 1*, Module 4.

Answers

1 e	2 c	3 b	4 a	5 d	6 f

4b Mira el cuadro de vocabulario otra vez y escribe una frase para cada dibujo. (AT4/2)

Exchange information/ideas, Level C

Writing. Pupils write sentences, using the three new structures, to describe a series of pictures.

Answers

➕ Some pupils could be encouraged to write and perform a dialogue between a host and a visitor, based on a combination of two or three of the pictures.

Answers

> **a** Necesito/Me hace falta champú. *or* Quiero lavarme el pelo.
> **b** Necesito/Me hace falta una toalla. *or* Quiero ducharme.
> **c** Necesito/Me hace falta una aspirina.
> **d** Quiero pasta de dientes *or* Necesito pasta de dientes.
> **e** Necesito/Quiero ducharme.
> **f** Quiero acostarme.

Plenary

Ask your class to write down how to say 'I need' and 'I want' (*Me hace falta/Quiero*). What can pupils tell you about the different positions of the pronoun in the following sentences: *Quiero acostarme a las diez/Me acuesto a las diez* and *Quiero ducharme a las siete/Me ducho a las siete*. What do these sentences mean in English?

Cuaderno B, page 6

1 Mira los dibujos y completa los globos usando las palabras en el cuadro. (AT4/2) [8S4]

✖ Exchange information/ideas, Level C

Writing. Pupils use the boxed phrases to write a speech bubble for each picture.

Answers

> **1** ¿Quieres un bocadillo?
> **2** ¿Necesitas ducharte?
> **3** Necesito llamar por teléfono.
> **4** Me hace falta bañarme.
> **5** ¿Quieres ver la tele?
> **6** Necesito acostarme.

2 Completa las frases con las palabras correctas. (AT3/2) [8W4, 5]

✖ Knowing about language

Writing. A multiple-choice exercise, based on grammatical accuracy.

Answers

> **1** toalla, cepillo **2** necesita **3** desodorante y jabón
> **4** Te **5** Quiere

Hojas de trabajo, Resource and Assessment File, pages 5 and 6

Cards for pairwork featuring items of toiletry and gifts: pupils match the pictures to the correct words.

5 Unos regalos

(Pupil's Book pages 14–15)

Main topics

- Buying gifts
- Describing someone's personality

Key Framework objectives

- Relaying gist and detail 8L3 (Launch)
- Word endings 8W4 (Reinforcement)
- Substituting and adding 8S6 (Reinforcement)

Grammar

- Indirect object pronouns
- Adjectives

Key language

Le compro …
Les compro …
una caja de chocolates
una camiseta (de Londres)
un CD de música clásica

gel de baño perfumado
una gorra (de Manchester United)
una lata de té
un llavero
una pluma
un teléfono móvil
un vídeo de 'Friends'

Es …

deportista	*simpático/a*
estudioso/a	*sociable*
hablador(a)	*trabajador(a)*
serio/a	*tranquilo/a*

Resources

Cassette A, side 1
CD1, tracks 12, 13 and 14
Cuaderno B, page 7
Hojas de trabajo, Resource and Assessment File, pages 5 and 6 (*una camiseta, un llavero, una gorra, dinero*)

Starter 1 [8W5]

Aim: to practise the endings of regular -*ar* verbs: *comprar, hablar.*

Use a dice, where dots correspond to each subject pronoun, e.g. one dot = *yo*, two dots = *tú*, three dots = *él*, etc., or dice with subject pronouns on them. Working in pairs, pupils take it in turns to throw the dice and conjugate the verbs.
Suggestion: You may wish to quickly revise the verb endings with your class beforehand.

1 Empareja los regalos con las personas. (1–4) (AT1/4) [8L3}

✄ Listening for information/instructions, Level D

Listening. Pupils listen to a series of dialogues in which a visitor discusses what presents to buy for members of the host's family. Pupils note down the number of each family member and the letter of the relevant present, as shown on page 14. The dialogues introduce indirect object pronouns, which are explained in the *Gramática* box on page 14, and teachers may wish to draw pupils' attention to this before they begin the listening task. Teachers should also ensure that pupils are familiar with the vocabulary used for the various presents.

✚ Some pupils could note down extra information, such as any suggested presents which the visitor decides against buying. There is also the opportunity to draw pupils' attention to some useful phrases for adding expression, such as *no sé, ya sé, no tengo ni idea, eso es difícil.*

Tapescript

1 – Voy a comprar regalos para la familia de Gerardo.
 – ¿Qué compras para la abuela de Gerardo?
 – Para su abuela, no sé.
 – ¿Por qué no le compras algo dulce como una caja de caramelos?
 – Ya sé. Le compro una caja de chocolates.
 – Buena idea.
2 – ¿Y para el hermano de Gerardo, qué le compras?
 – No tengo ni idea.
 – ¿Algo de ropa, como por ejemplo una camiseta o una gorra?
 – Le compro una camiseta de Londres.
3 – ¿Qué compras para los padres?
 – Eso es difícil.
 – Algo típico del Reino Unido.
 – ¿Cómo qué?
 – No sé, té, galletas, mermelada.
 – Buena idea. Les compro una caja grande de galletas.
4 – Y ¿qué compras para Gerardo?
 – Eso es más fácil porque le gusta el fútbol.
 – ¿Ah, sí?
 – Le compro una gorra del Manchester United.

Answers

1 c	2 b	3 e	4 a

2 Con tu compañero/a, pregunta y contesta. (AT2/3) [8W4]

✄ Speaking and interacting with others, Level C

Speaking. In pairs, pupils take it in turns to ask and answer questions about what they are planning to buy for various family members. Before tackling this, pupils need to have a clear understanding about indirect object pronouns, as explained in the *Gramática* box on page 14.

3a Escribe el orden en que se menciona el carácter de cada persona. (AT1/4) [8L3]

Listening for information/instructions, Level D/E

Listening. This activity introduces adjectives of personality. Pupils listen for the order in which the adjectives are mentioned and note down the letter of the picture which represents each adjective. Since the adjectives are embedded in longer dialogues, pupils should be encouraged to listen for gist, rather than expecting to understand every word. Equally, there are a number of clues, in addition to the adjective itself, in each of the dialogues, and some pupils may be able to spot these. If so, they should be encouraged to share this information with the rest of the class.

Tapescript

1 – ¿Cómo es tu hermana Pili?
  – Pues, siempre está por ahí. Nunca está en casa. Es muy sociable. Le gusta salir mucho y tiene muchos amigos.
2 – ¿Cómo es tu amiga Marta?
  – Marta es una persona muy seria. Me gusta mucho.
3 – ¿Cómo es tu primo Julio?
  – Todo el mundo quiere a Julio. Es un chico muy simpático y amable.
4 – Y Manuel, ¿cómo es?
  – Manuel trabaja mucho. Tiene un empleo con una compañía de ordenadores y estudia también. Es muy trabajador.
5 – Descríbeme a Elisa. ¿Cómo es su carácter?
  – Elisa hace mucho deporte, practica la natación, juega al baloncesto, es miembro de un equipo de fútbol. Es muy deportista y activa.
6 – ¿Cómo es el carácter de Belén?
  – Belén está siempre al teléfono hablando con sus amigas. Es muy habladora. Le encanta hablar con sus amigas.
7 – Y Enrique, ¿cómo es?
  – Enrique es estudioso, siempre hace sus deberes. Lee mucho. Quiere ser médico.
8 – ¿Cómo es el carácter de Mercedes?
  – Mercedes no es muy activa ni dinámica. Es tranquila. Le gusta la tranquilidad.

Answers

| 1 h | 2 d | 3 e | 4 a | 5 f | 6 b | 7 g | 8 c |

3b Escucha otra vez y empareja los nombres con los dibujos. (AT1/4) [8W4; 8L3]

Listening for information/instructions, Level D/E

Listening. Pupils listen again to the recording and match the letters of the adjectives with each name. As a follow-up, pupils could be asked to say or write a sentence about each of the people. Teachers should draw pupils' attention to the masculine and feminine forms of each adjective listed in **3a** and ask them to spot which adjective is the same in both the masculine and the feminine (*sociable*).

Tapescript

Tapescript as **3a**

Answers

Pili – h, **Mercedes** – c, **Elisa** – f, **Enrique** – g, **Belén** – b, **Marta** – d, **Manuel** – a, **Julio** – e

Starter 2 [8W4]

Aim: to recap vocabulary for describing personality and adjective endings.

Write on the board the following and ask pupils to replace the English with a suitable adjective in Spanish: *mi padre es* (chatty), *mi madre es* (sporty), *mis abuelos son* (nice), *mi hermana es* (very hard-working), *mis primos son* (sporty).

Ask pupils to fill in the appropriate form of *ser*.

4 Con tu compañero/a, describe el carácter de tus compañeros/as de clase. (AT2/3) [8S5]

Speaking and interacting with others, Level C/D

Speaking. Pairwork guessing-game. One pupil uses the adjectives to describe a member of the class and their partner has to guess who it is. They should be encouraged to use the negative (*No es …*) as well as the affirmative.

5 Empareja las personas con los regalos. (AT3/3)

Reading for information/instructions, Level D

Reading. Pupils read the description of family members' personality traits and interests, then write down the letter of a suitable present for each person.

Answers

hermano menor 2, hermano mayor 3, prima 6, padre 4, madre 5, abuela 1

6 Describe a cinco de tus amigos y elige un regalo ideal para cada uno. Utiliza un diccionario. (AT4/4) [8S6]

Exchange information/ideas, Level C/D

Writing. Pupils write a description of five friends and what present they would buy for each of them, using a direct object pronoun. They are encouraged to use a dictionary to look up extra vocabulary.

➕ Able pupils should be encouraged to go beyond the example on the page, by borrowing or adapting extra phrases from the text in exercise **5** and the tapescript in exercise **3a**, such as *En su tiempo libre … , le gusta/le encanta …* , etc.

Plenary

Ask someone to tell the rest of the class what the indirect object pronouns are (*me, te, le, nos, os, les*), where to place them (immediately before the verb), and when they are used (to replace the subject of the sentence). What do they mean in English: *le* (for him, for her), *les* (for them)? How are you going to remember them?

Cuaderno B, page 7

1 Empareja las descripciones con las personas. (AT3/2) [8S5]

✉ Reading for information/instructions, Level C/D

Reading. Pupils match a series of statements about people with descriptions of them.

Answers

1 d	2 b	3 h	4 a	5 g	6 e	7 f	8 c

2 Contesta a las preguntas. (AT4/3) [8W4]

✉ Exchange information/ideas, Level C/D

Writing. Pupils answer questions in Spanish, describing family members, friends and teachers.

3 ¿Qué compra Paloma a su familia para Navidad? Mira los dibujos y contesta a las preguntas. (AT4/3)

✉ Exchange information/ideas, Level C

Writing. Pupils answer questions in Spanish about Christmas presents, by looking at the pictures.

Answers

> **1** Le compra colonia.
> **2** Le compra un CD.
> **3** Le compra un video.
> **4** Le compra una camiseta.
> **5** Le compra una gorra.
> **6** Le compra un llavero.

Hojas de trabajo, Resource and Assessment File, pages 5 and 6

Cards for pairwork featuring items of toiletry and gifts: pupils match the pictures to the correct words.

6 Muchas gracias por el regalo

(Pupil's Book pages 16–17)

Main topics

● Writing a thank-you letter

Key Framework objectives

● Language and text types 8T3 (Launch)
● Dictionary use 8T4 (Launch)
● Text as a model and source 8T6 (Launch)
● Using support materials 9T4 (Launch)

Key language

Querido/a(s) …/¡Hola!
amigo/a(s)   *primo/a(s)*
familia   *abuelo/a(s)*   *tío/a*
Estimado/a(s), señor(es), señora(s)

(Muchas) gracias por …
el regalo   *el póster*
el dinero   *la foto*
el CD   *el llavero*
la camiseta   *la invitación*

Es muy/bastante …
interesante   *práctico/a*

fantástico/a   aburrido/a   horrible
bueno/a   malo/a
Me encanta.
(No) Me gusta (mucho/nada).
Lo/La odio/detesto.

Eres/Es (usted)/Sois/Son (ustedes) …
antipático/a(s)   *generoso/a(s)*
muy amable(s)   *poco amable(s)*
roñoso/a(s)   *simpático/a(s)*

Escríbeme pronto.   *¡Hasta pronto!*
Recuerdos a todos.   *No me escribas nunca más.*
Un saludo (cordial)   *Saludos*
Besos y abrazos   *Adiós*

Resources

Cassette A, side 1
CD1, track 15
Cuaderno B, page 8
Hojas de trabajo, Resource and Assessment File,
pages 5 and 6 (*una camiseta, un llavero, una gorra,*
dinero)

Starter 1 [8W5]

Aim: to recap the irregular verb *ser*.

Write the following paradigm on the board and ask
pupils to fill it in for *ser*: *yo, tu, él/ella/Ud, nosotros,*
vosotros, ellos/ellas/Uds.

Or, stick a yellow post-it under someone's chair
before the lesson starts with *ser* written on it. When
pupils come in, ask them to check under their seats.
The pupil with the yellow post-it has to conjugate *ser*.
Encourage the class to help if the pupil gets stuck.
Only use this technique with a confident, able class.

1a Escucha (1–3) y lee. Elige las palabras
apropiadas para Alejandro, Paulina y Fran.
(AT1/3, AT3/3) [8T2; 8L3]

✖ Listening for information/instructions, Level C

Listening. Pupils listen to three people thanking others
for presents they have received. They have to pick the
correct words for each speaker and note them down.
Pupils could first read through the options, in pairs,
looking up any unknown vocabulary in the back of the
Pupil's Book or in a dictionary. Teachers could then
check their understanding and answer any queries.

R Teachers may wish to provide the options on a
worksheet for pupils so that they can simply tick the
correct answers, rather than having to copy out
the words.

Tapescript

Alejandro
Queridos abuelos:

Gracias por el CD de Limp Bizkit. Es muy bueno. Me gusta
mucho. Sois muy amables. Hasta pronto. Besos y abrazos,
Alejandro

Paulina
Estimada señora Redondo:
Gracias por la camiseta. Es muy práctica. Me encanta. Es
usted muy amable. Recuerdos a todos. Un saludo cordial,
Paulina

Fran
¡Hola, primo!
Gracias por la foto pero es horrible. No me gusta nada. Eres
antipático. No me escribas nunca más. Adiós, Fran

Answers

Alejandro: 1 Queridos (**e**) abuelos   3 Gracias por (**c**) el
CD   4 Es muy (**c**) bueno   5 (**b**) Me gusta mucho   6 Sois
(**c**) muy amables   7 (**g**) Besos y abrazos

Paulina: 2 Estimada señora   3 Gracias por (**d**) la
camiseta   4 Es muy (**d**) práctica   5 (**a**) Me encanta
6 Es usted (**c**) muy amable   7 (**e**) Recuerdos a todos (**c**)
Un saludo cordial

Fran: 1 ¡Hola! (**d**) primo   3 Gracias por (**f**) la foto
4 Es (**f**) horrible   5 (**c**) No me gusta nada
6 Eres (**e**) antipático   7 (**f**) No me escribas nunca más

1b Elige regalos para tu compañero/a.
Comenta sobre cada regalo. (AT2/3) [8S6]

✖ Speaking about experiences/feelings/opinions,
Level C/D

Speaking pairwork. One pupil chooses a present and
their partner constructs appropriate 'thank you'

6 Muchas gracias por el regalo

phrases, using the boxes in **1a**. They should then swap roles.

1c Mira la postal en **1a** otra vez y escribe una similar. (AT4/4) [8T6]

✖ Writing to establish/maintain personal contact, Level C/D

Writing. Pupils use the phrases from **1a** to write a thank-you postcard.

Starter 2 [8W4; 8T4; 9T4]

Aim: looking words up in the glossary.

Get your pupils to have a quick look at pages 138–150 (glossary). Ask them what the glossary is for. Look for answers like: looking up unknown words; checking spellings of words you are unsure about; checking the gender of words.

Put up about 12 words on the OHP or on the board and ask them to work with a partner to use the glossary to answer the following: What do they mean? Are they spelled correctly (write up *cuidad, augusto, galetas, mokila*)? Are they masculine or feminine (write up *abuelo, palacio, tienda, chuletas*)?

2a Empareja las cartas con los dibujos. Utiliza un diccionario. (AT3/4) [8T2]

✖ Reading for information/instructions, Level D

Reading. Pupils read three letters written in response to an invitation to come and stay, then match each letter to the relevant picture. Pupils should be encouraged at this stage to skim-read the texts and look for clue words, such as *chalet en la costa, casa en las montañas* and *en tu piso.*

Answers

1 b	2 c	3 a

2b Lee las cartas otra vez. ¿Verdad (✓) o mentira (✗)? (AT3/4)

✖ Reading for information/instructions, Level D

Reading. Pupils re-read the letters and do a true/false exercise.

➕ As an extension, pupils could correct the false statements.

Answers

a ✗	b ✓	c ✗	d ✓	e ✗	f ✓	g ✓

2c Recibes una invitación de tu amigo/a español(a). Escribe una carta para aceptarla. Utiliza las cartas de **2a** para ayudarte. (AT4/4) [8S6]

✖ Writing to establish/maintain contact, Level D/E

Writing. Pupils write a letter of acceptance in response to an invitation to come and stay. They should adapt the letters in **2a**, adding their own ideas and vocabulary as appropriate.

R Some pupils might find the letter-writing task easier if they are given a sentence-building grid of key phrases, on copymaster or OHT.

Plenary

Ask pupils to write two things they have learned about understanding a letter in Spanish. Can they skim-read or do they have to pick out every piece of information?

Alternatively, you could ask pupils for three useful phrases they have learned to use when writing a letter.

Cuaderno B, page 8

1a Lee las cartas y rellena el cuadro. (AT3/3, AT4/1–2) [8S4]

✖ Reading for information/instructions, Level D

Reading and writing. After reading two letters, pupils complete a grid in Spanish.

Answers

> **Sofía:** dinero, sus abuelos, muy práctico, sí
> **Rosa:** camiseta de Puerto Rico, su tía Puri, bonita y graciosa, sí

1b Lee las cartas otra vez y empareja las dos partes de las frases. (AT3/2)

✖ Reading for information/instructions, Level D

Reading. Pupils re-read the letters and match up sentence halves.

Answers

1 a	2 d	3 b	4 f	5 e	6 c

2 Recibes una invitación de tu amigo español. Escribe una carta para aceptar esta invitación. (AT4/4) [8T3]

✖ Writing to establish/maintain contact, Level D/E

Writing. A letter-writing exercise, in which pupils accept an invitation to come and stay.

Hojas de trabajo, Resource and Assessment File, pages 5 and 6

Cards for pairwork featuring items of toiletry and gifts: pupils match the pictures to the correct words.

Resumen

This is a checklist of language covered in Module 1. There is a comprehensive **Resumen** list for Module 1 in the Pupil's Book (page 18) and a **Resumen** test sheet in Cuaderno B (page 12).

Prepárate

A revision test to give practice for the test itself at the end of the module.

Resources

Cassette A, side 1
CD1, track 16
Cuaderno B, pages 9–11
Skills, Resource and Assessment file, page 8
Resumen, Resource and Assessment File, page 9

1 Escucha las descripciones. Copia y rellena el cuadro. (AT1/4) [8L3]

✖ Listening for information/instructions, Level D

Listening. Pupils listen to three descriptions and note key information (age, where they live, nationality, family and description of family members) in a grid.

Tapescript

1 – *¿Cómo te llamas?*
– *Me llamo Vicente.*
– *¿Cuántos años tienes?*
– *Tengo 15 años.*
– *¿Dónde vives?*
– *Vivo en Madrid.*
– *¿Cuál es tu nacionalidad?*
– *Soy colombiano.*
– *¿Tienes hermanos?*
– *No, soy hijo único.*
– *¿Cómo eres?*
– *Soy bastante alto y soy moreno.*

2 – *¿Cómo te llamas?*
– *Me llamo Conchita.*
– *¿Cuántos años tienes?*
– *Tengo 13 años.*
– *¿Dónde vives?*
– *Vivo en Barcelona.*
– *¿Cuál es tu nacionalidad?*
– *Soy española.*
– *¿Tienes hermanos?*
– *Sí, tengo una hermana mayor.*
– *¿Cómo es tu pelo?*
– *Tengo el pelo rubio.*
– *¿De qué color son tus ojos?*
– *Tengo los ojos verdes.*

3 – *¿Cómo te llamas?*
– *Me llamo Sebastián.*
– *¿Cuántos años tienes?*
– *Tengo 16 años.*
– *¿Dónde vives?*
– *Vivo en Málaga.*
– *¿Cuál es tu nacionalidad?*
– *Soy francés.*
– *¿Tienes hermanos?*
– *Sí, tengo un hermano gemelo.*
– *¿Cómo eres?*
– *Tengo el pelo largo y los ojos marrones.*

Answers

Nombre	Edad	Vive en ...	Nacionalidad	Familia	Descrip-ción
Vicente	15	Madrid	colombiano	hijo único	bastante alto y moreno
Conchita	13	Barcelona	española	una hermana mayor	pelo rubio y ojos verdes
Sebastián	16	Málaga	francés	un hermano gemelo	pelo largo y ojos marrones

2 Presenta a Enrique o Fátima a tu compañero/a. (AT2/4)

✖ Speaking and interacting with others, Level C/D

Speaking. In pairs, pupils use the information given to introduce one of the two people to their partner.

3 Lee la carta y contesta a las preguntas. (AT3/4) [8S4]

✖ Reading for information/instructions, Level D

Reading. Pupils read a letter about someone's schoolday routine and answer questions in Spanish.

Answers

1 Se levanta a las seis y media.
2 Va al instituto en autobús.
3 Las clases empiezan a las ocho y terminan a la una y media.
4 Hace los deberes.
5 Practica la natación o juega al tenis.
6 Juega bien al tenis.
7 Toca la guitarra muy mal.
8 Su hermana es más musical que él.
9 Escucha música, lee un libro o ve la tele tranquilamente.
10 Se acuesta a las once.

4 Escribe sobre tu rutina diaria. (AT4/4) [8T6]

✖ Exchange information/ideas, Level D/E

Writing. Pupils describe their own daily routine.

Cuaderno B, page 9

Repaso

1 Contesta a las preguntas. (AT4/3) [8S4]

✕ Exchange information/ideas, Level C

Writing. Pupils answer personal information questions, in Spanish.

2a Lee el fichero de Raúl. ¿Verdad (✓) o mentira (✗)? (AT3/3) [8T3; 8C2]

✕ Reading for information/instructions, Level D

Reading. A true/false exercise, based on an identity card.

Answers

1 ✓	2 ✓	3 ✗	4 ✓	5 ✗	6 ✗

2b Corrige las frases falsas. (AT4/3)

✕ Exchange information/ideas, Level C

Writing. Pupils correct the false statements from **1a**.

Answers

1 Su lugar de nacimiento es Madrid.
2 Pesa 76 kg.
3 Mide 1,81 metros.

3 Empareja las dos partes de las frases. (AT3/2)

✕ Knowing about language

Reading. Pupils match up sentence halves.

Answers

1 f	2 d	3 a	4 g	5 c	6 e	7 b	8 h

Cuaderno B, page 10

Gramática 1

1 Write sentences using words from each list in the grid. (AT4/2) [8W4]

✕ Knowing about language

Writing. Pupils write sentences in the comparative, using the support grid and reminder box to help them.

2 Write five sentences using the words in the grid. (AT4/2)

✕ Knowing about language

Writing. This time, pupils use the support grid and reminder box to write sentences in the superlative.

Cuaderno B, page 11

Gramática 2

1 Choose the correct adverbs to complete the sentences. (AT3/2, AT4/1) [9W6]

✕ Knowing about language

Writing. Pupils should read the reminder box about making adjectives into adverbs, then complete the sentences using the picture prompts and list of words provided.

Answers

1 mal 2 bien 3 rápidamente
4 Normalmente 5 tranquilamente

2 Complete the sentences with the correct form of *éste*. (AT3/2, AT4/1) [8W4]

✕ Knowing about language

Writing. A gap-filling exercise using demonstrative adjectives, supported by a reminder box.

Answers

1 Éste	2 Éstos	3 Ésta	4 Éste	5 Ésta	6 Ésta

3 Choose the correct pronoun to complete each sentence. (AT3/2, AT4/1)

✕ Knowing about language

Reading and writing. Pupils should read the reminder box about indirect object pronouns, before completing the gap-filling exercise.

Answers

1 le	2 les	3 Me	4 Le	5 Me	6 Te

Skills, Resource and Assessment File, page 8 (Genders)

1

Answers

Masculine	Meaning	Feminine	Meaning
hermano	*brother*	*hermana*	*sister*
amigo	friend (m)	amiga	friend (f)
tío	uncle	tía	aunt
primo	cousin (m)	*prima*	cousin (f)
abuelo	grandfather	abuela	grandmother
hijo	son	*hija*	daughter

2

Answers

Word	Meaning 1	Meaning 2
a *hermanos*	*brothers*	*brothers and sisters*
b *amigos*	friends (m)	friends (m/f)
c *tíos*	uncles	aunts and uncles
d *primos*	cousins (m)	cousins (m/f)
e *abuelos*	grandfathers	grandparents (m/f)
f *hijos*	sons	sons and daughters

3a

Answers

One meaning

3b

Answers

Sisters

4

Answers

Masculine	Meaning	Feminine	Meaning
el padre			mother
el póster			city
el fútbol			t-shirt

5

Answer

The article: el = masculine   la = feminine

6

Answers

Masculine	Meaning	Feminine	Meaning
el padre	the father	la madre	the mother
el póster	the poster	la ciudad	the city
el fútbol	the football	la camiseta	the t-shirt

7

Answers

Masculine	Meaning	Feminine	Meaning
un padre	a father	una madre	a mother
un póster	a poster	una ciudad	a city
–	–	una camiseta	a t-shirt

(You may wish to explain to pupils that *fútbol* cannot take an indefinite article, as it refers to the game and not to the ball itself.)

módulo 1

7 ¡Extra! ¡Escríbeme pronto!

(Pupil's Book pages 20–21)

Main topics

This is an optional extension unit, which reviews some of the key language of the module. It consists of letters posted on a bulletin board at a website from young people interested in contacting others with similar interests or selling items.

Key Framework objectives

Daily life and young people 8C3 (Launch)

Verb tenses (and conditional) 9W5 (Launch)
Using grammar to understand words 9W8 (Launch)
Understanding complex language 9T1 (Launch)
Features for effect 9T2 (Launch)
Authentic texts as source 9T3 (Launch)

Resources

Cassette A, side 1
CD1, track 17

Starter 1

Aim: to revise some of language that comes up in the reading texts.

Write up *Me gusta(n) ...* , *Me encanta(n) ...* and *Estoy loco/a por ... .* (You will have to explain the meaning of this.) Give pupils two minutes to write a sentence beginning with each phrase.

1a Lee las cartas y contesta a las preguntas. (AT3/4) [8S4; 8T2; 8C3; 9W5,8; 9T1,2,3]

✖ Reading for information/instructions, Level E

Reading. Magazine-style page in which teenagers looking for penfriends describe themselves and their interests. Introduce the activity by asking pupils what sort of information they think is likely to be given in the 'looking for a penfriend' letters and the 'for sale' notices (name, age, personality, interests, etc.) Then give pupils three or four minutes to find as many adjectives as they can in the texts. Do they know the meaning of them? Which can they guess?

Next you could ask pupils to work in pairs. They should find one piece of information from each letter. Encourage them to find something their colleagues may not have found. Focus on two or three of the texts and ask the class to give their pieces of information. Point out the use of *Me gustaría* in the letters.

Pupils should now feel some familiarity with the texts and they can go on to answer a series of questions in Spanish.

Answers

a Pedro Gómez vive en Tenerife.
b Carlos Sánchez tiene 14 años.
c Creo que Carlos Sánchez es loco y divertido.
d Ana Luisa está loca por Brad Pitt.
e Le gusta la música; Valencia es su equipo preferido.
f Son simpáticas y abiertas.
g Vende 800 juegos.
h Vende órgano electrónico.

1b Empareja cada frase con la persona apropiada en **1a**. (AT3/4)

✖ Reading for information/instructions, Level E

Reading. Pupils match the sentences with people in exercise **1a**.

Answers

a *Pedro* b Ana Luisa c Isabel y Mireia
d Nieves Barreto e Wenceslas f Carlos Sánchez

1c Elige una de las cartas. Con tu compañero/a, pregunta y contesta para adivinar quién eres. (AT2/3)

✖ Speaking and interacting with others, Level C

Speaking. Pupils work in pairs: one makes a statement from one of the letters on page 20 and their partner guesses whose letter it comes from.

2 Escucha. Copia y rellena el cuadro. (AT1/4) [8L3]

✖ Listening for information/instructions, Level D

Listening. Pupils listen to a series of people describing themselves (age, eye colour, hair and interests) and complete the grid.

Tapescript

Ejemplo: ¡Hola! Me llamo Martín. Tengo 15 años. Tengo los ojos azules y el pelo negro. Me gustan la música y el baloncesto.

Me llamo Ester. Tengo 13 años. Tengo los ojos marrones y el pelo negro. Me gustan mucho los animales.

Mi nombre es Antonio. Tengo 16 años. Tengo los ojos verdes y el pelo castaño. Me encantan la música y el fútbol. Soy un aficionado de Deportivo de La Coruña. ¡Forza Depor!

¡Hola! Me llamo Carolina. Soy rubia y tengo los ojos azules. Me gusta el cine y me gusta salir con mis amigos. Mi actor preferido es Brad Pitt – es guapísimo.

Me llamo José. Tengo los ojos marrones y el pelo negro. Me gustan las motos y la música rock. Escríbeme o mándame un e-mail.

Answers

	Martín	Ester	Antonio	Carolina	José
edad	*15 años*	13 años	16 años	–	–
los ojos	*azules*	marrones	verdes	azules	marrones
el pelo	*negro*	negro	castaño	rubio	negro
le gusta	*la música, el balon-cesto*	los animales	la música, el fútbol	el cine, salir con sus amigos, Brad Pitt	las motos, la música rock

3 Write a letter in Spanish to *Mega Pop* magazine imagining either situation 'a' or 'b'. (AT4/4)

✕ Exchange information/ideas, Level D/E

Writing. Pupils choose 'a' or 'b' and write a letter using vocabulary they have learned in the unit.

Te toca a ti

(Pupil's Book pages 112–113)

● Self-access reading and writing at two levels

Key Framework objectives

Work of famous artists 9C2 (Launch)

A Reinforcement

1a Escribe una frase para cada dibujo. Elige los verbos de la lista. (AT4/3) [8W5; 9W5]

✉ Exchange information/ideas, Level B

Writing. Pupils write a sentence about daily routine, to go with each picture, using the infinitives given.

Answers

1 *Se levanta a las seis y media.*
2 Desayuna a las siete menos cuarto.
3 Llega a la escuela a las siete y cuarto.
4 Come a las dos.
5 Hace los deberes a las cuatro y veinte.
6 Juega al fútbol a las siete menos veinte.
7 Ve la televisión a las nueve y diez.
8 Se acuesta a las once.

1b Escribe frases similares sobre tu rutina. (AT4/3) [8W5; 9W5]

✉ Exchange information/ideas, Level C

Writing. Pupils write similar sentences about their own daily routine.

2 Empareja las dos partes de las frases. (AT3/2) [8W4]

✉ Knowing about language

Reading. Pupils pair up halves of sentences, drawn from a range of topics and language areas covered in the module.

Answers

1 *d* 2 g 3 b 4 f 5 a 6 e 7 c 8 j 9 i 10 h

B Extension

1a Lee la ficha. ¿Verdad (✓) o mentira (✗)? (AT3/4) [8C2; 9C2]

✉ Reading for information/instructions, Level D

Reading. Pupils read a profile of Antonio Banderas and do a true/false exercise.

Answers

1 ✓ 2 ✓ 3 ✓ 4 ✗ 5 ✗ 6 ✗ 7 ✗ 8 ✓

1b Escribe una ficha similar sobre otra persona famosa. (AT4/4)

✉ Writing imaginatively, Level D

Writing. Pupils write a similar profile of another famous person. They could use the Internet to look up relevant information.

2 Lee el test y elige las frases que te corresponden. Después suma el total de respuestas A y B y lee tus resultados. (AT3/4)

✉ Reading for pleasure

Reading. Pupils do a magazine-style quiz about personality.

Unit	Key Framework objectives	PoS	Key language and Grammar
1 ¿Qué comes? (pp. 24–25) Saying what you have to eat Talking about meal times in Spain and the UK	8W1 Adding abstract words [L] 8W2 Connectives [L] 8S6 Substituting and adding [R]	**1a** sounds and writing **2a** listen for gist and detail **2b** correct pronunciation/ intonation **2f** adapt language for different contexts **2g** dealing with the unpredictable **2i** report main points **4c** comparing cultures **5h** use TL for real purposes	Expressing likes and dislikes: *me encanta(n)* *me gusta(n) (mucho)* *no me gusta(n) (nada)* *odio* *¿Qué desayunas?* *Desayuno mariscos.* *¿Qué comes de primer plato?* *Como sopa.* *Ceno carne.* *Tomo fruta.* *a veces* *normalmente* *siempre*
2 ¿Qué te gusta comer? (pp. 26–27) Saying what type of food you like and why Using *¿Por qué?* and *porque*	8L4 Extending sentences [L] 8W4 Word endings [R]	**2a** listen for gist and detail **2c** ask and answer questions **2f** adapt language for different contexts **2h** scanning written texts **2i** report main points **3d** use reference materials **4b** communicating with native speakers **4c** compare cultures **5c** express opinions **5e** range of resources	Adjective agreements *El flan es delicioso.* *La ensalada es nutritiva.* *Los perritos calientes están ricos.* *Las salchichas son grasientas.* *soler* Food from different countries *¿Qué tipo de comida te gusta?* *Me gusta/Prefiero la comida india.* *¿Cuál es tu plato favorito?* *Mi plato favorito es chuletas.* *¿Por qué? Porque es (está)/son (están) …*
3 De compras (pp. 28–29) Buying fruit and vegetables Finding out how much things cost	8W1 Adding abstract words [R] 8L3 Relaying gist and detail [R] 8S6 Substituting and adding [R]	**1a** sounds and writing **2a** listen for gist and detail **2b** correct pronunciation and intonation **2c** ask and answer questions	*¿Qué desea?* *Déme un kilo de naranjas.* *¿Cuánto cuesta … ?* *Cuesta … euro(s).* *¿Algo más?* *Nada más, gracias.*
4 Cien gramos de jamón y una barra de pan (pp. 30–31) Buying food and drink in a shop Numbers 31–1000	8W1 Adding abstract words [R] 8L1 Listening for subtleties [R] 8L3 Relaying gist and detail [R]	**1a** sounds and writing **2b** correct pronunciation and intonation	Numbers 31–1000 *¿Qué desea?* *Una botella de limonada, por favor.* *¿Algo más? Sí, …* *No, nada más, gracias.*
5 ¡Qué aproveche! (pp. 32–33) Saying you are hungry and thirsty Ordering tapas and drinks	8T1 Meanings in context [L] 8C5 Colloquialisms [L] 8W5 Verbs (future) [L] 8T6 Text as model and source [R] 8L1 Listening for subtleties [R]	**1a** sounds and writing **2b** correct pronunciation and intonation **2c** ask and answer questions **2f** adapt language for different contexts **3a** memorising **4a** working with authentic materials **4c** compare cultures **5e** range of resources	Pronouns with prepositions *tener:* *¿Tienes hambre/sed?* *Tengo hambre/sed.* *No tiene mucha hambre.* *¿Qué va(n) a tomar?* *Para mí, aceitunas.* *¿De beber, qué va(n) a tomar?* *Para él, una cerveza.* *¿Va(n) a tomar algo más?* *Para ella, un flan.* *La cuenta, por favor.*

Unit	Key Framework objectives	PoS	Key language and Grammar
6 La comida sana (pp. 34–35) Talking about healthy eating	8T3 Language and text types [L] 8W5 Verbs (present) [R] 8S5 Negative forms and words [R]	**2j** redraft writing **3d** use knowledge of English **4a** working with authentic materials **5e** range of resources **5h** use TL for real purposes	*¿Con qué frecuencia comes carne (roja)?* *una vez a la semana/al año* *algunas veces a la semana/al mes* *todos los días* *¿Comes pescado?* *No como carne y no bebo leche.* *No me gustan mucho las verduras.* *Prefiero el pan integral.*
Resumen y Prepárate (pp. 36–37) Pupils' checklist and practice test			
7 ¡Extra! ¡Feliz Navidad! (pp. 38–39) Optional unit: Christmas	8W7 Dictionary detail [L] 9L4 Questions/text as stimulus to talk [L] 8W1 Adding abstract words [R] 9W8 Using grammar to understand words [R] 9T1 Understanding complex language [R] 9T3 Authentic texts as sources [R]	**2j** redraft writing **3b** use context to interpret meanings **4c** compare cultures **4d** consider experiences in other countries **5d** different types of language **5g** listening/reading for enjoyment	
Te toca a ti (pp. 114–115) Self-access reading and writing at two levels	9C4 Well-known features of the country [L]		

1 ¿Qué comes?

(Pupil's Book pages 24–25)

Main topics

- Saying what you have to eat
- Talking about meal times in Spain and the UK

Key Framework objectives

- Adding abstract words 8W1 (Launch)
- Connectives 8W2 (Launch)
- Substituting and adding 8S6 (Reinforcement)
- Dictionary use 8T4 (Reinforcement)
- Text as model and source 8T6 (Reinforcement)
- Using support materials 9T4 (Reinforcement)

Grammar

- Me encanta(n) …
- (No) Me gusta(n) …
- Odio …

Key language

¿Te gusta …?
Me encanta(n) …
Me gusta(n) (mucho)…
No me gusta(n) (nada)…

Odio …
el arroz   el pescado

la carne	*el pollo*
la ensalada	*las salchichas*
la fruta	*la sopa*
el helado	*la tarta*
los huevos	*las verduras*
los mariscos	

¿Qué desayunas/comes/cenas/tomas?
Desayuno/Como/Ceno/Tomo …
(de) primer plato
(de) segundo plato
(de) postre

a veces/normalmente/siempre

Resources

Cassette A, side 2
CD1, tracks 18 and 19
Cuaderno B, page 13
Starter 2, Resource and Assessment File, page 24
Hojas de trabajo, Resource and Assessment File, pages 26 and 27 (*los huevos, las verduras, la carne, un helado, el pescado, el pollo*)
Starter 2, Resource and Assessment File, page 24
OHTs 7 and 8
Flashcards 1–7 and 15, 18 (*¡Listos! 1*)

Starter 1 [8W4]

Aim: to talk about likes and dislikes in different contexts.

Write *Me encanta(n) … , (No) Me gusta(n) …, Odio …* on the board.

Ask pupils to write down two things they like or love and two things they dislike or hate. Ask a few pupils to read out one of their sentences.

1a ¿Qué comida le gusta o no le gusta a Rodrigo? Escribe la letra del dibujo y marca con ✓ o ✗. (1–8) (AT1/3) [8W1; 8L1]

✗ Listening for information/instructions, Level C

Listening. Before doing the listening activity, present the new food items to the class, for example by reading each one out loud, then saying them at random and asking pupils to give the letter of the correct picture. You can then say the letter and ask pupils to give you the word. Pay attention to pronunciation. This is a good opportunity to revise short vowel sounds and also the mute 'h' (in *helado* and *huevos*).

Pupils hear Rodrigo answering a series of questions about whether he likes specific food items. They must note down the letter of each item of food shown on the page and put either a tick or a cross next to it, to show whether he likes or dislikes it. The *Gramática* box on page 24 reminds pupils of *(No) Me gusta(n)*, *Me encanta(n)* and *Odio*, which were introduced in *¡Listos! 1*, Module 3.

Tapescript

1 – ¿Rodrigo, te gusta el pollo?
  – Sí, me gusta mucho el pollo, también me gusta mucho el arroz.
2 – ¿Te gustan los mariscos?
  – No, no me gustan los mariscos, prefiero las verduras.
3 – ¿Te gusta la sopa?
  – No, no me gusta nada la sopa, prefiero la ensalada.
4 – ¿Te gustan los huevos?
  – Me encantan los huevos.
5 – ¿Te gustan las salchichas?
  – No, no me gustan nada las salchichas.
6 – ¿Te gusta el pescado?
  – No, odio el pescado. Prefiero la carne.
7 – ¿Te gusta el helado?
  – Sí, me encanta.
8 – ¿Te gusta la fruta?
  – No me gusta la fruta. Prefiero la tarta.

Answers

1 e✓ f✓	**2** a✗ c✓	**3** d✗ b✓	**4** h✓	**5** g✗
6 i✗ m✓	**7** l✓	**8** k✗ j✓		

1b Con tu compañero/a, pregunta y contesta. (AT2/3) [8S4]

✗ Speaking about experiences/feelings/opinions, Level C

Speaking. Pupils work in pairs, taking it in turns to ask one another whether they like certain food items. Before pupils tackle this activity, teachers should give the class oral practice of saying the new food vocabulary and reinforce this through repetition games. For example, pupils close their books, teachers choose the letter of one of the pictures on page 24 and give pupils two options: b – *la ensalada o las verduras?* Pupils must then say the correct option. This could be played as a team memory game, to add a competitive edge. Following this, teachers could simply give a letter and pupils have to say the name of the food item.

2a ¿Qué comen o cenan estas personas? Copia y rellena el cuadro. (1–4) (AT1/4) [8L3]

⚐ Listening for information/instructions, Level D

Listening. This exercise introduces a range of new language for talking about what you eat, including the first and second person singular of *comer, tomar* and *cenar,* the expressions *de primer plato, de segundo plato, de postre* and the adverbs or adverbial expressions *normalmente, generalmente, a veces* and *siempre.* Teachers should ensure pupils understand the names of the three courses on the grid, which pupils have to copy out and complete. However, pupils should be encouraged to listen for key words they need to do the task, rather than trying to understand everything they hear. As a follow-up, teachers may wish to check pupils' understanding of the three verbs and adverbs/adverbial expressions listed above.

Tapescript

1 – ¿Qué comes de primer plato, Pablo?
 – Normalmente como verduras de primer plato.
 – ¿Y de segundo plato?
 – Pues, a veces arroz con pollo y ensalada.
 – ¿Y de postre?
 – Siempre como fruta.
2 – ¿Qué cenas, Ester?
 – De primer plato siempre tomo sopa.
 – ¿Y qué tomas de segundo plato?
 – A veces tomo pescado, pescado con un poco de ensalada.
 – ¿Y de postre?
 – De postre tomo helado.
3 – ¿Qué comes, Rubén?
 – A veces como mariscos de primer plato.
 – ¿Y de segundo plato?
 – De segundo plato normalmente como carne.
 – ¿Y de postre?
 – No como postre.
4 – ¿Qué cenas, Patricia?
 – No tomo primer plato. A veces ceno salchichas y huevos.
 – ¿Y de postre?
 – No tomo postre generalmente, pero a veces tomo tarta.

Answers

	primer plato			segundo plato							postre		
	a	b	c	d	e	f	g	h	i	j	k	l	m
Pablo		✓		✓	✓	✓							✓
Ester			✓		✓				✓		✓		
Rubén	✓		.							✓			
Patricia							✓	✓				✓	

Starter 2 [8W1]

Aim: to revise food vocabulary.

Using *Resource and Assessment File,* page 24, ask pupils to work out the following words which have their vowels missing: p*sc*d* (*pescado*), s*p* (*sopa*), h**v*s (*huevos*), *ns*l*d* (*ensalada*), t*rt* (*tarta*), p*ll* (*pollo*), h*l*d* (*helado*), fr*t* (*fruta*), s*lch*ch*s (*salchichas*), v*rd*r*s (*verduras*). When asking for the answers, pay attention to short vowel sounds and the silent '*h*' in *helado* and *huevos*.

2b Con tu compañero/a, pregunta y contesta. (AT2/3) [8W1]

⚐ Speaking and interacting with others, Level C/D

Speaking. Pupils ask and answer questions about what they have for breakfast and their main meal of the day, following a model dialogue. The grid on page 24 also gives them support and teachers should check that pupils are confident with the pronunciation of these key phrases, as well as of the questions, before beginning the pairwork. Pupils may also need reminding of the breakfast food and drink vocabulary first introduced in *¡Listos! 1,* Module 3. This could be done via a brainstorming or a dictionary activity. Able pupils, in particular, should be encouraged to use a range of adverbs/adverbial expressions in the pairwork task.

3a Lee el correo electrónico de Fátima. ¿Verdad (✓) o mentira (✗)? Utiliza un diccionario. (AT3/4) [8T4; 9T4]

⚐ Listening for information/instructions, Level D

Reading. Pupils read an email in which a girl describes her mealtimes and what she eats, then do a true/false exercise. They should first read the text for gist, then use a dictionary, if necessary, to help them answer the questions.

Answers

1✗	2✗	3✓	4✗	5✓	6✗	7✓	8✓	9✗	10✗

3b Corrige las frases falsas. (AT4/4) [8S6]

⚐ Exchange information/ideas, Level C

Writing. Pupils correct the false sentences in **3a**.

Answers

1	Fátima no desayuna mucho.
2	Toma café con leche.
4	Fátima come a las dos.
6	Los domingos Fátima come mariscos de primer plato.
9	De primer plato toma tortilla.
10	De postre hay fruta.

3c Contesta al correo electrónico de Fátima. (AT4/4) [8S6; 8T6]

✖ Writing to establish/maintain contact, Level D/E

Writing. Pupils write a reply to the email, describing their mealtimes and what they eat.

✚ Able students should be encouraged to adapt and supplement the email text in **3a**, making use of a range of adverbs/adverbial expressions and giving opinions about food items, where appropriate.

R Less able pupils might benefit from being given a writing frame of key expressions, perhaps in the form of a sentence- or paragraph-building grid, on a worksheet or OHT.

Plenary [8W2]

Talk about the words/phrases in the reading text in **3a** that you can use in other contexts to lengthen your sentences and to make your writing more interesting. With an able group you could ask pupils for suggestions. With other groups you could ask them to find the Spanish for: normally (*normalmente*), always (*siempre*), sometimes (*a veces*), for example (*por ejemplo*), or (*o*), and (*y*), a lot of (*mucho/a*).

Cuaderno B, page 13

1a Lee los globos, mira los dibujos y escribe los números en el cuadro. (AT3/3)

✖ Reading for information/instructions, Level D

Reading. Pupils read about people's eating habits and fill in the numbers of the correct pictures on a grid.

Answers

	primer plato	segundo plato	postre
Carlota	3	4	9
Fernando	–	6, 8	11
Paco	1	5	–
Amanda	1	7, 8	10

1b Rellena el globo sobre ti. (AT4/4) [8W2; 8S6; 8T6]

✖ Exchange information/ideas, Level D/E

Writing. Pupils use the texts in **1a** as models to write about their own eating habits.

Hojas de trabajo, Resource and Assessment File, pages 26 and 27

Cards for pairwork featuring various foods: pupils match the pictures to the correct words.

módulo 2 — 2 ¿Qué te gusta comer?

(Pupil's Book pages 26–27)

Main topics and objectives
Saying what type of food you like and why

Key Framework objectives
- Extending sentences 8L4 (Launch)
- Word endings 8W4 (Reinforcement)

Grammar
- Agreement of adjectives
- *soler*

Key language

¿Qué tipo de comida te gusta?
Me gusta/Prefiero la comida ...

caribeña	*italiana*
china	*mexicana*
india	*rápida*
vegetariana	

¿Cuál es tu plato preferido?
Mi plato preferido es ...

las chuletas	*los perritos calientes*
el flan	*las salchichas*
las gambas	

¿Por qué?
Porque es (está)/son (están) ...

delicioso/a(s)	*rico/a(s)*
dulce(s)	*sabroso/a(s)*
grasiento/a(s)	*salado/a(s)*
nutritivo/a(s)	*sano/a(s)*
picante(s)	

¿Sueles comer ... ?
Sí, suelo comer ...
No, no suelo comer ...

Resources
Cassette A, side 1
CD1, tracks 20 and 21
Cuaderno B, page 14
Starter 2, Resource and Assessment File, page 24
Grammar, Resource and Assessment File, page 28
Flashcards 8–11

Starter 1 [8W4]

Aim: to recap the use of the definite article with nouns.

First you may wish to brainstorm the definite article with your class.

Write the following on the board, or prepare an OHT and ask pupils to fill in the gaps with the correct form of the definite article: ... *comida italiana*, ... *perritos calientes*, ... *flan*, ... *chuletas*, ... *manzana*, ... *ciudad*, ... *chocolate*, ... *plátanos*.

1a ¿Qué tipo de comida les gusta a estas personas? (1–6) (AT1/3) [8L3]

✂ Listening for information/instructions, Level D

Listening. Pupils listen to a series of people saying what type of food they like and note down the letter of the relevant photograph. Teachers should first familiarise pupils with the sound of the seven types of food listed on page 26. As a follow-up, teachers may wish to play the recording again and see how many names of specific food items pupils can recognise.

Tapescript

1 – ¿Qué tipo de comida te gusta?
  – Me encanta la comida rápida, el chocolate, las patatas fritas, los caramelos. Todo tipo de comida rápida. Suelo comer chocolate y patatas fritas todos los días.
2 – ¿Qué tipo de comida te gusta?
  – Me encanta la comida mexicana, me encantan las fajitas, las tortillas, el guacamole ...

3 – ¿Qué tipo de comida te gusta a ti?
  – Pues, a mi me gusta la comida china, el arroz, los fideos, todo tipo de comida china.
4 – ¿Qué tipo de comida te gusta?
  – Soy de Cuba en el Caribe. Prefiero la comida caribeña.
5 – ¿Qué tipo de comida te gusta?
  – Soy vegetariana. No como carne ni pescado. Prefiero legumbres y verduras.
6 – ¿Qué tipo de comida te gusta a ti?
  – Adoro la comida italiana. Suelo comer macarrones o espaguetis todos los días de primer plato.

Answers

1 *a*	2 e	3 c	4 f	5 g	6 d

1b Haz un sondeo. Pregunta a tus compañeros/as de clase. Copia y rellena el cuadro. (AT2/4) [8S4, 6]

Speaking. Pupils conduct a class survey about the types of food people prefer, using the grid provided.

💾 As a follow-up, pupils could enter the results of their survey into an Excel spreadsheet and create a bar graph or pie chart, using the chart wizard.

2a Escucha y elige las opiniones apropiadas de Martín para cada plato. (AT1/4) [8L4]

✂ Listening for information/instructions, Level D

Listening. Pupils listen to a boy answering questions about why he likes or dislikes certain food items and note down the adjectives he uses. A number of new adjectives for describing food are used and these are

44

listed on page 26. Before undertaking the listening exercise, pupils could work in pairs with a dictionary to establish the meaning of the nine adjectives. Teachers should also ensure pupils are familiar with the sound of these new words and direct them to the *Gramática* box on page 26, which reminds them about adjectival agreement.

Tapescript

1 – ¿Cuál es tu plato preferido, Martín?
 – Adoro los perritos calientes. Están muy ricos.
2 – ¿Te gustan las salchichas?
 – No, no me gustan.
 – ¿Por qué?
 – Porque son muy grasientas.
3 – ¿Cuál es tu postre preferido?
 – Mi postre preferido es el flan. Suelo comer flan los domingos.
 – ¿Por qué?
 – Porque es dulce. Me gustan las cosas dulces.
4 – ¿Te gustan las gambas?
 – Me encantan las gambas, especialmente al ajillo. Son deliciosas.
5 – ¿Te gustan las chuletas?
 – Me encantan las chuletas. Son sabrosas. Suelo comer chuletas una vez a la semana.
6 – ¿Te gustan las sardinas?
 – No me gustan mucho pero son muy nutritivas.

Answers

1 *ricos* 2 grasientas 3 dulce 4 deliciosas
5 sabrosas 6 nutritivas

Starter 2 [8W4]

Aim: categorising adjectives.

Using *Resource and Assessment File*, page 24, ask pupils to categorise the following adjectives under the headings masculine singular/masculine plural/feminine singular/feminine plural:
sano, rica, grasientos, nutritivas, sabrosos, sana, deliciosa, deliciosos, grasienta, saladas, sabroso, picante, dulces.

Ask pupils to write down the meaning of each.

2b Con tu compañero/a, pregunta y contesta. (AT2/3) [8S4]

Speaking about experiences/feelings/opinions, Level D

Speaking. Pupils work in pairs to ask each other what their favourite dish is and why, following the model dialogue. Teachers should first give pupils oral practice of using the adjectives and making these agree with various food items.

3a Lee las opiniones de las personas. Empareja los dibujos con las descripciones. (AT3/3) [8T2; 9T2]

Reading for information/instructions, Level D

Reading. Pupils read three texts about Spanish, Caribbean and Mexican food, then match each one to the correct picture. In this first reading task, pupils should be encouraged to skim the texts for information, rather than trying to understand every word, or to use a dictionary. The verb *soler* is used in the first text and teachers may wish to direct pupils initially to the *Gramática* box on page 27, which explains it.

Answers

1 c 2 a 3 b

3b Contesta a las preguntas. (AT3/3)

Reading for information/instructions, Level D

Reading. Pupils now read the texts for more detail and answer questions in English. They may need to use a dictionary at this point. As a follow-up, teachers may wish to do a 'find the Spanish for … ' exercise, to draw pupils' attention to key phrases, which could be used in the writing task **3c**, below. Phrases such as (*La paella es*) *un plato de … y … ; Un plato típico* (*cubano*) *es … ; No es … ni …* and *¡Qué rico!* could all be useful.

Answers

1 rice, seafood, fish
2 Spanish people eat a lot of fish.
3 He thinks Caribbean food is tasty/delicious.
4 fried chicken with rice and black beans and fried plantain
5 It's salty and greasy.
6 She likes Mexican food.
7 avocados and tomatoes, with a little chilli
8 It's spicy.

3c Escribe frases sobre la comida y los platos que te gustan y no te gustan. (AT4/4) [8S6; 8T6]

Exchange information/ideas, Level C/D

Writing. Pupils write about what food they like and dislike and why, following the model texts in **3a**. They should pay particular attention to adjectival agreement. Before pupils start writing, teachers may wish to show them how they can adapt key phrases, lifted from the texts in **3a** to write about their own preferences, for example, by asking how you would say 'A typical (English) meal is … ', or 'Spaghetti bolognese is a dish of … with … '.

Some pupils could be encouraged to use the verb *soler* in their written work.

Plenary [8W4]
Give the beginning of a sentence about an item of food and ask pupils to write down a suitable adjective for it. Remind the class that the adjective will have to agree with the food in both number and gender.

el flan es … , la ensalada es … , los perritos calientes son … , las salchichas son … , el chocolate es … , el pescado es … , la sopa es … , la comida rápida es … , la comida india es … , la comida mexicana es …

Cuaderno B, page 14

1 Empareja las dos partes de las frases. (AT3/2) [8W4; 8S5]

✕ Knowing about language

Reading. Pupils match sentence halves about food preferences.

Answers

1 c	2 e	3 a	4 d	5 g	6 f	7 b

2a Empareja las descripciones con los dibujos. (AT3/3)

✕ Reading for information/instructions, Level D

Reading. Pupils match shorts texts about food preferences to the pictures.

Answers

1 d	2 b	3 a	4 c

2b ¿Verdad (✓) o mentira (✗)? (AT3/2)

✕ Reading for information/instructions, Level D

Reading. A true/false exercise, based on the texts in 2a.

Answers

1 ✓	2 ✓	3 ✓	4 ✗	5 ✗	6 ✗

2c Corrige las frases que son falsas. (AT4/3) [8S6]

✕ Exchange information/ideas, Level C

Writing. Pupils correct the false phrases in **2b**.

Answers

1 A Amalia le gusta la comida italiana porque es deliciosa.
2 Siempre come macarrones de primer plato.
3 A Santiago le gusta la comida española.

Grammar, Resource and Assessment File, page 28

How to talk about likes and dislikes

1

Pupils look at the prompts to decide on the correct form of the verb *gustar* and write sentences about their opinions.

Answers

a No me gusta el pescado.
b Me gustan los tomates.
c Me encanta el queso.
d No me gustan las hamburguesas.
e Me gusta la carne.

2

Pupils write their own opinions using *gusta/gustan*.

Using adjectives

3

Pupils fill in a grid with the correct forms of the adjectives according to whether they are masculine (sing. or pl.) or feminine (sing. or pl.).

Answers

Masculine	Masc. pl	Feminine	Fem. pl	Meaning
delicioso	deliciosos	*deliciosa*	deliciosos	*delicious*
dulce	dulces	*dulce*	dulces	sweet
grasiento	grasientos	grasienta	*grasientas*	fatty
nutritivo	*nutritivos*	nutritiva	nutritivas	nutritious
rico	ricos	rica	ricas	tasty
sano	sanos	sana	sanas	*healthy*

4

Pupils are given various foods (masc./fem./sing./pl.) plus an adjective and must make a sentence, using the correct form of each adjective.

Answers

a El arroz es nutritivo.
b Las verduras son sanas.
c Los caramelos son dulces.
d La hamburguesa es grasienta.
e El flan está rico.

5

Pupils now write sentences of their own using the rules they have practised.

3 De compras

(Pupil's Book pages 28–29)

Main topics

- Buying fruit and vegetables
- Finding out how much things cost

Key Framework objectives

- Adding abstract words 8W1 (Reinforcement)
- Relaying gist and detail 8L3 (Reinforcement)
- Substituting and adding 8S6 (Reinforcement)

Other aims

- Pronounciation

Key language

¿Qué desea?
Deme …
un kilo de …
un cuarto kilo de …
medio kilo de …
un kilo y medio de …
dos kilos de …

¿Cuánto cuesta …?
Cuesta … euro(s).

las cebollas	*las peras*
las lechugas	*los plátanos*
las manzanas	*los tomates*
las naranjas	*las uvas*
las patatas	*las zanahorias*

¿Algo más?
Nada más, gracias.

Resources

Cassette A, side 2
CD1, tracks 22, 23, 24 and 25
Cuaderno B, page 15
Starter 1, Resource and Assessment File, page 25
Hojas de trabajo, Resource and Assessment File, pages 26 and 27 (*las uvas, las naranjas, los plátanos, las patatas, una lechuga*)
OHTs 9 and 10
Flashcards 12–16

Starter 1 [8W1; 8L1]

Aim: vocabulary work: fruit and vegetables.

Using *Resource and Assessment File*, page 25, tell pupils that you are going to read a list of new words. They must use their knowledge of how letters sound to pick the appropriate ending for each word. (With an able group you could read the beginnings out in a different order so that they have to find both parts of each word.)

Text to read: *las cebollas, las lechugas, las manzanas, las naranjas, las patatas, las peras, los plátanos, los tomates, las uvas, las zanahorias*

Reveal the third column showing the complete words. Ask pupils to guess at the meanings. (Some are cognates.)

1a Escucha y escribe las frutas y verduras en el orden correcto. (1–10) (AT1/1)

✉ Listening for information/instructions, Level A

Listening. Pupils list the fruit and vegetables shown on page 28 in the order in which they are mentioned in the recording. Teachers may wish to familiarise pupils with the sound of each item, using the photograph on the page, before they listen to the recording.

Tapescript

1 *las peras*
2 *las patatas*
3 *los tomates*
4 *los plátanos*
5 *las zanahorias*
6 *las cebollas*
7 *las naranjas*
8 *las uvas*
9 *las manzanas*
10 *las lechugas*

Answers

1 c	2 g	3 f	4 a	5 j	6 i	7 b	8 d	9 e	10 h

1b Escucha otra vez y repite. Pon atención a la pronunciación. (AT1/1) [8L1]

✉ Listening for information/instructions, Level A

Speaking. Pupils listen again to the text in **1a** and repeat after the recording to practise pronouncing the vocabulary correctly.

Tapescript

Tapescript as **1a**

2a ¿Qué compran los clientes y en qué cantidades? (1–5) (AT1/3) [8L3]

✉ Listening for information/instructions, Level D

Listening. Pupils hear a series of dialogues in which people buy fruit and vegetables. They note down what is bought and the quantity. The support box on page 28 lists key quantities used and teachers should refer pupils to this before beginning the exercise. As a follow-up, teachers may wish to play the recording again and ask pupils to listen out for key shopping expressions (*¿Qué desea?, Deme … , ¿Tiene … ?, Tome usted, ¿Algo más?* and *Nada más*), asking them what they think each one means.

módulo 2

3 De compras

Tapescript

1 – Buenos días. ¿Qué desea?
  – Un kilo de naranjas.
  – ¿Algo más?
  – No, nada más, gracias.
2 – Buenos días, señora. ¿Qué desea?
  – Medio kilo de peras.
  – Muy bien, medio kilo de peras. ¿Algo más?
  – Sí, deme dos lechugas y medio kilo de tomates.
  – Medio kilo de tomates y dos lechugas. Tome usted.
3 – Buenas tardes, señor. ¿Qué desea?
  – ¿Tiene plátanos?
  – Sí, hay plátanos.
  – Pues, un cuarto kilo de plátanos.
  – ¿Algo más?
  – Sí, dos kilos de manzanas.
4 – Buenos días. ¿Qué desea?
  – ¿Hay zanahorias?
  – Sí, son muy buenas.
  – Medio kilo de zanahorias.
  – ¿Algo más?
  – Sí, un cuarto kilo de uvas.
  – Tome usted, medio kilo de zanahorias y un cuarto kilo de uvas.
5 – Buenas tardes. ¿Qué desea?
  – Un kilo y medio de cebollas y dos kilos de patatas.
  – Tome usted, kilo y medio de cebollas y dos kilos de patatas. ¿Algo más?
  – Nada más, gracias.

Answers

1 un kilo de naranjas
2 medio kilo de peras, dos lechugas, medio kilo de tomates
3 un cuarto kilo de plátanos, dos kilos de manzanas
4 medio kilo de zanahorias, un cuarto kilo de uvas
5 un kilo y medio de cebollas, dos kilos de patatas

2b Mira los dibujos. Con tu compañero/a, pregunta y contesta. (AT2/3) [8S6]

✕ Speaking and interacting with others, Level D

Speaking. A role-play in which pupils must ask for fruit and vegetables, in the quantities shown, following a model dialogue. In addition to the expressions used in the model, teachers may wish to encourage pupils to use others, such as *deme* and *tome usted*.

Starter 2

Aim: to revise numbers between 100 and 500.

Use mini-whiteboards or pen and paper. Call out a series of numbers between 100 and 500. Ask pupils to write these down as you call them out and hold up their whiteboard or pieces of paper for you to see.

3a ¿En qué orden se mencionan los precios y cuáles son? (1–6) (AT1/3) [8L3]

✕ Listening for information/instructions, Level C

Listening. Pupils listen to customers asking the prices of fruit and vegetables. They must note down what the customer asks for and the price.

Tapescript

1 – ¿Cuánto cuesta un kilo de tomates?
  – Cuesta tres euros.
2 – ¿Cuánto cuesta un kilo de zanahorias?
  – Cuesta dos euros.
3 – ¿Cuánto cuesta un kilo de manzanas?
  – Cuesta tres euros.
4 – ¿Cuánto cuesta un kilo de uvas?
  – Cuesta cuatro euros.
5 – ¿Cuánto cuesta un kilo de plátanos?
  – Cuesta dos euros.
6 – ¿Cuánto cuesta una lechuga?
  – Cuesta un euro.

Answers

1	tomates – 3 euros		4	uvas – 4 euros
2	zanahorias – 2 euros		5	plátanos – 2 euros
3	manzanas – 3 euros		6	lechuga – 1 euro

3b Con tu compañero/a, pregunta y contesta. (AT2/3) [8S4, 6]

✕ Speaking and interacting with others, Level D

Speaking. Pupils work in pairs, taking it in turns to ask each other the prices of items shown on the market stall in the picture. The support box on page 29 reminds them of the question ¿Cuánto cuesta/es … ? and the answer *Cuesta … euro(s)*.

➕ Pupils could be encouraged to extend their dialogues using some of the shopping phrases included on page 28 and listed above.

4 Escribe un diálogo entre un(a) cliente y un(a) tendero/a en el mercado. (AT4/4) [8S6]

✕ Writing imaginatively, Level C/E

Writing. Pupils write a dialogue between a customer and a market-stall holder. They should be encouraged to include as many of the new shopping phrases as possible. Teachers may also wish to draw pupils' attention to the visual showing the range of euro notes and coins and demonstrate how to give prices that include céntimos. Pupils could also be encouraged to record their dialogues, once they have been checked and practised for pronunciation, accuracy and fluency. These could then be played to the rest of the class, for comprehension work, or simply for interest and celebration of achievement.

Plenary [8C1]

Brainstorm: find out what your class knows about the euro. Take feedback. Spain joined the euro system in January 2002, along with many other European countries such as France, Germany and Italy. The euro conversion from pesetas, the old currency of Spain, is approximately 100 pesetas = 0.60 euros (or 60 céntimos) (the conversion to sterling is approximately £1 = 0.60 euros). There are seven euro notes, all with the same design, common to all member states. There are also eight coins, all with a common European face but decorated with each country's own motifs on the reverse, although all will be accepted in any member state.

Alternatively, you could ask pupils about key shopping expressions that they have learned. (See list in notes for exercise **2a**).

Cuaderno B, page 15

1 Empareja las palabras con los dibujos. (AT3/2)

✖ Reading for information/instructions, Level C

Reading. Pupils match labels to pictures of fruit and vegetables.

Answers

1 f	**2** h	**3** i	**4** c	**5** e	**6** d	**7** a	**8** j	**9** b	**10** g

2a Completa el diálogo. (AT3/3, AT4/3)

✖ Enlarge information/ideas, Level B

Reading and writing. A gap-filling exercise, replacing picture prompts in a shopping dialogue.

Answers

- Un kilo de naranjas.
- ¿Hay plátanos?
- Pues, medio kilo de plátanos.
- Kilo y medio de cebollas y un cuarto kilo de zanahorias.
- Son diez euros.

2b Escribe una conversación similar. Cambia los productos y las cantidades. (AT4/4) [8S6]

✖ Writing imaginatively, Level C/D

Writing. Pupils adapt the text in **2a** to create their own dialogue.

Hojas de trabajo, Resource and Assessment File, pages 26 and 27

Cards for pairwork featuring various foods: pupils match the pictures to the correct words.

4 Cien gramos de jamón y una barra de pan

(Pupil's Book pages 30–31)

Main topics

- Buying food and drink in a shop
- Numbers 31–1000

Key Framework objectives

- Adding abstract words 8W1 (Reinforcement)
- Listening for subtleties 8L1 (Reinforcement)
- Relaying gist and detail 8L3 (Reinforcement)

Other aims

- Pronunciation ('c')

Grammar

Numbers 31–1000

Key language

cero	*treinta*
diez	*treinta y cinco*
quince	*cuarenta*
veinte	*cincuenta*
veinticinco	*sesenta*
setenta	*cuatrocientos*
ochenta	*quinientos*

noventa	*seiscientos*
cien	*setecientos*
ciento diez	*ochocientos*
doscientos	*novecientos*
trescientos	*mil*

una barra de pan
una botella de limonada
una caja de pasteles
un cartón de leche
una docena de huevos
una lata de sardinas
un paquete de galletas
doscientos gramos de queso
doscientos cincuenta gramos de chorizo
quinientos gramos de jamón

Resources

Cassette A, side 2
CD1, tracks 26, 27, and 28
Cuaderno B, page 16
Hojas de trabajo, Resource and Assessment File, pages 26 and 27 (*el queso, el pan, las galletas, un pastel*)
Flashcards 18–25

Starter 1 [8W1]

Aim: number practice (100–1000).

Put the words/numbers below on the board. Ask pupils to fill in the gaps with the appropriate numerals or words. They should be able to deduce the answers from the information you have given them. Pupils can use the box at the top of page 30 to check their answers. Which will they find hardest to remember? Ask for suggestions of how to remember the numbers.

cien ...	*... 600*
doscientos ...	*... 700*
tres cientos ...	*... 800*
... 400	*... 900*
quinientos ...	*mil ...*

1a Escucha y escribe los números. (AT1/1) [8L1]

✉ Listening for information/instructions, Level B

Listening. Pupils listen to a series of numbers between zero and one thousand and note them down. The support box reminds pupils of how numbers up to 100 (covered in *¡Listos! 1*) are formed and demonstrates the formation of numbers from 100 to 1000. Before using the recorded item, teachers may wish to give pupils aural practice of higher numbers, for example by playing various number games (see page 7 of the Introduction to this Teacher's Guide).

The numbers provide an opportunity to contrast the hard and soft 'c' sounds. You could put up the transcript below, play the recording again and get pupils to repeat each item. All but *quinientos* include 'c'.

Tapescript

treinta y cinco
setenta y cinco
cien
ciento diez
cincuenta
noventa y cinco
doscientos
cuatrocientos diez
quinientos
setecientos cincuenta

Answers

35, 75, 100, 110, 50, 95, 200, 410, 500, 750

1b Escribe los números. (AT4/1)

✉ Exchange information/ideas, Level B

4 Cien gramos de jamón y una barra de pan

Writing. Pupils read a series of high numbers given as words, and write them as numerals. Teachers could make this a timed pairwork challenge, with a reward or prize for the pair who write down all the numbers correctly in the shortest time.

Answers

a *66*	b 72	c 83	d 99	e 111	f 150
g 198	h 250	i 520	j 675		

1c Escribe diez números del 31 al 1000. Lee los números a tu compañero/a. Tu compañero/a los escribe. (AT2/1)

✖ Speaking to convey information, Level B

Speaking. Pupils write down and read out ten high numbers to their partner who must write them down correctly as numerals.

2a Lee la lista de la compra y empareja las cosas con los artículos en la foto. (AT3/3) [8T4; 9T4]

✖ Reading for information/instructions, Level C

Reading. Pupils read a shopping list and must match each item to its equivalent in the photograph. Teachers may wish to give pupils a few moments before doing the matching exercise to check that they know all the items of shopping listed and to look up in a dictionary any that they are unsure about. After the matching exercise, pupils could be encouraged to guess the meaning of the various packages mentioned: *una barra, un cartón, una docena, un paquete, una botella, una caja* and *una lata.*

Answers

a 2	b 8	c 4	d 6	e 5	f 1	g 7
h 10	i 3	j 9				

2b Escucha y comprueba tus respuestas. (AT1/3)

Listening. Pupils listen to the list of items and check that they have matched them up correctly.

Tapescript

1 un cartón de leche
2 una botella de limonada
3 una caja de pasteles
4 250 gramos de chorizo
5 una barra de pan
6 500 gramos de jamón
7 una docena de huevos
8 200 gramos de queso
9 una lata de sardinas
10 un paquete de galletas

Starter 2

Aim: more number practice. Gaining confidence listening to and understanding numbers.

Call out numbers between 10 and 1000. Ask pupils to write these down. Increase the pace so you reach the speed at which prices would be called out in a shop or at the market. Suggestion: keep a note of all the numbers you call out. Go over with the class.

2c Escucha las conversaciones. ¿Qué desean los clientes? Copia y rellena el cuadro con las cantidades apropiadas. (AT1/4) [8L3]

✖ Listening for information/instructions, Level D

Listening. Pupils copy out the grid, then listen to a series of shopping dialogues and fill in on the grid the quantity of each item purchased.

Tapescript

1 – ¿Qué desea?
– Una lata de sardinas y dos barras de pan, por favor.
– ¿Algo más?
– Sí, media docena de huevos.
2 – ¿Qué desea, señora?
– Dos paquetes de galletas y una botella de limonada.
– Tome usted.
3 – Buenos días. ¿Qué desea?
– Doscientos gramos de chorizo, una docena de huevos y un cartón de leche, por favor.
– Tome usted, doscientos gramos de chorizo, una docena de huevos y un cartón de leche.
4 – Buenas tardes. ¿Qué desea señor?
– Una barra de pan y una botella de limonada.
– ¿Algo más?
– Nada más gracias.
5 – ¡Hola!
– Hola. Doscientos cincuenta gramos de jamón, por favor, y cien gramos de queso.
– Doscientos cincuenta de jamón y cien de queso.
– Eso es.
– Muy bien.

Answers

	sardinas	galletas	limonada	chorizo	huevos	jamón	leche	pan	queso
1	1				6			2	
2		2	1						
3				200g	12		1		
4			1					1	
5						250g			100g

3 Con tu compañero/a, haz un diálogo entre un(a) cliente y un(a) tendero/a en la tienda de comestibles. (AT2/4) [8S6]

✗ Speaking and interacting with others, Level D

Speaking. Pupils work in pairs with a partner to create dialogues in a grocer's shop. As with exercise **3b** on page 29, pupils should be encouraged to use a wide range of shopping expressions and could record their dialogues, once perfected.

4 Escribe una lista de la compra para una merienda para diez amigos. (AT4/3) [8T6]

✗ Writing imaginatively, Level C

Writing. Pupils write a shopping list (including quantities) for a tea/snack for ten friends. For an added challenge, teachers could provide pupils with a price list and tell them they can only spend a certain amount, or include special dietary requirements, such as a number of vegetarians in the group, or people who are allergic to certain food items.

Plenary [8W1]

Numbers sound quite daunting in Spanish. Ask if someone can explain to the rest of the class the patterns of bigger numbers (*ciento(s)* is added to the basic numeral – *doscientos,* etc.) and which is the odd one out (*quinientos*).

Cuaderno B, page 16

1 Escribe los números. (AT3/1)

✗ Reading for information/instructions, Level B

Reading. Pupils write numerals next to the numbers in words.

Answers

1 85	**2** 59	**3** 200	**4** 500	**5** 360			
6 700	**7** 171	**8** 903					

2 Escribe los números en español. (AT4/2)

✗ Exchange information/ideas, Level B

Writing. This time, pupils write out numbers in Spanish, to match the numerals.

Answers

1 sesenta y ocho
2 ciento veintitrés
3 quinientos noventa y uno
4 setecientos ochenta y cuatro
5 novecientos veintisiete
6 ochocientos nueve
7 seiscientos treinta y seis
8 cuatrocientos cincuenta

3 Lee los diálogos y escribe las cantidades en las columnas apropiadas del cuadro. (AT3/3)

✗ Reading for information/instructions, Level D

Reading. After reading four dialogues, pupils complete a grid with quantities.

	cheese	sardines	lemonade	meat	bread	chorizo	cakes	biscuits	eggs	milk
1		1	1			250g		1		
2			2	500g	1				12	1
3	750g						1			
4					2	500g			6	

Hojas de trabajo, Resource and Assessment File, pages 26 and 27

Cards for pairwork featuring various foods: pupils match the pictures to the correct words.

5 ¡Que aproveche!

(Pupil's Book pages 32–33)

Main topics

- Saying you are hungry and thirsty
- Ordering tapas and drinks

Key Framework objectives

- Meanings in context 8T1 (Launch)
- Colloquialisms 8C5 (Launch)
- Verb tenses 8W5 (near-future) (Part-launch)
- Text as model and source 8T6 (Reinforcement)
- Listening for subtleties 8L1 (Reinforcement)

Grammar

- Phrases with *tener*
- Pronouns with prepositions

Key language

¿Tienes hambre/sed?
Tengo hambre/sed.
No tiene mucha hambre.

¿Qué va(n) a tomar?
¿Qué va(n) a beber?
¿Va(n) a tomar algo más?
Para mí/él/ella …

las aceitunas	*el jamón serrano*
los calamares	*las patatas bravas*
el chorizo	*la tortilla española*
las gambas	

agua con gas	*el flan*
agua sin gas	*el helado de vainilla/fresa/*
la cerveza	*chocolate*
la naranjada	
La cuenta, por favor.	

Resources

Cassette A, side 2
CD1, tracks 29 and 30
Cuaderno B, page 17
OHTs 11 and 12
Flashcards 5, 10, 11, 17 and 19, 21 (*¡Listos! 1*)

Starter 1 [8L1]

Aim: pronunciation of 'g' and 'j', 'll' and hard and soft 'c'.

Before starting the unit, put the above letters on the board and ask pupils if they can provide examples for each from previous work. Then look at the menu at the top of page 32. Ask pupils to look for further examples of the sounds. Now go through all the items on the menu, paying particular attention to pronunciation. You could make this into a class game with two teams. One team says the number of a menu item (in Spanish!) and a member of the other team must pronounce the word. Award marks for good pronunciation. Finally, check that pupils understand the meaning of the menu items.

An alternative starter would be to revise the irregular verb *tener*. Write the subject pronouns on the board and ask pupils to work with a partner and fill in the paradigm for *tener*. [8W5; 9W5]

1a Lee y escucha. (AT1/4, AT3/4) [8T1, 4; 9T4]

✖ Reading for information/instructions, Level D

Listening and reading. Pupils read and listen to a conversation in which Gerardo and Oscar order food and drinks in a tapas bar. Teachers should first give pupils time to familiarise themselves with the menu on page 32 and to ensure they understand everything on it, looking up any unknown vocabulary in a dictionary. After reading and listening to the dialogue, teachers should check pupils' understanding of who ordered what. They should also draw pupils'

attention to the expressions *tener hambre* and *tener sed* (explained in the *Gramática* on page 32), as well as to other new phrases such as *¿Qué vas/van a tomar/beber?*, *Voy a pedir …* , *La cuenta, por favor* and *En seguida.*

Tapescript

Gerardo:	*¿Tienes hambre?*
Oscar:	*Bueno … no tengo mucha hambre.*
Gerardo:	*Bueno, voy a pedir unas tapas. ¿Tienes sed?*
Oscar:	*Sí, tengo sed.*
Gerardo:	*¿Qué vas a beber?*
Oscar:	*Agua con gas.*
El camarero:	*¿Qué van a tomar?*
Gerardo:	*Calamares, unas patatas bravas … y jamón serrano.*
El camarero:	*¿Y qué van a beber?*
Gerardo:	*Una naranjada para mí. Y para él, agua con gas.*
El camarero:	*¿Van a tomar algo más?*
Gerardo:	*Un helado de vainilla, fresa y chocolate.*
El camarero:	*¿Algo más?*
Oscar:	*¡Y dos cucharas!*
El camarero:	*¡Vale!*
Gerardo:	*Y la cuenta, por favor.*
El camarero:	*Claro. En seguida.*

1b Lee el texto otra vez y completa las frases con Oscar o Gerardo. (AT3/4)

✖ Reading for information/instructions, Level D

Reading. Pupils copy and complete a series of sentences in Spanish to show comprehension of the text in 1a.

módulo 2 — 5 ¡Que aproveche!

Answers

1 *Gerardo*	**2** Oscar	**3** Oscar	**4** Gerardo
5 Oscar	**6** Oscar, Gerardo		

1c Mira el menú otra vez. Escucha y escribe los números de las cosas mencionadas. (1–6) (AT1/4) [8L3]

✕ Listening for information/instructions, Level D

Listening. Pupils listen to a series of dialogues in a tapas bar and write down the numbers of the items on the menu which are ordered.

Tapescript

1	Waiter:	Hola. ¿Qué van a tomar?
	Customer 1:	Unas tapas … a ver … gambas y calamares.
2	Waiter:	¿Y qué van a beber?
	Customer 1:	Para mí, una cerveza.
	Customer 2:	Y para mí, agua con gas.
3	Waiter:	¿Qué va a tomar?
	Customer 3:	No tengo mucha hambre. Unas aceitunas y un agua con gas.
4	Waiter:	Bueno, de tapas tenemos gambas, tortilla española y …
	Customer 4:	Tortilla española. ¡Qué bien! Para mi la tortilla.
	Customer 5:	Y para mí, gambas.
5	Waiter:	¿Qué van a beber?
	Customer 4:	Para mí, una naranjada.
	Customer 5:	Y para mí, agua sin gas.
6	Customer 1:	¿Qué hay de postre?
	Waiter:	Hay helado y flan.
	Customer 1:	Un flan, para mí.
	Customer 2:	Nada para mí.

Answers

1 *1, 3*	**2** 11, 9	**3** 7, 9	**4** 4, 1	**5** 8, 10	**6** 13

Starter 2 [8W5; 9W5]

Aim: to reinforce the idea that high-frequency words (here, the verb *tener*) will be useful in many different contexts and topics.

Ask pupils to work with a partner and to think up as many expressions as they can that take *tener*, for example: *Tengo hambre, Tengo sed, Tengo calor, Tengo frio, Tengo una hermana, Tengo trece años*, etc.

2 Con tu compañero/a, haz un diálogo entre un camarero y un cliente. (AT2/4) [8S6]

✕ Speaking and interacting with others, Level D

Speaking. Pupils work with a partner to make up a dialogue in a tapas bar. The support grid on page 33 reminds them of key expressions. As before, pupils could be encouraged to record their dialogue, once polished, as a record of achievement. Pupils who enjoy drama could also learn their dialogue off by heart and perform it for the rest of the class, perhaps using some simple props.

3 Lee los textos. Escribe una frase para pedir dos cosas para cada persona. (AT3/3) [8S5; 9W5]

✕ Reading for information/instructions, Level D

Reading and writing. Pupils write sentences to show how they would order the relevant food and drink for various people, using *para él/ella*. The use of pronouns with prepositions is explained in the *Gramática* box on page 33.

Answers

Pupils to supply two, where more options given.
1 Para ella, chorizo y jamón serrano.
2 Para él, patatas bravas/tortilla española/aceitunas.
3 Para ella, patatas bravas/tortilla española/jamón serrano/chorizo.
4 Para él, naranjada/agua con gas/agua sin gas/ cerveza/helado/flan.
5 Para ella, gambas/patatas bravas/calamares/tortilla española/jamón serrano/chorizo/aceitunas/helado de vainilla/fresa.
6 Para él, naranjada/tortilla español.

✑ As a follow-up to work on this unit, pupils could use a graphics or desktop publishing programme to create their own tapas bar menus. The finished menus could be used for display purposes, or as props in role-play activities. [8T6]

Plenary [8W1; 8C6]

Ask pupils to tell you how to say: for me, for him, for her (also how to say 'nothing for me'). Ask for ideas about how pupils might memorise these.

If time allows, you could ask pupils for some of the colloquialisms they have learned, e.g. *¡Vale!, en seguida, bueno.*

Cuaderno B, page 17

1 Mira los dibujos y completa el crucigrama.
(AT4/2)

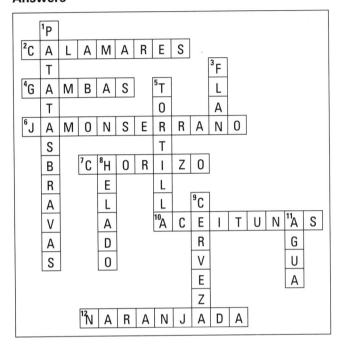 Knowing about language

Writing. Pupils complete the crossword puzzle based on food and drink.

Answers

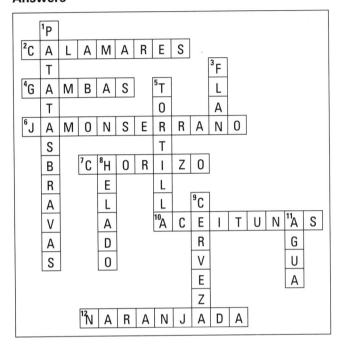

2 Elige platos del crucigrama y completa el diálogo sobre ti y un(a) amigo/a. (AT4/4)

Exchange information/ideas, Level B

Writing. Pupils write a dialogue, using items from the crossword puzzle.

módulo 2
6 La comida sana
(Pupil's Book pages 34–35)

Main topics

- Talking about healthy eating

Key Framework objectives

- Language and text types 8T3 (Launch)
- Verb tenses 8W5 (Reinforcement)
- Negative forms and words 8S5 (Reinforcement)

Grammar

The present tense singular of *comer* and *beber*
Expressions of frequency: *una vez al año, algunas veces a la semana*

Key language

¿Con qué frecuencia comes carne (roja)?
una vez a la semana/al año
algunas veces a la semana/al mes
todos los días
¿Comes (pescado)?
No como (carne) y no bebo (leche).
No me gusta(n) mucho (las verduras).
Prefiero (el pan integral).

Resources

Cassette A, side 2
CD1, track 31
Cuaderno B, page 18

Starter 1 [8W5; 9W5]

Aim: to revise regular -er verbs: *comer, beber.*

Before your class comes in, write the following on the board, or prepare an OHT. Ask pupils to fill in the endings. *Yo com, Tú… com…, Él com…, Nosotros com…, Vosotros com…, Ellos com…*. Ask pupils to write out the paradigm for *beber*.

1 Lee la información. ¿Verdad (✓) o mentira (✗)? (AT3/4) [8T3]

✉ Reading for information/instructions, Level E

Reading. Pupils read a text about why the Mediterranean diet is believed to be healthy and do a true/false exercise. Some vocabulary help is given and pupils should be encouraged to do as much of the task as they can before using a dictionary to look up any unknown words. The text includes several expressions of frequency, which are explained in the *Gramática* on page 34.

➕ As an extension, pupils could correct the incorrect statements in 1.

Answers

1 ✓	2 ✗	3 ✓	4 ✓	5 ✗	6 ✓	7 ✓	8 ✓

2 ¿Con qué frecuencia comen estas personas los alimentos mencionados? Copia y rellena el cuadro. (AT1/4) [8S5; 8L3]

✉ Listening for information/instructions, Level D

Listening. Pupils listen to people talking about how often they eat or drink certain things, then copy and fill in a grid, using ticks to show how often each speaker eats or drinks the items shown on the grid.

Tapescript

1 – ¿Comes carne todos los días?
  – No, no todos los días. Como carne algunas veces a la semana.
  – ¿Y el pescado?
  – Como pescado algunas veces al mes.
  – ¿Comes ensalada, verduras o fruta todos los días?
  – Sí, todos los días. ¡Me encanta la fruta!
  – ¿Bebes leche todos los días?
  – Sí, todos los días.
  – ¿Comes pan, cereales o arroz todos los días?
  – Sí. Siempre tomo cereales para el desayuno.

2 – ¿Comes carne todos los días?
  – Sí, sí, todos los días. ¡Soy muy carnívoro!
  – ¿Con qué frecuencia comes pescado?
  – El pescado no me gusta mucho. Como pescado algunas veces al mes.
  – ¿Comes verduras, ensalada o fruta todos los días?
  – No, no todos los días. Algunas veces a la semana.
  – ¿Bebes leche o comes queso o yogur?
  – Sí, bebo leche todos los días.
  – ¿Comes pan, cereales o arroz todos los días?
  – El arroz no tanto, pero como pan y cereales todos los días.

3 – ¿Con qué frecuencia comes carne roja? ¿Algunas veces al mes? ¿Algunas veces a la semana? ¿O todos los días?
  – No me gusta mucho la carne, prefiero el pollo o el pescado. Como carne roja algunas veces al mes.
  – ¿Y el pescado?
  – El pescado, algunas veces a la semana.
  – ¿Te gusta la fruta, la ensalada y las verduras?
  – Sí. Como estos alimentos todos los días.
  – ¿Bebes leche o comes queso?
  – Sí, todos los días.
  – ¿Comes pan, cereales o arroz todos los días o algunas veces a la semana?
  – Todos los días.

Answers

	meat	fish	fruit & veg	milk, yoghurt, cheese	cereal, bread, rice
1	✓✓	✓	✓✓✓	✓✓✓	✓✓✓
2	✓✓✓	✓	✓✓	✓✓✓	✓✓✓
3	✓	✓✓	✓✓✓	✓✓✓	✓✓✓

Starter [8W2]

Aim: expressions of frequency.

Text manipulation. Ask pupils to unscramble the following three phrases, then write down what they mean in English: **1** *mes algunas al veces* **2** *días los todos* **3** *a la veces semana algunas*. You could ask for an example of a sentence containing each phrase.

3 Haz un sondeo. Copia y completa el cuadro de **2** para diez compañeros/as de clase. (AT2/4) [8S4]

✕ Speaking and interacting with others, Level D

Speaking. Pupils conduct a class survey on healthy eating using a further copy of the grid from exercise **2**. A sample dialogue is provided to guide them.

👄 Pupils could enter the results of their survey into an Excel spreadsheet, then produce a bar graph or pie chart using the chart wizard.

4a Lee los textos. Explica quién tiene la dieta más sana y la dieta menos sana y por qué. (AT3/4) [8S5; 9W5]

✕ Reading for information/instructions, Level D

Reading. Pupils read three texts and decide which writer has the most and least healthy diet and why. Teachers may wish to remind pupils of the use and formation of the superlative, introduced in Module 1, Unit 1 (page 7) and reused here.

Answers *(examples)*

> *Roberto tiene la dieta menos sana porque come carne todos los días, no come mucha ensalada ni verduras; come fruta algunas veces al mes; no bebe leche – bebe Coca-Cola o naranjada.*
>
> *Juan tiene la dieta más sana porque come pasta, ensalada y arroz. Siempre desayuna cereales con leche y fruta y pan integral. Come pescado o pollo – no come mucho la carne roja.*

4b Escribe frases sobre tu dieta. (AT4/4) [8W5; 8S5; 8T6; 9W5]

✕ Exchange information/ideas, Level C/E

Writing. Pupils write a similar text to those in **4a** about their own diet, including expressions of frequency.

The *Gramática* box on page 35 highlights the first, second and third person singular of *comer* and *beber*.

➕ Able pupils should be encouraged to adapt the texts in **4a**, adding their own ideas and vocabulary.

🄡 Some pupils might benefit from being given a writing frame, in the form of a sentence-building grid on a worksheet or OHT. This could include key phrases such as *(No) Como/Bebo …* (+ expressions of frequency), *porque … ; (No) Me gusta mucho … ; Odio … ; Prefiero …* and *Mi plato preferido es … .*

Plenary [8W5; 9W5]

Quick-fire questions. Go round the class and ask pupils how to say: I eat, you eat, he eats. I drink, you drink, he drinks (mix these up if pupils are confident conjugating *comer* and *beber*). Can pupils spot a pattern with regular -*er* verbs? Ask someone to explain what it is.

Cuaderno B, page 18

1a Lee los textos. ¿Con qué frecuencia comen las personas los alimentos mencionados? (AT3/3)

✕ Reading for information/instructions, Level D

Reading. Pupils read two texts and fill in a grid, to shown how often people eat and drink each item.

Answers

	meat	chicken/ fish	fruit & veg	milk, yoghurt, cheese	cereal, bread, rice
Timeu	✓✓✓	✓✓	✓✓	✓✓✓	✓✓✓
Patricia	✓✓✓	✗	✓	✗	✓✓✓

1b Contesta a las preguntas. ¿Patricia o Timeu? (AT3/3) [8S4]

✕ Reading for information/instructions, Level D

Reading. Pupils answer questions in Spanish about the texts in **1a**, noting down the correct names.

Answers

1	Timeu, Patricia	**5**	algunas veces al mes
2	Timeu	**6**	todos los días
3	Timeu	**7**	Timeu
4	Patricia	**8**	Patricia

1c Escribe unas frases para describir la dieta de Susana. (AT4/4)

✕ Exchange information/ideas, Level D

Writing. Pupils write a description of Susana's diet, using information from the grid in **1a.**

Resumen y Prepárate

(Pupil's Book pages 36–37)

Resumen

This is a checklist of language covered in Module 2. There is a comprehensive **Resumen** list for Module 2 in the Pupil's Book (page 36) and a **Resumen** test sheet in Cuaderno B (page 22).

Prepárate

A revision test to give practice for the test itself at the end of the module.

Resources

Cassette A, side 2
CD1, track 32
Cuaderno B, pages 19, 20 and 21
Skills, Resource and Assessment File, page 29
Resumen, Resource and Assessment File, page 30

1 Escucha las conversaciones. Copia y rellena el cuadro. (AT1/4) [8L3]

✖ Listening for information/instructions, Level D

Listening. Pupils listen to shopping dialogues and note down the items purchased, the quantity and price.

Tapescript

1 – *Buenos días.*
   – *Buenos días. ¿Qué desea?*
   – *Medio kilo de manzanas, por favor.*
   – *¿Algo más?*
   – *Kilo y medio de naranjas.*
   – *Aquí tiene.*
   – *¿Cuánto es en total?*
   – *Son tres euros cincuenta.*
   – *Tome usted.*
2 – *Buenos días.*
   – *Hola. ¿Qué desea?*
   – *Doscientos (200) gramos de queso.*
   – *¿Algo más?*
   – *Sí, quinientos (500) gramos de jamón serrano, por favor.*
   – *Tome usted.*
   – *¿Cuánto cuesta en total?*
   – *Son cinco euros setenta cinco.*
   – *Aquí tiene.*
   – *Gracias.*
3 – *Buenos días. ¿Qué desea?*
   – *Un kilo de cebollas, por favor.*
   – *¿Algo más?*
   – *Dos kilos de zanahorias.*
   – *Tome.*
   – *¿Cuánto es?*
   – *Son dos euros.*
   – *Tenga.*
   – *Gracias. Adiós.*

Answers

Cliente	¿Qué compra?	¿Cantidades?	¿Cuánto es?
1	manzanas, naranjas	$\frac{1}{2}$ kg, $1\frac{1}{2}$ kg	3,50 euros
2	queso, jamón serrano	200g, 500g	5,75 euros
3	cebollas, zanahorias	1kg, 2kg	2 euros

2 Mira los dibujos. Con tu compañero/a, haz un diálogo entre un camarero y un(a) cliente. (AT2/4)

✖ Speaking and interacting with others, Level D

Speaking. Pupils use the pictures to create a dialogue between a customer and waiter in a tapas bar.

3 Lee la carta y contesta a las preguntas. (AT3/4) [8S4; 8T2; 9T2]

✖ Reading for information/instructions, Level D

Reading. Pupils read a letter about what Julia eats and drinks for breakfast, lunch and evening meal, then answer questions in Spanish.

Answers

1 Desayuna zumo de naranja, cereales y té con leche.
2 La comida en el instituto es a las dos.
3 Come una hamburguesa con patatas fritas o pizza.
4 Cenan a las nueve y media.
5 Hay sopa o ensalada.
6 Comen carne o pescado con patatas.
7 Come pan.
8 Bebe agua.
9 Suele tomar fruta.
10 Porque es sana.

4 Escribe una carta y contesta a las preguntas de Julia. (AT4/4) [8T6]

✖ Writing to establish/maintain contact, Level D

Writing. Pupils answer the questions in the letter in exercise 3, by writing a similar piece about their own eating habits.

Cuaderno B, page 19

Repaso

1 Mira el anuncio del supermercado y contesta a las preguntas. (AT3/4) [8T3]

✖ Reading for information/instructions, Level D

Reading. Pupils read a supermarket leaflet and answer questions about prices.

Answers

1 1,45 euros
2 2,69 euros
3 1,08 euros
4 89 céntimos/0,89 euros
5 83 céntimos/0,83 euros
6 53 céntimos/0,53 euros
7 91 céntimos/0,91 euros
8 72 céntimos/0,72 euros

2 Busca las palabras en el anuncio. (AT3/4, AT4/1) [8W1; 8T4; 9T4]

✖ Reading for information/instructions, Level D

Reading and writing. Pupils find the Spanish for key words in the leaflet.

Answers

1 rasca y gana
2 bebidas
3 ultramarinos
4 congelados
5 almíbar
6 melocotón

3 Diseña un folleto de tus productos favoritos con precios. Busca las palabras que no conoces en el diccionario. (AT4/4) [8T3; 8T6]

✖ Writing imaginatively, Level C/D

Writing. Pupils create their own supermarket leaflet, using a dictionary for support.

Cuaderno B, page 20

Gramática 1

1 ¿Qué opinas de estos planos? (AT4/3) [8W4]

✖ Knowing about language

Reading and writing. Pupils use the support and reminder boxes to write their opinion of food items.

2 ¿Qué opinas de estos platos y productos? Elige las palabras de la lista para completar las frases. (AT3/2, AT4/1) [8W4]

✖ Knowing about language

Reading and writing. A gap-filling exercise about food, using the adjectives listed. Pupils must remember to make the adjectives agree.

Possible answers

1 deliciosos
2 sanas
3 saladas
4 ricas
5 dulces
6 nutritiva
7 grasienta
8 picante

Cuaderno B, page 21

Gramática 2

1 Contesta a las preguntas. (AT4/3) [8W5; 8S4; 9W5]

✖ Knowing about language

Writing. Pupils answer questions about their eating habits, using the verb *soler*.

2 Mira los dibujos y completa las frases en los globos con las palabras apropiadas de la lista. (AT3/2, AT4/2)

✖ Knowing about language

Writing. A dialogue-completion exercise, using para *mí/él* or *ella*.

Answers

1 Para mí **2** Para él **3** Para mí **4** Para ella

Skills, Resource and Assessment File, page 29 (Pronunciation and spelling)

1a
Answers

3

1b
Answers

4

2
Answers

a 3	**b** 2	**c** 1	**d** 2	**e** 4	**f** 4
g 3	**h** 4	**i** 3	**j** 2		

3a

Answers

They all contain *vowels*.

3b

Answers

a patatas
b fruta
c pan
d agua
e hamburguesas
f ensalada
g pescado
h naranjada
i verduras
j queso

4

Answers

a pescado
b comida
c desayuno
d lechuga
e pollo
f sopa
g helado

5

Answers

a ver du ras
b sar di nas
c chul et as
d en sal ad a
e pa ell a
f nar an jas
g ce boll as
h tom at es
i que so
j cho ri zo

6

Answers

Pupils' own anagrams.

Main topics

This is an optional unit which reviews some of the key language of the module: it focuses on Christmas.

Key Framework objectives

- Dictionary detail 8W7 (Launch)
- Questions/text as stimulus to talk 9L4 (Launch)
- Adding abstract words 8W1 (Reinforcement)
- Using grammar to understand words 9W8 (Reinforcement)
- Understanding complex language 9T1 (Reinforcement)
- Authentic texts as sources 9T3 (Reinforcement)

Resources

Cassette A, side 2
CD1, tracks 33 and 34

Starter 1 [8W7]

Aim: glossary/dictionary practice.

Write the following words on the board (or prepare an OHT) and ask pupils to group them into verbs and nouns. Pupils use the glossary or dictionaries and 1 confirm whether the word is a verb or a noun 2 write down the meaning and 3 if it's a noun, identify the gender.

adorna, canta, manda, pavo, regalo, belén, tarjeta (plus any others you wish to add).

Do this starter without introducing the fact that you'll be working on pages 38–39.

1 Lee sobre las tradiciones de Navidad en España y contesta a las preguntas. Utiliza un diccionario. (AT3/4) [8T3; 9W8; 9T1, 3]

✕ Reading for information/instructions, Level E

Reading. Begin by asking pupils to predict what sorts of things might be talked about in a text entitled *¿Cómo se celebra la Navidad en España?*. They could then scan the text for familiar words (including those encountered in the starter activity) and cognates. Can they identify some of the topics covered, e.g. food, presents? Pupils go on to answer questions in Spanish. The text contains examples of the use of the passive, which is explained in the *Gramática* box on page 39.

Answers

1 Se celebra la Nochebuena el 24 de diciembre.
2 Se celebra más la Nochebuena que el día de Navidad en España.
3 Se cena pescado o a veces pavo y de postre se come turrón.
4 Se celebra la misa del gallo a medianoche.
5 Se montan nacimientos en casa, en plazas y en las iglesias.
6 Se reciben los regalos el 6 de enero.
7 Se ponen los zapatos en el balcón.
8 Se comen doce uvas en Nochevieja.

2 Escucha la conversación y completa las frases con las palabras apropiadas. (AT1/4) [8L3]

✕ Listening for information/instructions, Level E

Listening. Pupils listen to a dialogue about Christmas traditions in the UK and Spain and do a multiple-choice exercise.

Tapescript

– ¿Cómo se celebra Navidad en el Reino Unido? ¿Qué se celebra más, Nochebuena o el día de Navidad?
– En el Reino Unido se celebra más el veinticinco de diciembre.
– ¿Se montan belenes?
– Sí, algunas veces. Pero en las casas y las tiendas se pone un árbol y se adorna. En la Plaza de Trafalgar en Londres se pone un árbol enorme.
– ¿Se cantan villancicos?
– Sí, muchos como Silent Night.
– ¿Se mandan tarjetas?
– Sí, se mandan muchas tarjetas. ¿Y en España se mandan tarjetas?
– En España no se mandan muchas. ¿Cuándo se dan los regalos?
– Los regalos se dan el día de Navidad. Es tradición poner los regalos en los calcetines de los niños.
– ¡En los calcetines! En España se ponen en los zapatos. ¿Hay una cena especial el Día de Navidad?
– No, el día de Navidad se celebra con una comida en casa con la familia.
– ¿Qué se come?
– Se come pavo y pudín. Después se ve la televisión.
– ¿Se celebra Nochevieja?
– Sí, especialmente en Escocia. Nochevieja se celebra mucho en Escocia.

Answers

1 a	2 b	3 a	4 a	5 c
6 b	7 c	8 b	9 a	10 c

➕ Using the multiple-choice questions as support, you could ask pupils to summarise the information in the listening text.

módulo 2 — 7 ¡Extra! ¡Feliz Navidad!

Starter 2 [8W1]

Aim: vocabulary extension.

Ask pupils to find the Spanish for the following words in the the text on page 38: church, Christmas carols, almonds and honey, midnight mass, turkey, Christmas Eve (plus any others you wish to add).

3a Elige una fiesta. Con tu compañero/a, haz y contesta a las preguntas. (AT2/4) [8S4; 9L4]

✉ Speaking and interacting with others, Level E/F

Speaking. In pairs, pupils ask and answer questions about how festivals are celebrated in their home.

3b ¿Qué fiesta se celebra en tu casa? Escribe unas frases describiendo cómo se celebra en tu casa. (AT4/4)

✉ Exchange information/ideas, Level D/E

Writing. Pupils write about how a chosen festival is celebrated in their home.

Plenary [8W5; 9W5]

Ask a volunteer to explain what the 'passive' means. Ask everyone to write down an example from the text.

Escucha y lee la canción y busca las palabras que no conoces en el diccionario. [8C4]

✉ Listening for enjoyment

Listening: Pupils listen to the song and look up any unfamiliar words in the dictionary.

Tapescript

Un villancico

*Campana sobre campana
y sobre campana una,
asómate a la ventana
verás al Niño en la cuna.*

*Belén, campanas de Belén,
que los ángeles tocan
¿qué nuevas me traéis?*

*Recogido tu rebaño
¿adónde vas pastorcillo?
Voy a llevar al portal
requesón, manteca y vino.*

*Belén, campanas de Belén,
que los ángeles tocan
¿qué nuevas me traéis?*

*Campana sobre campana
y sobre campana dos,
asómate a la ventana
porque está naciendo Dios.*

*Belén, campanas de Belén,
que los ángeles tocan
¿qué nuevas me traéis?*

Aprende y canta el villancico.

Reading: Pupils can then learn the song and sing it together!

módulo 2
Te toca a ti
(Pupil's Book pages 114–115)

● Self-access reading and writing at two levels

Key Framework objectives

Well-known features of the country 9C4 (Launch)

A Reinforcement

1a Empareja los números. (AT3/1)

✕ Reading for information/instructions, Level C

Reading. Pupils match up high numbers in Spanish with numerals.

Answers

1 j	2 a	3 g	4 e	5 f	6 i	7 d	8 h	9 c	10 b

1b Escribe los números en palabras. (AT4/1)

✕ Exchange information/ideas, Level B

Writing. Pupils write high numbers as words in Spanish.

Answers

> **a** trescientos cincuenta y siete
> **b** quinientos setenta y nueve
> **c** ciento catorce
> **d** setecientos veintiséis
> **e** mil cuatrocientos ochenta y nueve
> **f** dos mil seiscientos treinta y seis
> **g** doscientos cuarenta y seis
> **h** ochocientos noventa y uno

2a Pon las frases en el orden correcto. (AT3/2)

✕ Reading for information/instructions, Level D

Reading. Pupils copy out lines from a dialogue in a tapas bar in the correct order.

Answers

> e, f, d, c, h, b, a, g

2b Escribe una conversación similar entre un(a) camarero/a y dos clientes. (AT4/4)

✕ Writing imaginatively, Level D

Writing. Pupils write a tapas bar conversation between a waiter and two customers.

B Extension

1a Empareja los dibujos con las descripciones. (AT3/4) [9C4]

✕ Reading for information/instructions, Level D

Reading. Pupils read for gist a series of statements about different food items and match them with the correct pictures.

Answers

1 d	2 f	3 a	4 g	5 c	6 b	7 h	8 e

1b Contesta a las preguntas. (AT3/4)

✕ Reading for information/instructions, Level E

Reading. Pupils re-read the sentences in **1a**, skimming for information and answering a series of questions in English. They may need to look up unknown vocabulary in a dictionary.

Answers

> **1** chocolate, vanilla and banana
> **2** in Colombia, Cuba, Costa Rica and Nicaragua
> **3** a delicious, spicy sausage
> **4** cold
> **5** crushed ice
> **6** Valencia
> **7** 'papa'
> **8** the Spanish
> **9** eggs and potatoes
> **10** corn

1c Escribe una descripción de dos de tus platos o bebidas favoritos. (AT4/4) [8T6]

✕ Exchange information/ideas, Level D/E

Writing. Pupils write a description of two of their favourite dishes or drinks.

Unit	Key Framework objectives	PoS	Key language and Grammar
1 ¿Qué ropa llevan? (pp. 42–43) Talking about clothes Comparing prices	8S1 Word, phrase and clause sequencing [L] 8W1 Adding abstract words [R] 8T4 Dictionary use [R]	**2g** dealing with the unpredictable **3b** use context to interpret meaning **3c** use knowledge of English **4a** working with authentic materials	Comparatives: *más* + adjective + *que* Adjectives: *barato/a(s), caro/a(s), grandes, pequeño/a(s)* *Ester lleva botas, una blusa, …*
2 Me gusta aquella camiseta roja (pp. 44–45) Talking about what clothes you like and what suits you	8W4 Word endings [R] 8S1 Word, phrase and clause sequencing [R]	**1a** sounds and writing **2b** correct pronunciation/ intonation **5c** express opinions	Demonstrative adjectives: *este, ese, aquel,* etc. *¿Qué tal me queda(n) el jersey (los pantalones)?* *La chaqueta me queda ajustada.* *Los vaqueros me quedan pequeños.* *No, te queda mal el color.*
3 ¿Me lo puedo probar? (pp. 46–47) Shopping for clothes	9L1 Listening for inferences [L] 8W4 Word endings [R] 8S1 Word, phrase and clause sequencing [R]	**2a** listen for gist and detail **2g** dealing with the unpredictable **5c** express opinions	Direct object pronouns: *lo, la, los, las* *Me gusta aquella camiseta. ¿Me la puedo probar?* *Me gustan los vaqueros. ¿Me los puedo probar?*
4 ¿Qué vas a llevar para ir a la fiesta? (pp. 48–49) Describing clothes Asking what someone is wearing Saying what you are wearing	8S7 Present, past, *future* [L] 9W4 Main inflections [L] 9L2 Recognising rhetorical devices [L] 8W5 Verbs [R]	**2a** listen for gist and detail	The immediate future *ir + a +* infinitive *Lleva un traje gris y una corbata.* *Para ir a la fiesta voy a llevar pantalones y un top.*
5 ¿Llevas uniforme? (pp. 50–51) Talking about your school uniform	8C3 Daily life and young people [L] 8W2 Connectives [R] 8W4 Word endings [R] 8L3 Relaying gist and detail [R] 9W4 Main inflections [R]	**2c** ask and answer questions **4c** compare cultures **5c** express opinions	Adjectival agreements: *claro/oscuro* *¿Llevas uniforme?* *Sí, llevo pantalones negros y una camisa blanca.* *¿Cuál prefieres, una camisa o una camiseta?* *¿Cuáles prefieres, las faldas o los pantalones?*
6 En la calle principal (pp. 52–53) Talking about types of shops Saying where you can buy things	8W8 Non-literal meanings [L] 8S8 High-frequency words [L] 9S2 Order of elements in sentences [L] 8S2 Connectives [R]	**3c** use knowledge of English	Present tense of *poder: puedo, puedes, …* Direct object pronouns: *comprar lo/la/los/las* *¿Dónde puedo comprar pan?* *Puedes comprarlo en la panadería.*
Resumen y Prepárate (pp. 54–55) Pupils' checklist and practice test			

Unit	Key Framework objectives	PoS	Key language and Grammar
7 ¡Extra! ¿Cuál es tu estilo? (pp. 56–57) Optional unit: personal style	9C3 Youth attitudes to sport and culture [L] 9W8 Using grammar to understand words [R] 9S2 Order of elements in sentences [R] 9T3 Authentic texts as sources [R] 9T4 Using support materials [R]	**2h** scanning texts **3b** use context to interpret meaning **3c** use knowledge of English **4a** working with authentic materials **5d** respond to different types of language	
Te toca a ti (pp. 116–117) Self-access reading and writing at two levels			

1 ¿Qué ropa llevan?

(Pupil's Book pages 42–43)

Main topics and objectives

- Talking about clothes
- Comparing prices

Key Framework objectives

- Word, phrase and clause sequencing 8S1 (Launch)
- Adding abstract words 8W1 (Reinforcement)
- Dictionary use 8T4 (Reinforcement)

Other aims

- Pronunciation practice

Grammar

- Comparatives: *más* + adjective + *que*
- Adjectives: *barato/a(s)*, *caro/a(s)*, *grande(s)*, *pequeño/a(s)*

Key language

Lleva …
una blusa   una falda

unas botas   un jersey
unos calcetines   unos pantalones
una camisa   unos vaqueros
una camiseta   unas zapatillas de deporte
una chaqueta   unos zapatos

Los pantalones son más baratos que los vaqueros.
Las camisas son más caras que los calcetines.

Resources

Cassette B, side 1
CD2, tracks 2 and 3
Cuaderno B, page 23
Starter 1, Resource and Assessment File, page 45
Hojas de trabajo, Resource and Assessment File, pages 48 and 49 (*la camisa, la falda, las botas, el jersey, los pantalones, los zapatos, los vaqueros, los calcetines, la chaqueta, las zapatillas de deporte*)
OHTs 13 and 14

Starter 1 [8S1]

Aim: revision of 'comparisons' – *más* + adjective + *que*; pronunciation practice.

Text manipulation: Using *Resource and Assessment File*, page 45, ask pupils to unjumble the following:

1 Que más La Torre Eiffel es alta Big Ben el (*La Torre Eiffel es más alta el Big Ben.*)

2 La es nutritiva que más los paella perritos calientes (*La paella es más nutritiva que los perritos calientes.*)

3 es deporte El más que interesante la geografía (*El deporte es más interesante que la geografía.*)

If time allows, when pupils have finished unjumbling, ask them to work with a partner and practise saying these sentences. They will either agree with the statement (*Estoy de acuerdo*) or disagree (*No estoy de acuerdo*).

➕ If they disagree, pupils must rejig the statements. For example, 2 *No estoy de acuerdo. Los perritos calientes son más nutritivos que la paella.*

1a Mira los dibujos y escucha. ¿Verdad (✓) o mentira (✗)? (1–10) (AT1/2) [8L1]

✖ Listening for information/instructions, Level B

Listening. Pupils look at pictures of three people, listen to a series of statements about what each person is wearing and decide whether each statement is true or false. Teachers should first introduce the clothes vocabulary. This could be done using realia, or pupils

could work in pairs to find out what the 12 items listed on page 42 mean. If the latter option is used, teachers should ensure pupils receive aural practice of the new vocabulary before tackling the listening comprehension exercise. The vocabulary gives an opportunity to revise the *que* and the *ll* sound.

Tapescript

1 *Ester lleva una blusa.*
2 *Martín lleva una camisa.*
3 *Ester lleva unos pantalones.*
4 *Isabel lleva un jersey.*
5 *Martín lleva zapatos y calcetines.*
6 *Isabel lleva una chaqueta.*
7 *Martín lleva una falda.*
8 *Isabel lleva una camiseta.*
9 *Ester lleva botas.*
10 *Isabel lleva vaqueros y zapatillas de deporte.*

Answers

1 ✓	2 ✓	3 ✗	4 ✗	5 ✓	6 ✓	7 ✗	8 ✓
9 ✓	10 ✓						

1b Describe lo que llevan Ester, Martín e Isabel. Tu compañero/a dice 'verdad' o 'mentira'. (AT2/2)

✖ Speaking and interacting with others, Level C

Speaking pairwork. Pupils take it in turns to make statements to their partner about what one of the three people on page 42 is wearing and their partner must decide whether the statement is true or false.

2a Escucha y contesta a las preguntas. (AT1/3) [8L3]

❌ Listening for information/instructions, Level D

Listening. Pupils listen to a dialogue in a sportswear shop and answer questions in English. Once they have completed the exercise, teachers may wish to play the recording again and ask pupils about the meaning of some of the key shopping phrases used, such as *¿Qué vas a comprar?*, *Voy a comprar …* , *Es muy cara*, *Es más barata* and *Cuesta sólo … .*

Tapescript

– ¿Qué vas a comprar, Oscar?
– Voy a comprar una camisa del Real Madrid para mi hermana.
– ¿Cuánto es?
– Vamos a ver … el precio es sesenta y cinco euros. Es muy cara.
– La gorra es más barata. Cuesta sólo quince euros.
– Vale. Entonces, voy a comprar una gorra … y unos pantalones cortos.

Answers

1 65 euros	**2** 15 euros **3** a cap and some shorts

2b Mira la foto y tus respuestas de **2a** y completa las frases. (AT3/2) [8W4]

❌ Knowing about language

Reading. Pupils read the prices on the photograph tags and complete a series of sentences, using the comparative (introduced in Module 1, Unit 1). Pupils need to be familiar with the adjectives *caro* and *barato* to do this exercise and should be reminded about the rules governing adjective agreement.

Answers

> 1 *Las camisas son más caras que las botas.*
> 2 La gorra es más barata que la camisa.
> 3 Las botas son más caras que los pantalones cortos.
> 4 Los pantalones cortos son más baratos que las camisas.
> 5 Una camisa es mucho más cara que una gorra.

Starter 2 [8W1]

Aim: vocabulary extension (thinking about words). To get pupils to work out vocabulary through context, cognates, picture clues, knowledge of other words, etc., before using a dictionary.

Ask pupils to work out the meaning of the following words without looking them up in the glossary: *rebeca, rebeca con cremallera, vaqueros, sandalias, zapatillas de deporte, bolsillo* (plus any others you wish to add).

3a Mira el catálogo y busca las palabras en español para: (AT3/3) [8W1; 8T4]

❌ Reading for information/instructions, Level E

Reading. Pupils read an extract from a clothing catalogue and then find the Spanish for ten items of vocabulary. They should be encouraged to use a range of reading skills and strategies – such as context, logic, prediction, picture clues and cognates/near-cognates – to work out as many answers as possible, before being allowed to check or look up words up in a dictionary.

Answers

1 mangas	**2** cremallera	**3** 100% algodón
4 cuello alto	**5** sandalias	**6** (de) cuero
7 cinturón	**8** parte delantera	**9** bolsillos **10** precio

3b Empareja las dos partes de las frases. (AT3/3) [8S1]

❌ Reading for information/instructions, Level E

Reading. Pupils pair up sentence halves, using information from the text in **3a**. All the sentences involve use of the comparative or the superlative. The *¡Ojo!* feature explains the two Spanish words for size (*número* and *talla*).

Answers

1 c **2** a **3** d **4** b **5** f **6** e **7** h **8** g	

3c Escribe cinco frases similares. (AT4/4) [8S6]

❌ Exchange information/ideas, Level C

Writing. Pupils write five more sentences, like those in **3b**, about the clothing in the catalogue text.

Plenary

Ask pupils to write down three strategies they use to help them work out the meaning of words without looking them up in a dictionary. See exercise **3a** in the *Teacher's Guide* for strategies. Take feedback.

Cuaderno B, page 23

1a Empareja las descripciones con las personas. (AT3/2)

❌ Reading for information/instructions, Level C

Reading. Pupils match descriptions of what people are wearing to the relevant pictures.

Answers

a 2 **b** 3 **c** 1 **d** 4	

1 ¿Qué ropa llevan?

1b Mira el dibujo y describe lo que lleva Carmen. (AT4/3)

✖ Exchange information/ideas, Level C

Writing. Pupils write a description of what someone is wearing, from a picture prompt.

Answers

Carmen lleva una falda, una camiseta (ajustada) y unas botas.

2a Lee las frases y mira los dibujos. ¿Verdad (✓) o mentira (✗)? (AT3/2) [8W4]

✖ Reading for information/instructions, Level D

Reading. A true/false exercise, based on statements about clothing, using the comparative.

Answers

1 ✗ 2 ✓ 3 ✓ 4 ✓ 5 ✗

2b Escribe cinco frases similares. (AT4/3) [8W4]

✖ Exchange information/instructions, Level C

Writing. Pupils must write five statements similar to those in **2a**.

Hojas de trabajo, Resource and Assessment File, pages 48 and 49

Cards for pairwork featuring items of clothing: pupils match the pictures to the correct words.

2 Me gusta aquella camiseta roja

(Pupil's Book pages 44–45)

Main topics

- Talking about what clothes you like and what suits you

Key Framework objectives

- Word endings 8W4 (Reinforcement)
- Word, phrase and clause sequencing 8S1 (Reinforcement)

Grammar

Demonstrative adjectives:
este, esta, estos, estas
ese, esa, esos, esas
aquel, aquella, aquellos, aquellas

Key language

¿Qué tal me queda (el jersey)?
La chaqueta me queda ajustada.
Los vaqueros me quedan pequeños.

Te queda pequeño/a.
Te quedan grandes.
No, te queda mal el color.

amarillo/a(s)	*naranja*
azul(es)	*negro/a(s)*
beige	*rojo/a(s)*
blanco/a(s)	*verde(s)*
gris(es)	*violeta*
marrón(es)	

este/ese/aquel jersey
esta/esa/aquella chaqueta
estos/esos/aquellos pantalones
estas/esas/aquellas sandalias

Resources

Cassette B, side 1
CD2, tracks 4 and 5
Cuaderno B, page 24
Starter 1, Resource and Assessment File, page 46
OHTs 15 and 16

Starter 1 [8W4]

Aim: to introduce demonstrative adjectives *este, esta, estos, estas* in another familiar context before introducing them with clothes. Looking for patterns.

Write the following on the board: *… flan, … plátanos, … chuletas, … pera.*

Then tell pupils you are going to write up the four words for 'this' and 'these' (*este, esta, estos, estas*). Working in pairs, ask pupils to match up the demonstrative adjectives with the nouns. How did they decide which adjective to put with which noun?

✚ Pupils produce sentences such as *Esta pera es deliciosa*, etc.

Alternative starter 1 [8W4]

Aim: to revise adjective agreement.

Using *Resource and Assessment File*, page 46, prepare an OHT or write up the following on the board.

amarilla	*roja*	*(fem. sing.)*
naranja	*beige*	*(don't change)*
negras	*rojas*	*(fem pl.)*
blanco	*negro*	*(masc. sing.)*
verdes	*grises*	*(fem. or masc. pl.)*
rojos	*amarillos*	*(masc. pl.)*

Below, put a list of adjectives which pupils must place in the correct row – they must be able to justify their choice!

negra, rosa, verdes, amarillo, azules, blancas

1 Escucha y escribe el orden en que se menciona la ropa. (1–8) (AT1/2) [8W4; 8L3]

✖ Listening for information/instructions, Level C

Listening and writing. Pupils listen to a series of statements and identify the item of clothing mentioned in each one. A number of different colours are mentioned in the recording and the colour chart on page 44 supports pupils' understanding of these. The recording also presents the three demonstrative adjectives *este, ese* and *aquel*, which are explained in the *Gramática* box on page 44. Teachers may wish to refer pupils to the *Gramática before* undertaking the listening task, if it is felt that the new grammar might hamper pupils' understanding of the recording. Alternatively, teachers might prefer to wait until exercise 1 has been completed, then use the *Gramática* and play the recording again, asking pupils to spot which demonstrative adjective is used in each statement, in which form and why.

Tapescript

1 *Me gusta aquella camiseta roja.*
2 *A mí, no. Pero me gustan esos pantalones azules.*
3 *Me gusta ese jersey en negro.*
4 *Me gusta este jersey.*
5 *Aquellos vaqueros son baratos.*
6 *Me gustan estos zapatos marrones.*
7 *Yo prefiero ~~esas~~ zapatillas blancas.* *aquellas*
8 *A mí me encanta aquel cinturón.*

Answers

1 b	**2** g	**3** e	**4** i	**5** c	**6** k	**7** h	**8** a

2 Me gusta aquella camiseta roja

2a Completa las frases con la forma apropiada de 'aquel', 'ese' o 'este'. (AT3/3) [8W4]

✕ Knowing about language

Reading. A grammar gap-filling exercise, in which pupils must use the correct form of the three demonstrative adjectives.

Answers

1 *aquella* **2** aquella **3** este **4** esas **5** aquellas **6** esos **7** aquellos **8** esta

2b Mira los dibujos en **1** otra vez y escribe tus opiniones sobre cuatro cosas. (AT4/4) [8W4; 8S1]

✕ Exchange information/ideas, Level C

Writing. Pupils write sentences, giving their opinion of each item of clothing shown in the drawing for exercise 1. They must use a demonstrative adjective and colour in each sentence, taking care to make both agree with the noun.

R Some pupils might benefit from being given a sentence-building grid, on a worksheet or OHT, as support for this exercise. For example:

	este	ese	aquel	jersey (etc.)	negro (etc.)
Me encanta ... (No) Me gusta ... Odio ...	esta	esa	aquella	falda (etc.)	negra (etc.)
	estos	esos	aquellos	vaqueros (etc.)	negros (etc.)
	estas	esas	aquellas	botas (etc.)	negras (etc.)

Starter 2 [8W4]

Aim: recap agreement of colours with clothes.

Using mini-whiteboards or pen and paper, call out a list of clothes. Ask pupils to write down a suitable colour for each: it doesn't matter what colour as long as it agrees with the noun. For example: *una camiseta (roja, negra, blanca).* Ask pupils to hold up their board/paper for you to see and check.

3a Escucha y elige la frase apropiada para cada dibujo. (1–5) (AT1/3) [8L3]

✕ Listening for information/instructions, Level C

Listening. Pupils match short dialogues to the drawings on the page. This introduces *me/te queda(n)* and teachers should first refer pupils to the *Gramática* box on page 44, which explains this point.

Tapescript

1 – ¿Qué tal me queda este jersey?

– Te queda grande.
2 – Esta camiseta me queda pequeña.
3 – ¿Me queda bien el chándal?
   – No, te queda mal el color.
4 – ¿Qué tal me quedan las botas?
   – Te quedan muy grandes.
5 – Te queda muy bien.

Answers

1 c 2 d 3 b 4 e 5 a

3b Con tu compañero/a, elige un dibujo de **3a** y di la frase apropiada. (AT2/3) [8W4; 8S4]

✕ Speaking and interacting with others, Level C

Speaking. In pairs, pupils practise asking and answering questions, using *quedar*, referring to the pictures in **3a**. Teachers should first give pupils whole-class oral practice of making questions and statements with *quedar*, to ensure accurate pronunciation.

Plenary [8W4]

Ask a pupil to describe what an adjective is to the rest of the class.

What endings do you add to make it agree with the noun ? (*-o, -a, -os, -as, -s* if the adjective ends in *e*).

However, some colours do not change. Can anyone name them (*naranja, rosa, beige*)?

Cuaderno B, page 24

1 Completa las frases con la forma apropiada del color. (AT4/1–2) [8W4]

✕ Knowing about language

Writing. A gap-filling exercise, using adjectives of colour. Pupils should read the information box about adjectival agreement before tackling the exercise.

Answers

1 negros **2** blanco **3** verdes **4** azul **5** amarillo **6** gris **7** roja **8** marrones

2 Completa las frases con las palabras apropiadas de la lista. (AT4/1–2) [8W4; 8S1]

✕ Knowing about language

Writing. A second gap-filling exercise, based on adjectives (including demonstrative adjectives).

Answers

1 blusa **2** ese **3** botas **4** preciosos **5** cinturones **6** gorro **7** esta **8** Aquellas

3 Empareja las frases con los dibujos. (AT3/2)

Knowing about language

Reading. Pupils match sentences using *me queda(n)* to the relevant pictures.

Answers

1 b	**2** d	**3** a	**4** c	**5** e					

(Pupil's Book pages 46–47)

Main topics

- Shopping for clothes

Key Framework objectives

- Listening for inferences 9L1 (Launch)
- Word endings 8W4 (Reinforcement)
- Word, phrase and clause sequencing 8S1 (Reinforcement)

Grammar

Direct object pronouns:
¿Me lo/la/los/las puedo probar?

Key language

Este vestido es bonito. ¿Me lo puedo probar?
La chaqueta me queda bien. ¿Me la puedo probar?
Me gustan los vaqueros. ¿Me los puedo probar?
Aquellas sandalias son estupendas. ¿Me las puedo probar?
¿Qué número usa Ud?
El (treinta y nueve).
¿Qué tal le quedan?
Me quedan (preciosas).
Me lo/la/los/las llevo.

Resources

Cassette B, side 1
CD2, tracks 6 and 7
Cuaderno B, page 25
Starter 1, Resource and Assessment File, page 47
OHTs 17 and 18

Starter 1 [8S1]

Aim: to revise pronouns and demonstrative adjectives and building up a sentence in the correct sequence.

Using *Resource and Assessment File*, page 47, give pupils a card with a word on it and ask them to make a sentence in the correct order. Clap hands: pupils move round to form another sentence. Alternatively, provide a set of cards per group (no more than four pupils).

1 Escucha y escribe la letra de la ropa que quieren probarse. (1–6) (AT1/3) [9L1; 8W4; 8L3]

✖ Listening for information/instructions, Level C

Listening. Pupils listen to a series of questions and statements about trying on clothes and note down the letter of the relevant item of clothing in each case. After completing this exercise, it is suggested that teachers refer pupils to the *Gramática* on page 46, which explains direct object pronouns, then play the recording again, asking pupils to spot which pronoun is used in each case and why.

Tapescript

1 *Me gusta aquella falda azul. ¿Me la puedo probar?*
2 *Ese vestido es muy bonito. ¿Me lo puedo probar?*
3 *Quiero probarme este jersey.*
4 *Me encanta esa camiseta. ¿Me la puedo probar?*
5 *Estos vaqueros no son caros. ¿Me los puedo probar?*
6 *Aquellas botas son preciosas. ¿Me las puedo probar?*

Answers

1 b	2 e	3 c	4 a	5 d	6 f

2 Con tu compañero/a, pregunta y contesta. (AT2/4) [8L4]

✖ Speaking and interacting with others, Level C

Speaking. Pupils take turns with a partner, asking to try on the items of clothing shown in the pictures and using the correct direct object pronoun.

Starter 2 [8W4]

Aim: to recap direct object pronouns.

Write on the board or call out the following sentences. Ask pupils to write the appropriate form of 'Can I try it on? *¿Me lo puedo probar?*' for each. You may wish to write the various combinations of the above on the board for pupils to choose from.

1 *Me gusta este jersey. (¿Me lo puedo probar?)*
2 *Me gustan estos vaqueros. (¿Me los puedo probar?)*
3 *Me encanta esta chaqueta. (¿Me la puedo probar?)*
4 *Me encantan estas botas. (¿Me las puedo probar?)*

3 Lee y escucha el diálogo entre la dependienta y el cliente. Contesta a las preguntas. (AT3/4) [8S4; 9L1]

✖ Reading for information/instructions, Level D

Reading. Pupils read a clothes shop dialogue and answer questions in Spanish. As a follow-up, teachers may wish to draw pupils' attention to key shopping phrases, for example, by doing a 'find the Spanish for ... ' exercise. Useful phrases to look for might include: 'What size do you take?', 'Here you are', 'May I try them in a size 40?', 'I'm sorry, we don't have them in a 40', 'They are very comfortable', 'I'll take them', etc. Following this, teachers may also wish pupils to practise the dialogue, orally, in pairs.

Tapescript

Dependienta: ¡Hola!

Cliente: ¡Hola! Me gustan aquellas botas negras. ¿Me las puedo probar?

Dependienta: Claro. ¿Qué número usa Ud?

Cliente: Un treinta y nueve.

Dependienta: Vale. Aquí las tiene.

Dependienta: ¿Qué tal le quedan?

Cliente: Me quedan pequeñas. ¿Me las puedo probar en un cuarenta?

Dependienta: Lo siento. No las tengo en un cuarenta. Pero tenemos estas botas marrones.

Cliente: Me las pruebo. A ver … Son muy cómodas. ¿Son más caras o más baratas que las botas negras?

Dependienta: Son más caras. Son ciento doce euros. Pero son de cuero. Le quedan preciosas.

Cliente: Me las llevo.

Answers

a Quiere probarse unas botas negras.
b Le quedan pequeñas.
c Son un treinta y nueve.
d Le quedan bien en un cuarenta.
e Cuestan 112 euros.
f Las botas negras cuestan menos que las botas marrones.
g El cliente compra las botas marrones.

4a Copia y completa las frases con las palabras apropiadas. (AT4/4)

✖ Knowing about language

Writing. Pupils complete a similar dialogue to the one in exercise 3, replacing the pictures with words chosen from a 'menu' of missing words on the page.

Answers

| vaqueros | treinta y ocho | pequeños |
| cuarenta | bien | |

4b Con tu compañero/a, haz la conversación entre un(a) cliente y un(a) dependiente/a. (AT2/4) [8L4]

✖ Speaking and interacting with others, Level D

Speaking. Pupils work in pairs to practise the dialogue in **4a**.

➕ Able pupils could be encouraged to create a new dialogue, adapting elements of the conversation in exercise 3 and adding their own ideas, paying careful attention to accuracy with direct object pronouns and adjectival agreement.

Cuaderno B, page 25

1 Empareja las frases. (AT3/2) [8W4]

✖ Knowing about language

Reading. Pupils match statements about clothes to questions using the direct object pronoun.

Answers

| 1 f/c | 2 a/e | 3 b | 4 d | 5 f/c | 6 e/a |

2 Pon las frases de conversación en el orden correcto. (AT3/3) [8T2]

✖ Reading for information/instructions, Level D

Reading. Pupils must place sentences in the correct order, to create a dialogue in a shoe shop.

Answers

| 1 b | 2 f | 3 a | 4 d | 5 c | 6 e |
| 7 h | 8 l | 9 g | 10 j | 11 k | 12 i |

3 Escribe un diálogo similar. (AT4/4) [8T2]

✖ Writing imaginatively, Level D

Writing. Pupils adapt the model dialogue in exercise 2, to create a similar dialogue.

módulo 3

4 ¿Qué vas a llevar para ir a la fiesta?

(Pupil's Book pages 48–49)

Main topics

- Describing clothes
- Asking what someone is wearing
- Saying what you are wearing

Key Framework objectives

- Present, past, *future* 8S7 (Launch)
- Main inflections 9W4 (Launch)
- Recognising rhetorical devices 9L2 (Launch)
- Verb tenses (near future) 8W5 (Reinforcement)

Grammar

The immediate future: *ir* + *a* + infinitive

Key language

Para ir a la fiesta/a la playa, voy a llevar

un abrigo	*unos zapatos de tacón alto*
una camisa	*unas zapatillas (de deporte)*

una corbata	*un top*
una gorra	*un traje*
una sudadera (con capucha)	*un vestido*
ajustado/a	*corto/a*
ancho/a	*elegante*

Resources

Cassette B, side 1
CD2, tracks 8 and 9
Cuaderno B, page 26
Hojas de trabajo, Resource and Assessment File, pages 48 and 49 (*el cinturón, la corbata, la gorra, el abrigo, el traje*)
Grammar, Resource and Assessment File, page 50

Starter 1 [8W4; 8L1]

Aim: practising the indefinite article – *un, una, unos, unas.*

Write the following items of clothing on the board and ask pupils to fill in the gaps with the appropriate form of the indefinite article: *abrigo, corbata, sudadera, zapatos, pantalones, zapatillas de deporte, gorra*. Ask pupils to write down what these items of clothing are. When going through the answers, there is an opportunity to work on the pronunciation of 'j' in *un traje* and *ajustado*.

1a Mira las fotos y lee. ¿A quién se describe? (AT3/3) [8S1]

✕ Reading for information/instructions, Level D

Reading. Pupils match photos of famous personalities to descriptions of what each person is wearing.

Answers

1	Will Smith	3	Eminem
2	Kylie Minogue	4	Christina Aguilera

1b Escucha y comprueba tus respuestas. (AT1/3)

✕ Listening for information/instructions, Level C

Listening. Pupils check their answers to **1a** by listening to descriptions of who is wearing what.

Tapescript

1 *Will Smith lleva un traje gris y una corbata. También lleva una camisa negra.*
2 *Kylie Minogue lleva un vestido elegante y zapatos de tacón alto.*
3 *Eminem lleva una gorra, una sudadera y pantalones anchos.*
4 *Christina Aguilera lleva un top de lycra y una falda corta y ajustada. También un abrigo estampado de leopardo.*

2 Describe a una persona de las fotos. Tu compañero/a dice quién es. (AT2/3) [8S6]

✕ Speaking to convey information, Level C

Speaking. Pupils take it in turns to describe what one of the famous people is wearing and their partner has to say who is being referred to.

3 ¿Qué van a llevar? Escucha y elige los dibujos apropiados. (1–5) (AT1/5) [8W5; 9W5]

✕ Listening for information/instructions, Level C/D

Listening. Pupils listen to a series of dialogues in which people discuss what they are going to wear to various events and write down the letters of the relevant pictures. The *Gramática* on page 48 reminds pupils about the use of *ir a* + infinitive to talk about the immediate future.

➕ You could play the final item again and draw pupils' attention to the colloquialisms – *Sí, claro, Lo de siempre, Entonces, ¡Por supuesto!* [8C5; 9L2]

4 ¿Qué vas a llevar para ir a la fiesta?

Tapescript

1 – ¿Qué vas a llevar para ir a la fiesta?
– Voy a llevar pantalones negros … y un top ajustado.
2 – ¿Y tú? ¿Qué vas a llevar para ir a la fiesta?
– Voy a llevar una falda corta y una camiseta.
3 – ¿Qué vas a llevar para ir a la boda?
– Voy a llevar un traje y una corbata.
4 – ¿Y tú? ¿Qué vas a llevar a la boda?
– Voy a llevar un vestido muy elegante y zapatos de tacón alto.
5 – ¿Vas a ir a la discoteca mañana?
– Sí, claro.
– ¿Qué te vas a poner?
– Lo de siempre.
– Entonces te vas a poner una sudadera … con capucha.
– ¡Por supuesto!
– Zapatillas … y una gorra.

Answers

1 a,b	2 e,j	3 f,h	4 g,c	5 d,i,k

Starter 2 [8W5; 9W5]

Aim: to recap *ir*.

Write the following on the board and ask pupils to match up.

First column: I am going, you are going, he is going, they are going, she is going.

Scond column: *ellos van, ella va, tú vas, yo voy, él va.*

4 Empareja las dos partes correctas de cada frase. (AT3/5) [8W5; 9W5]

⚑ Reading for information/instructions, Level D

Reading. Pupils match up sentence halves about what people are going to wear to various events. The *¡Ojo!* box points out the two words for 'to wear' in Spanish (*llevar* and *ponerse*).

Answers

1 d	2 c	3 e	4 b	5 a	6 f

5 Escribe sobre la ropa que vas a llevar. (AT4/5) [8W4; 9W4]

⚑ Exchange information/ideas, Level C/E

Writing. Pupils write about what they are going to wear to go to a party and a disco. The *Gramática* box on page 49 reminds them about adjectival agreement.

Plenary [8W5; 9W5]

Ask a pupil to explain when you use the immediate future. How is it formed? Give pupils two minutes to think about the following question: *¿Qué vas a llevar a la fiesta?* Take class feedback or ask pupils to work with a partner.

Cuaderno B, page 26

1a Elige la descripción apropiada para cada dibujo. (AT3/2)

⚑ Reading for information/instructions, Level C

Reading. Pupils match descriptions of clothing to the relevant pictures.

Answers

1 a	2 a	3 a	4 a	5 b	6 a

1b Escribe una descripción de cada artículo. (AT4/3)

⚑ Exchange information/ideas, Level C

Writing. Pupils write descriptions of pictures of clothing.

Answers

1	una chaqueta negra
2	una corbata rayada
3	una falda de rayas
4	un vestido elegante
5	vaqueros
6	un traje negro

2a Empareja las preguntas con las respuetas. (AT3/2) [8W5; 8S4; 9W5]

⚑ Reading for information/instructions, Level C/D

Reading. A matching exercise, linking questions to answers about what you are going to wear for different occasions.

Answers

1 b	2 e	3 a	4 c	5 d

2b Contesta a las preguntas. (AT4/3) [8S4]

⚑ Exchange information/ideas, Level C/E

Writing. Pupils write their own answers to questions about what they are going to wear.

Hojas de trabajo, Resource and Assessment File, pages 48 and 49

Cards for pairwork featuring items of clothing: pupils match the pictures to the correct words.

Grammar, Resource and Assessment File, page 50

Using pronouns

1 Pupils complete sentences using the pronouns appropriate to the items to which they are referring.

Answers

> **a** Me encanta la camiseta, ¿me la puedo probar?
> **b** Odio los pantalones, no los quiero.
> **c** ¿Dónde está la falda azul?, no la veo.
> **d** Tengo una gorra negra, la llevo en invierno.
> **e** Me gustan las zapatillas, ¿me las puedo probar?
> **f** El uniforme es obligatorio, lo llevo en el instituto.

Infinitives

2 Pupils match up the 1st person singular form of each verb with its infinitive.

Answers

First Person	Infinitive
Voy	ir
Hago	hacer
Practico	practicar
Monto	montar
Salgo	salir
Llevo	llevar

Present and future

3 Pupils complete the grid giving the meaning of each verb in the 1st person singular and then putting them into the immediate future tense with the appropriate translation.

Answers

Present	Meaning	Immediate future	Meaning
Llevo	*I wear*	*Voy a llevar*	*I'm going to wear*
Voy a la discoteca	I go to the disco	Voy a ir a la discoteca	I'm going to go to the disco
Monto a caballo	I go horseriding	Voy a montar a caballo	I'm going to go horseriding
Hago camping	I go camping	Voy a hacer camping	I'm going to go camping
Salgo con amigos	I go out with friends	Voy a salir con amigos	I'm going to go out with friends
Practico el ciclismo	I go cycling	Voy a practicar el ciclismo	I'm going to go cycling

4 Pupils write their own sentences about what they are going to do over the coming weekend using the immediate future tense.

5 ¿Llevas uniforme?

(Pupil's Book pages 50–51)

Main topics

- Talking about your school uniform

Key Framework objectives

- Connectives 8W2 (Reinforcement)
- Word endings 8W4 (Reinforcement)
- Relaying gist and detail 8L3 (Reinforcement)
- Daily life and young people 8C3 (Reinforcement)
- Main inflections 9W4 (Reinforcement)

Grammar

- ¿Cuál …?/¿Cuáles …?
- Adjectival agreements: claro/oscuro

Key language

¿Llevas uniforme?
Sí, llevo (pantalones negros) y (una camisa blanca).
No llevo uniforme.

¿Cuál prefieres, (una camisa) o (una camiseta)?
¿Cuáles prefieres, (las faldas) o (los pantalones)?
Prefiero …
Porque son más/menos …
cómodo/a(s)   elegante(s)
práctico/a(s)   barato/a(s)

Resources

Cassette B, side 1
CD2, tracks 10 and 11
Cuaderno B, page 27

Starter 1 [8W4; 9W4]

Aim: revision of comparisons (nouns and adjectives).

Write a list of nouns and a list of adjectives on the board. You could brainstorm these with your class. Then ask pupils to make sentences using the structure: *más* + adjective + *que*/*menos* + adjective + *que*.

For example. Column 1 (nouns) person in class, food, school subject, etc. Column 2 (adjectives) any they have met so far: colours, food description, description of school subjects, personal characteristics, etc.

1a Mira los dibujos. Escucha e identifica los uniformes de los diferentes países. (1–4) (AT1/3) [8L3]

✕ Listening for information/instructions, Level C/D

Listening. Pupils listen to people from four different countries describing their school uniforms and match each one to the relevant picture. The recording introduces *claro* and *oscuro* and the *Gramática* on page 50 explains that when these are used the adjective is invariable.

Tapescript

1 – ¿Llevas uniforme?
  – Sí, llevo una camisa blanca, una falda naranja y calcetines blancos.
2 – ¿Llevas uniforme?
  – Sí, llevo una camisa blanca, un jersey azul y pantalones negros.
3 – ¿Llevas uniforme?
  – Sí, llevo una camisa blanca y una falda azul.
4 – ¿Llevas uniforme al instituto?
  – No, no llevo uniforme.
  – Pues, ¿qué llevas?
  – Llevo vaqueros, una camiseta y zapatillas de deporte.

Answers

1 c	2 a	3 b	4 d

2 Mira los dibujos. Con tu compañero/a, pregunta y contesta. (AT2/3) [8L4]

✕ Speaking and interacting with others, Level C

Speaking. Pupils work in pairs to ask and answer questions about school uniform, describing the pictures on the page. The vocabulary box gives help with how to say 'checked' and 'striped'.

3a Escucha y lee las frases. Juan habla de la ropa. ¿Verdad (✓) o mentira (✗)? (AT1/4, AT3/3) [8C3]

✕ Listening for information/instructions, Level E

Listening. Pupils listen to a boy being interviewed about his clothing preferences and do a true/false exercise. This exercise uses a number of examples of the comparative, introduced in Module 1, Unit 1. Teachers should ensure pupils understand the six statements on the page before undertaking the listening task.

Tapescript

1 – ¿Qué prefieres llevar, zapatillas de deporte o zapatos?
  – Prefiero llevar zapatillas de deporte.
  – ¿Por qué?
  – En mi opinión las zapatillas de deporte son más cómodas que los zapatos.
2 – ¿Qué prefieres llevar, uniforme o vaqueros?
  – Prefiero llevar uniforme.
  – ¿Por qué?
  – Porque el uniforme es más práctico que los vaqueros.
3 – ¿En tu opinión, cuáles son más elegantes, las faldas o los pantalones?
  – Yo creo que los pantalones son más elegantes.
4 – ¿Cuál es más práctico, una camisa o una camiseta?
  – Naturalmente, es más práctico llevar una camiseta que una camisa.
5 – ¿Qué prefieres llevar, una chaqueta o un jersey?
  – Prefiero llevar una chaqueta. Un jersey es menos elegante que una chaqueta.

6 – *Una sudadera es más cómoda que un jersey.*
  – *Estoy de acuerdo. Es mucho más cómoda que un jersey.*

Answers

1 ✓ 2 ✗ 3 ✗ 4 ✗ 5 ✓ 6 ✗

3b Con tu compañero/a, pregunta y contesta. (AT2/4) [8W4; 8S4]

❌ Speaking about experiences/feelings/opinions, Level D

Speaking. Pupils discuss their clothing preferences, adapting the model dialogue on the page. The *Gramática* on page 51 reminds them of how to use *¿Cuál?*.

Starter 2 [8W2; 8L4]

Aim: recap use of *prefiero*, items of clothing, agreement of adjectives and *porque*.

Write a selection of clothes on the board. Ask pupils to choose two items and write down why they prefer them, e.g. *Prefiero la camiseta porque es más práctica.*

4a Lee los textos y contesta a las preguntas. (AT3/4) [8S4]

❌ Reading for information/instructions, Level D

Reading. Pupils read two texts about school uniforms and answer questions in Spanish. As before, they should be encouraged to use reading skills and strategies to make sense of the text, only looking words up in a dictionary as a last resort.

Answers

1 Sólo hay uniforme en algunos colegios privados.
2 Lleva unos vaqueros, una camisa o camiseta y zapatillas de deporte.
3 Llevar uniforme es menos cómodo.
4 Llevar vaqueros es más barato.
5 Es privado.
6 Es a cuadros.
7 Llevan pantalones grises.
8 Llevan todos un jersey verde.
9 Le gusta porque es elegante.
10 Llevar vaqueros es menos cómodo.

4b Lee los textos otra vez y escribe unas frases similares para describir tu uniforme. (AT4/4) [8W2; 8T6]

❌ Exchange information/ideas, Level C/E

Writing. Pupils adapt the texts in **4a** to write about their own school uniform.

R Some pupils might benefit from being give a writing frame for this task on a worksheet or OHT.

Plenary [8W4]

Ask a volunteer to explain the difference between the two questions: *¿Cuál prefieres?* and *¿Cuáles prefieres?* Ask pupils to write down an example for each.

Cuaderno B, page 27

1a Lee las cartas y escribe M (Mariano) o S (Santiago) para cada dibujo. (AT3/3) [8T2]

❌ Reading for information/instructions, Level D

Reading. After reading two texts about clothing, pupils must allocate each picture to either Mariano or Santiago.

Answers

1 S 2 M 3 M 4 S 5 M 6 S 7 M

1b Subraya los adjetivos en las cartas. (AT3/3) [8S1]

❌ Knowing about language

Reading. Pupils must find and underline the adjectives in the two texts in **1a**.

Answers

Mariano: azul marino, blanca, de rayas azules, amarillas, de cuero negros, negros, incómodo, no es práctico
Santiago: vaquera, de deporte, cómodo, práctico

1c ¿Verdad (✓) o mentira (✗)? (AT3/3)

❌ Reading for information/instructions, Level D

Reading. A true/false exercise, based on the texts in **1a**.

Answers

1 ✓ 2 ✗ 3 ✗ 4 ✓ 5 ✓ 6 ✓ 7 ✓

2 Mira el dibujo y describe el uniforme de Jacobo. (AT4/4) [8W4]

❌ Exchange information/ideas, Level C/E

Writing. Pupils write a description of Jacobo's school uniform, as shown in the picture. The *¡Ojo!* feature reminds them to use adjectives to enhance their writing.

Answers *(to include)*

un jersey gris
una corbata de rayas
una chaqueta negra
unos pantalones negros
unas zapatos negros

6 En la calle principal

(Pupil's Book pages 52–53)

Main topics

- Talking about types of shops
- Saying where you can buy things

Key Framework objectives

- Non-literal meanings 8W8 (Launch)
- Connectives 8S2 (Launch)
- High-frequency words 8S8 (Launch)
- Order of elements in sentences 9S2 (Launch)

Grammar

- Present tense of *poder*: *puedo*, *puedes*, etc.
- Direct object pronouns: *comprarlo/la/los/las*

Key language

¿Dónde puedo comprar …?
Puedes comprarlo/la/los/las en …
la bombonería	la librería
la carnicería	la panadería
la droguería	la pastelería
la farmacia	la pescadería
la frutería	la zapatería
la joyería	

Resources

Cassette B, side 1
CD2, tracks 12 and 13
Cuaderno B, page 28
Starter 1, Resource and Assessment File, page 47
OHTs 19 and 20

Starter 1 [8W1,8]

Aim: vocabulary extension: working out the meaning of words by using cognates, near-cognates, knowledge of other vocabulary.

Using *Resource and Assessment File*, page 47, ask pupils to deduce the meaning of the following places (cognates): *la librería, la farmacia, la frutería, la tienda de discos.*

They can then try to work out the following places by relating them to words they already know in Spanish: *la panadería, la carnicería, la zapatería.*

1a Escribe el orden en que se mencionan las tiendas. (AT1/1)

✕ Listening for information/instructions, Level A

Listening. Pupils note down the order in which they hear different types of shops mentioned. Teachers should first familiarise pupils with the shops listed on page 52, the meaning of most of which pupils should be able to guess or work out from their knowledge of food vocabulary, or because the words are near-cognates of English.

Tapescript

1 la librería
2 la panadería
3 la zapatería
4 la farmacia
5 la frutería
6 la droguería
7 la carnicería
8 la pescadería
9 la pastelería
10 la bombonería

Answers

1 e	2 g	3 a	4 j	5 k	6 c	7 h	8 i	9 f	10 d

1b Escucha. ¿En qué tiendas puedes comprar estos artículos? (AT1/2) [8L3]

✕ Listening for information/instructions, Level C

Listening. Pupils listen and write down in which type of shop the items listed can be bought.

Tapescript

1 – ¿Dónde puedo comprar pan?
  – Puedes comprarlo en la panadería.
2 – ¿Dónde puedo comprar pasteles?
  – Puedes comprarlos en una pastelería.
3 – ¿Dónde puedo comprar zapatos?
  – Puedes comprarlos en una zapatería.
4 – ¿Dónde puedo comprar libros?
  – Puedes comprarlos en una librería.
5 – ¿Dónde puedo comprar aspirinas?
  – Puedes comprarlas en una farmacia.
6 – ¿Dónde puedo comprar pasta de dientes?
  – Puedes comprarla en una droguería.
7 – ¿Dónde puedo comprar manzanas?
  – Puedes comprarlas en una frutería.
8 – ¿Dónde puedo comprar chuletas?
  – Puedes comprarlas en la carnicería.
9 – ¿Dónde puedo comprar chocolates?
  – Puedes comprarlos en una bombonería.
10 – ¿Dónde puedo comprar sardinas?
  – Puedes comprarlas en la pescadería.

Answers

Answers as tapescript

6 En la calle principal

1c Con tu compañero/a, pregunta y contesta. (AT2/3) [8W4; 9W4]

✖ Speaking and interacting with others, Level C

Speaking. In pairs, pupils take it in turns to ask and answer questions about where various items can be bought. Teachers should draw attention to the support grid on page 52, which shows pupils how to form and answer the question. In particular, teachers should point out the position and agreement of the direct object in the phrase *puedes comprarlo/la/los/las en …* and how this relates to the use of the direct object pronoun which they met in Unit 3 (page 46). The grid also lists the complete paradigm of *poder*, parts of which are used at different points on this spread.

Starter 2 [8L1]

Aim: pronunciation practice.

Remind pupils to use short vowels to achieve authentic Spanish pronunciation. Also remind them that an accent is used to show where stress falls when a word doesn't follow the usual stress patterns. Give examples. Ask pupils to work in pairs and take it in turns to say the list of shops on page 52, concentrating on short vowels and stress. You could extend this exercise by writing up the shops without any accents and asking pupils to add them in.

2a Lee la tarjeta de Charo. Copia y rellena el cuadro. (AT3/5) [8S8; 9S2]

✖ Reading for information/instructions, Level D

Reading. Pupils read about what gifts Charo is planning to buy and where, then copy out and complete the grid, in Spanish. As before, pupils should be encouraged to use a range of reading skills and strategies before looking up words in a dictionary.

Answers

Persona	Regalo	Tienda	Más información
madre de Charo	abanico	tienda de recuerdos	muchas en las calles principales
abuela de Charo	castañuelas	tienda de recuerdos	las calles principales
padres de Teresa	cerámica	tienda de recuerdos	las calles principales
padre de Charo	CD de flamenco	tienda de discos	FNAC
hermana de Charo	camiseta	tienda de moda	Mango o Zara

2b ¿Qué vas a comprar, para quién y dónde? Ecribe una lista. (AT4/5) [8S2,6]

✖ Exchange information/ideas, Level C/E

Writing. Pupils write sentences about what gifts they are going to buy for whom and where they can buy them, using the correct direct object pronoun.

➕ Able pupils could be encouraged to write a more substantial and continuous piece, similar to Charo's text on page 53, perhaps imagining they are on holiday in a chosen Spanish or Latin American location.

Plenary

Ask pupils to write down two strategies they use to help them understand native speakers when listening to recordings. Take feedback. Are pupils finding it easier to understand the recordings as they progress through the course?

Cuaderno B, page 28

1 Empareja los artículos con las tiendas. (AT3/1)

✖ Reading for information/instructions, Level A

Reading. A matching exercise, linking types of shops to the items which they sell.

Answers

1 e	2 j	3 g	4 b	5 f	6 h	7 i	8 c	9 d	10 a

2a Rellena los espacios en blanco con las palabras apropiadas. (AT3/3, AT4/1) [8W4; 9W4]

✖ Reading for information/instructions, Level C

Reading and writing. A gap-filling exercise, based on buying presents.

Answers

1 castañuelas, abanico, regalos
2 pelota, deportes
3 gorra, camiseta, ropa
4 disco compacto, discos

2b ¿Qué regalos vas a comprar a tu familia? ¿Donde vas a comprarlos? Escribe unas frases como las de **2a**. (AT4/3-4) [8S2]

✖ Exchange information/ideas, Level C/E [8T6]

Writing. Pupils write sentences about the presents they are going to buy for their family and where they are going to buy them, using the model in **2a**.

Resumen y Prepárate

(Pupil's Book pages 54–55)

Resumen

This is a checklist of language covered in Module 3. There is a comprehensive **Resumen** list for Module 3 in the Pupil's Book (page 54) and a **Resumen** test sheet in Cuaderno (page 32).

Prepárate

A revision test to give practice for the test itself at the end of the module.

Resources

Cassette B, side 1
CD2, track 14
Cuaderno B, page 29–31
Skills, Resource and Assessment File, page 51
Resumen, Resource and Assessment File, page 52

---

1 Escucha las conversaciones. Copia y rellena el cuadro. (AT1/3) [8L3; 9L2]

✂ Listening for information/instructions, Level D

Listening. Pupils listen to dialogues in a clothes shop and write down on a grid what the customer wants to buy, the size, whether they buy it and why/why not.

Tapescript

1 – ¿Me puedo probar esas botas?
 – ¿Qué número usa usted?
 – El 42.
 – Aquí tiene.
 – ...
 – ¿Qué tal le quedan?
 – Me están muy ajustadas.
 – ¿Muy ajustadas?
 – Sí. No me las llevo.
 – Vale.
2 – Me encanta esa camisa. ¿Me la puedo probar?
 – ¿Qué talla lleva?
 – La 36.
 – La 36 ... Tome usted.
 – ...
 – ¿Qué tal le queda?
 – Estupenda. ¿Cuánto es?
 – 20 euros.
 – ¡Uff! ¡Qué caro! Es demasiado. La dejo.
3 – Aquellos vaqueros no son caros. ¿Me los puedo probar?
 – ¿Qué talla llevas?
 – La 40.
 – ...
 – ¿Qué tal me quedan?
 – Te quedan muy bien.
 – ¿Me quedan bien? Estupendo, me los llevo.
4 – Aquel vestido verde es precioso.
 – ¿Se lo quiere probar?
 – ¡Ay, sí!
 – ¿Qué talla lleva?
 – La 34.
 – La 34. Tome usted.
 – ...
 – ¿Qué tal?
 – Me queda pequeño. ¿Lo tiene en la talla 36?
 – Lo siento, no tenemos en la 36.
 – Pues, lo dejo.

Answers

	Artículo	número/talla	¿Lo compra?	¿Por qué?/¿Por qué no?
1	*botas*	42	*No*	*ajustadas*
2	camisa	36	No	caro
3	vaqueros	40	Sí	le quedan muy bien
4	vestido	34	No	pequeño

2a Mira los dibujos. Con tu compañero/a, pregunta y contesta. ¿Qué vas a llevar para ir a los lugares? (AT2/5) [8S2]

✂ Speaking to convey information, Level C/D

Speaking. Pupils work in pairs using the pictures to ask and answer questions about what they are going to wear to various events.

2b Mira los dibujos y compara la ropa. ¿Cuál de los artículos de ropa prefieres en cada caso? ¿Por qué? (AT2/4) [8S2]

✂ Speaking about experiences/feelings/opinions, Level D

Speaking. Pupils express opinions about the clothes shown in the pictures, saying which they prefer and why.

3 Lee la carta de Óscar. ¿Verdad (✓) o mentira (✗)? (AT3/4) [8C3]

✂ Reading for information/instructions, Level D

Reading. Pupils read a letter about school uniform and do a true/false exercise.

Answers

1 ✗	2 ✗	3 ✗	4 ✗	5 ✓	6 ✓	7 ✗	8 ✓

4 Escribe un párrafo para describir lo que llevas los fines de semana. (AT4/4)

✂ Exchange information/ideas, Level C/E

Writing. Pupils write about what they like to wear at the weekend.

R Teachers may wish to give pupils some 'starter' sentences for this task.

módulo 3 Resumen y Prepárate

Cuaderno B, page 29

Repaso 1

1a Mira el dibujo y marca los artículos de la lista. (AT3/1)

✕ Reading for information/instructions, Level C

Reading. Pupils tick items of clothing in a list, according to which are shown in the picture.

Answers

1 ✓	3 ✓	5 ✓	6 ✓	10 ✓	12 ✓	14 ✓

1b Escribe dos listas. (AT4/3) [8W5; 8S2; 9W5]

✕ Exchange information/ideas, Level C/D

Writing. Pupils write two lists of clothes which they are going to wear for different occasions.

Cuaderno B, page 30

Repaso 2

1a Lee la conversación ¿Verdad (✓) o mentira (✗)? (AT3/3)

✕ Reading for information/instructions, Level C

Reading. A true/false exercise, based on a dialogue in a clothes shop.

Answers

1 ✓	2 ✓	3 ✓	4 ✗	5 ✗	6 ✗	7 ✓

1b Mira los dibujos y escribe una conversación similar. (AT4/3-4) [8T6]

✕ Exchange information/ideas, Level D

Writing. Pupils adapt the model dialogue in **1a**, using picture prompts to write a similar dialogue.

Answers

> Me gusta esta camiseta blanca.
> Claro. ¿Qué talla tiene?
> La 42.
> ¿Qué tal me queda la camiseta?
> Le queda grande.
> ¿Me la puedo probar en 40?
> Lo siento. En 40 no la tenemos en blanca.
> ¿Me la puedo probar en negra?
> Sí, tome usted.
> Me queda muy bien. ¿Cuánto cuesta?
> 15 euros.
> Me la llevo.

Cuaderno B, page 31

Gramática

1a Write *este, esta, estos* or *estas*. (AT4/1) [8W4; 9W4]

✕ Knowing about language

Writing. A gap-filling exercise, using *este*, etc. The information box reminds pupils that all demonstrative adjectives must agree with the noun.

Answers

1 esta	2 estas	3 estos	4 este

1b Write *ese, esa, esos* or *esas*. (AT4/1) [8W4; 9W4]

✕ Knowing about language

Writing. A similar exercise, using *ese*, etc.

Answers

1 esos	2 ese	3 esas	4 esa

1c Write *aquel, aquella, aquellos* or *aquellas*. (AT4/1) [8W4; 8S1; 9W4]

✕ Knowing about language

Writing. A third exercise, using *aquello*, etc.

Answers

1 aquel	2 aquellos	3 aquella	4 aquellas

2 Write *lo, la, los* or *las*. (AT4/1)

✕ Knowing about language

Writing. A gap-filling exercise, using direct object pronouns. The information box offers a brief reminder.

Answers

1 la	2 las	3 los	4 lo	5 las	6 lo

3 Answer the questions. (AT4/3) [8W5; 8S4; 9W5]

✕ Knowing about language

Writing. Pupils answer questions about what they are going to wear. The information box reminds them of how to use *ir + a* + infinitive.

Possible answers

1 Voy a comprar la comida.
2 Voy a comprar los regalos.
3 Voy a llevar una minifalda, una chaqueta vaquera y zapatos verdes.
4 Voy a llevar una falda de deporte, los calcetines de deporte y zapatillas de deporte.
5 Voy a ponerme una camisa blanca y los pantalones negros. *or* Voy a ponerme una camiseta, los vaqueros y las zapatillas.

Skills, Resource and Assessment File, page 51 (Ordering and sorting words)

1

Answers

1	*amarillo*	*yellow*
2	azul	blue
3	blanco	white
4	gris	grey
5	marrón	brown
6	naranja	orange
7	negro	black
8	rojo	red
9	rosa	pink
10	verde	green
11	violeta	purple

2

Answers

Carnicería	Farmacia	Frutería	Ropa	Deportes
chuletas	*aspirinas*	peras	camiseta	fútbol
pollo	*champú*	plátanos	camisa	natación
carne	colonia	naranjas	gorra	baloncesto
jamón	desodorante	uvas	pantalones	voleibol

3 Pupils fill in the grid giving three examples of words that fall into each grouping: animals, family, colours, hobbies.

4a

Answers

1	*zapatos*
2	lechuga
3	cafetería
4	azul
5	cuatro
6	pájaro

4b

Answers

1 Wear on your feet; plural
2 It's a vegetable – the others are fruits/It's singular, the others are plural
3 You buy food to eat there. In the other two you buy food to eat somewhere else.
4 It's a colour – the others are sizes
5 It's a cardinal number – the others are ordinal numbers.
6 It's a bird – the others are animals

4c

Answers

1 You wear them.
2 You eat them.
3 They are adjectives.
4 They are numbers.
5 They are pets.

7 ¡Extra! ¿Cuál es tu estilo?

(Pupil's Book pages 56–57)

Main topics and objectives

This is an optional extension unit which reviews some of the key language of the module: it focuses on personal style (attitudes to clothes, accessories, appearance, etc.).

Key Framework objectives

- Youth attitudes to sport/culture 9C3 (Launch)
- Using grammar to understand words 9W8 (Reinforcement)
- Order of elements in sentences 9S2 (Reinforcement)
- Authentic texts as sources 9T3 (Reinforcement)
- Using support materials 9T4 (Reinforcement)

Resources

Cassette B, side 1
CD2, track 15

Starter 1 [8T4; 9T4]

Aim: vocabulary extension and glossary work.

Ask pupils to try to work out the meaning of the following words through knowledge, cognates, logic and prediction. Failing this they can then look the word up in the glossary.

la música étnica, cómodo, color, prefiero, saco de dormir, teléfono móvil, organizar, el top estampado, las botas de senderismo, la vela

1a Lee el test. Elige las letras de las respuestas apropiadas para ti. (AT3/4) [8T3; 9W8; 9S2; 9T1,3]

✗ Reading for enjoyment

Reading. Pupils do a magazine-style quiz about clothing preferences and opinions.

1b Escucha y busca el estilo personal según las respuestas. (AT1/4) [8C3; 9C3]

✗ Listening for information/instructions, Level C

Listening. Pupils listen to people answering questions from the quiz in **1a** and find the correct option in the quiz question for each speaker.

Tapescript

1 – ¿Cuáles son tus colores preferidos?
 – Por el momento prefiero el negro, el rojo y el violeta.
2 – ¿Tienes un par de zapatos favoritos? ¿Cómo son?
 – Tengo unas zapatillas Nike super cómodas y de moda.
3 – ¿Qué te gusta más hacer los fines de semana?
 – Me gusta salir a bailar.
4 – ¿Qué tipo de música prefieres?
 – Me gusta Moby y trip hop.
5 – ¿Cuáles son tus accesorios imprescindibles?
 – Mi teléfono móvil.
6 – ¿Cuál es tu opinión sobre el uniforme escolar?
 – Creo que el uniforme escolar es feo. No está de moda.

Answers

1 c	2 d	3 c	4 a	5 c	6 b

2 Con tu compañero/a, contesta a las preguntas del test y busca su estilo en el análisis. (AT2/4) [8S4; 9L4]

✗ Speaking about experiences/feelings/opinions, Level C/D

Speaking. Pupils work in pairs to ask and answer the quiz questions, then read the *Análisis* on page 57 to try to identify their own style of dress, preferred social activities, etc. A support box offers help with some of the new language.

Starter 2 [8W5; 9W5]

Aim: matching verbs with their infinitives.

Ask pupils to find four verbs in the text, write down which infinitive each comes from and what the infinitive means. Encourage pupils to use a dictionary if they are unsure.

3a Escribe seis frases del test que corresponden a tu estilo personal. (AT4/4) [8S6; 8T6]

✗ Exchange information/ideas, Level C/D

Writing. Pupils adapt and write down six sentences from the quiz to describe their style of dress, etc.

3b Escribe cuatro frases que corresponden a tu compañero/a. (AT4/4) [8T6]

✗ Exchange information/ideas, Level C/D

Writing. Pupils write four sentences to describe their partner, including what they look like, what they like to wear and what they do in their social life.

Plenary

Brainstorm. Ask pupils what strategies they used to help them read the 'test'. Did they dive straight in and start answering questions? Did they try skim-reading? Did they look up words in the dictionary? Did they work out words through context and cognates or use grammar they have learned to help decipher something?

What should they do next time when tackling a similar task? Write ideas down on the board and ask pupils to copy them down and keep for reference.

módulo 3 Te toca a ti

(Pupil's Book pages 116–117)

● Self-access reading and writing at two levels.

A Reinforcement

1a Une las dos partes de las frases y emparéjalas con los dibujos. (AT3/2) [8S1]

✖ Knowing about language

Reading. Pupils join up sentence halves to form questions used when shopping for clothes.

Answers

1	f5	**2**	c3	**3**	e1	**4**	a2	**5**	g4	**6**	b6	**7**	d7

2 Mira los dibujos. Lee y completa la descripción. (AT4/5) [8W4; 9W4]

✖ Exchange information/ideas, Level B

Writing. Pupils copy and complete six descriptions of what people in the pictures are wearing.

Answers

1	**a** pantalones	**b** sudadera	**c** de deportes
2	**a** negro	**b** blanca	**c** corbata
3	**a** cortos	**b** camiseta	**c** sandalias
4	**a** falda	**b** top	**c** zapatos
5	**a** gorra	**b** botas	**c** gafas
6	**a** vaqueros	**b** camisa	**c** de deportes

B Extension

1 Mira esta página de la tienda Mango On-line. Contesta a las preguntas. (AT3/4) [8S4; 8T3]

✖ Reading for information/instructions, Level D/E

Reading. Pupils read a page from the website of an online clothes store and answer questions in Spanish.

Answers

1 azules
2 los vaqueros
3 una camiseta naranja, una camiseta amarilla, un jersey amarillo, una falda rosa, una sudadera amarilla, verde y naranja
4 30 euros
5 una falda roja, una camisa tejana clara y una gorra verde
6 38
7 mediana
8 verde
9 24 euros
10 87 euros

2 Mira los dibujos y elige uno de cada par. Escribe cuál prefieres y por qué. (AT4/4) [8S2]

✖ Exchange information/ideas, Level D/E

Writing. Pupils look at pairs of contrasting pictures showing items of clothing, then complete questions and answers about which they prefer and why.

módulo 4

El turismo

(Pupil's Book pages 60–77)

Unit	Key Framework objectives	PoS	Key language and Grammar
1 ¿Qué hay de interés? (pp. 60–61) Asking what is of interest in a place and what you can do there	8S3 Modal verbs [L] 9C5 Regions of the country [L] 8S8 High-frequency words and punctuation clues [R] 8T6 Text as model and source [R] 8C3 Daily life and young people [R] 9C4 Well-known features of the country [R]	2b correct pronunciation/ intonation 2e adapt language 2g dealing with the unpredicable 2h scanning texts 3b use context to interpret meaning 4c compare cultures 5e range of resources 5f using the TL creatively 5h using the TL for real purposes	*se puede* + infinitive *¿Qué hay de interés en … ?* *Hay una plaza de toros.* *¿Dónde se puede (practicar el golf)?* *Se puede (practicar el golf) en …* *Se pueden (ver animales y practicar deportes).*
2 Tus vacaciones (pp. 62–63) Talking about where you go and what you do on holiday	8S1 Word, phrase and clause sequencing [R] 8S2 Connectives [R] 8T6 Text as model and source [R] 8L3 Relaying gist and detail [R] 9L4 Questions and text as stimulus to talk [R]	2a listen for gist and detail 2c ask and answer questions 2d initiate/develop conversations 3c use knowledge of English 4c compare cultures	*¿Dónde vas de vacaciones?* *Voy a la costa.* *¿Cómo vas?* *Voy en coche.* *¿Qué haces?* *Descanso.* *Me baño en el mar.*
3 ¿Dónde fuiste? (pp. 64–65) Saying where you went, what for and who with	9S3 Different tense modals [L] 8W5 Verbs (preterite) [L] 8S1 Verb, phrase and clause sequencing [R] 8S2 Connectives [R] 8T2 Expression in text [R] 8T4 Dictionary use [R] 8T6 Text as model and source [R] 9T2 Features for effect [R]	1a sounds and writing 2a listen for gist and detail 2b correct pronunciation/ intonation 3b use context to interpret meaning 3c use knowledge of English 3d use reference materials 4b communicating with native speakers 4d consider experiences in other countries 5d respond to different types of language	Preterite tense of *ir* Days of the week *¿Dónde fuiste el sábado?* *Fui a la piscina.* *¿A qué fuiste?* *Fui al cine a ver una película.* *¿Con quién fuiste?* *Fui con mi hermana.*
4 ¿Adónde fueron? (pp. 66–67) Talking about where other people went	8W4 Word endings [R] 8W5 Verbs (preterite) [R] 8S4 Question types [R] 9W4 Main inflections [R]	4d consider experiences in other countries	Revision of places in town The preterite of *ir: fui, fuiste*, etc.
5 ¿Lo pasaste bien? (pp. 68–69) Saying what you did on holiday	8S7 Present, past and future [L] 8W5 Verbs (preterite)[R] 8S1 Word, phrase and clause sequencing [R] 8S2 Connectives [R] 8T2 Expression in text [R] 9W5 Verbs [R]	2c ask and answer questions 3a memorising	Preterite tense *Fui a España.* *Fui en avión.* *Me alojé en un hotel.* *Visité una catedral.* *Compré una camiseta.* *Nadé en el mar.* *Lo pasé muy bien.*
6 Fueron de excursión (pp. 70–71) Saying what other people did on holiday	8W5 Verbs [R] 8S2 Connectives [R] 8S7 Present, past and future [R] 9L4 Questions and text as stimulus to talk	5d respond to different types of language	Preterite tense – 3rd person singular and plural *Miguel descansó.* *Se despertaron temprano.*

Unit	Key Framework objectives	PoS	Key language and Grammar
Resumen y Prepárate (pp. 72–73) Pupils' checklist and practice test			
7 ¡Extra! ¡Cuba! (pp. 74–75) Optional unit: Cuba	9S8 Inflections as aid to comprehension [L] 9L3 Reporting and paraphrasing [L] 8W7 Dictionary detail [R] 8T4 Dictionary use [R] 9W8 Using grammar to understand words [R] 9S3 Different tense modals [R]	**2g** dealing with the unpredictable **2h** scanning texts **3b** use context to interpret meaning **3d** use reference materials	
Te toca a ti (pp. 118–119) Self-access reading and writing at two levels			

1 ¿Qué hay de interés?

(Pupil's Book pages 60–61)

Main topics

- Asking what is of interest in a place
- Asking what you can do there

Key Framework objectives

- Modal verbs 8S3 (Launch)
- Region of the country 9C5 (Launch)
- High-frequency words and punctuation clues 8S8 (Reinforcement)
- Text as model and source 8T6 (Reinforcement)
- Daily life and young people 8C3 (Reinforcement)
- Well-known features of the country 9C4 (Reinforcement)

Grammar

- *se puede(n)* + infinitive

Key language

¿Qué hay de interés en Jerez de la Frontera?
Hay …

un campo de golf
una escuela de caballos
un espectáculo de flamenco
un parque temático
un paseo marítimo
una playa
una plaza de toros
un puerto

centros comerciales   *un parque natural*
discotecas   *un zoo*

¿Dónde se puede practicar el golf?
Se puede practicar el golf en …
Se pueden ver animales y practicar deportes.

Resources

Cassette B, side 2
CD2, tracks 16 and 17
Cuaderno B, page 33
Flashcards 26–30

Starter 1 [8S6]

Aim: using the high-frequency word *hay* in different contexts.

Have ready on the board one or both of the following questions: *¿Qué hay en tu dormitorio?* *¿Qué hay en tu pueblo?*

Ask pupils to give a description of their room or their town starting with: *En mi dormitorio hay …* *En mi pueblo hay …*

Alternative starter [8W1; 8L1]

Aim: presentation of new vocabulary and highlighting use of accents.

Present the eight places on the map on page 60. When you have established meaning you could go on to specific pronunciation practice. Point out the use of accents to denote stress in Spanish. You could go on to play a game. Write the words up and challenge pupils to say as many as they can with correct pronunciation.

1a Escucha y escribe los lugares en el orden correcto. (AT1/3) [8L3; 9C5]

✖ Listening for information/instructions, Level D

Listening. Pupils listen to a description of what there is in Jerez de la Frontera and Málaga, noting down the places of interest in the order in which they are mentioned. Teachers should check pupils' understanding of the places of interest shown on page 60 and give them aural practice of the new vocabulary before playing the recording, if not done

in the starter exercise above. The recording includes some further new items of vocabulary, which are picked up on in exercise **1b**.

Tapescript

¿Qué hay de interés en Jerez de la Frontera?
Bastante cerca hay un parque temático y un parque natural.
También hay un zoo.
¿Hay playas?
No, pero hay espectáculos de flamenco. Hay una escuela de caballos y hay una plaza de toros.

¿Qué hay de interés en Málaga?
Hay muchas playas, un puerto y paseos marítimos.
¿Hay un parque natural?
No, pero hay centros comerciales, campos de golf y discotecas.

Answers

Jerez de la Frontera: *4*, 1, 3, 2
Málaga: 1, 4, 3, 2

1b Escucha otra vez. ¿Qué otros lugares de interés hay en las ciudades? (AT1/3) [9C4]

✖ Listening for information/instructions, Level D

Listening. Pupils listen to the recording again and try to identify the extra places of interest which are mentioned.

Tapescript

Tapescript as **1a**

Answers

Jerez de la Frontera: *parque natural,* un zoo
Málaga: centros comerciales, discotecas

1c Con tu compañero/a, pregunta y contesta. (AT2/4) [8S4; 9C4]

✖ Speaking and interacting with others, Level C/D

Speaking pairwork. Pupils take it in turns to ask and answer questions about what there is in the two resorts.

> **Starter 2** [8W1]
>
> *Aim:* revising new vocabulary.
>
> Text manipulation. Ask pupils to unjumble the following places: *golfcampodeun, marítimounpaseo, untemáticoparque, unflamencodeespectáculo, torosunadeplaza.*

> **Alternative starter 2** [8T3]
>
> *Aim:* to prepare pupils for answering the questions in reading exercise **2a**.
>
> Ask pupils what sort of information is likely to be in a text entitled *¿Qué se puede hacer en Jerez de la Frontera?* (activities; names of places, etc.)
>
> Ask pupils, in pairs, to identify as many infinitives as they can in the text. Do they know what they mean?
>
> Now do a search for nouns. Which nouns do they know? Which can they work out? Encourage them to look up the remaining ones in a dictionary.

2a Lee los textos y contesta a las preguntas. Utiliza un diccionario. (AT3/4) [8S3,8; 8T4; 9T4]

✖ Reading for information/instructions, Level D/E

Reading. Pupils read two texts about facilities in Jerez de la Frontera and Málaga, then answer questions in Spanish. They should be given access to dictionaries to look up unknown vocabulary. However, they should be encouraged to use reading skills and strategies first (see *Alternative starter 2* above for suggestions) only using the dictionary either as a last resort or to check their assumptions. A number of the questions use the expression *se puede(n)* and this is explained in the *Gramática* box on the page.

Answers

1	el jerez
2	el flamenco
3	a la plaza de toros
4	la fiesta de la feria del caballo
5	el ballet con caballos
6	alpinismo, montar a caballo
7	los deportes acuáticos (el surfing, la pesca, el buceo), el golf
8	por el puerto y los paseos marítimos
9	los campos de golf
10	Isla Mágica

2b Con tu compañero/a, pregunta y contesta. (AT2/3)

✖ Speaking and interacting with others, Level C/D

Speaking. Pupils work in pairs to ask each other questions about which resort you can do certain things in. Teachers should ensure that pupils are confident about pronouncing and using *se puede(n)* accurately before they tackle this exercise.

2c En el ordenador diseña un folleto sobre tu ciudad/pueblo. Describe lo que hay de interés y lo que se puede hacer. (AT4/4) [8W2; 8T6]

✖ Writing imaginatively, Level D/E

Writing. Pupils design a promotional leaflet for their town or village (or for another place in Spain), listing places of interest and things to do.

Encourage pupils to use useful words and phrases from the text. In particular, you could draw their attention to connectives by doing a 'find the Spanish for …' activity (e.g. also (*también*), and (*y*), where you can (*donde se puede …*), which is (*que es*), such as (*como*)).

If possible, they should use a graphics or desktop publishing programme to produce their leaflet, giving them access to a range of layouts, type styles and sizes, and images. If the school has links with one in Spain, the finished leaflets could be sent to the Spanish school and, ideally, similar leaflets from the Spanish school would be sent to the UK, for display purposes and reading for interest or enjoyment. [8C3]

> **Plenary**
>
> Discuss with pupils the strategies they used for the reading exercise **2a**, and/or for the extended writing exercise **2c**.

Cuaderno B, page 33

1 ¿Qué hay de interés en Cádiz? Lee el texto y elige los dibujos apropiados. (AT3/3) [8S8]

✕ Reading for information/instructions, Level D

Reading. Pupils read a short text about what Cádiz has to offer and tick the relevant pictures.

Answers

1 ✓	2 ✓	5 ✓	6 ✓	8 ✓	10 ✓

2a Escribe sobre lo que se puede hacer en Cádiz. (AT4/2) [8S1,3]

✕ Exchange information/ideas, Level C

Writing. Pupils write a description of what there is to do in Cádiz, using the sentences provided.

Answers

> Se puede ir a la playa.
> Se puede ir a una corrida de toros.
> Se puede ir de paseo al lado del mar.
> Se puede visitar la catedral.
> Se pueden ver los cuadros en el museo de arte.
> Se puede comer en un restaurante.
> Se puede bañar en el mar.

2b Escribe sobre lo que se puede hacer en tu ciudad. (AT4/3-4) [8S3]

✕ Exchange information/ideas, Level D/F

Writing. Pupils write about what there is to do in their own town.

2 Tus vacaciones

(Pupil's Book pages 62–63)

Main topics

- Talking about where you go and what you do on holiday

Key Framework objectives

- Word, phrase and clause sequencing 8S1 (Reinforcement)
- Connectives 8S2 (Reinforcement)
- Relaying gist and detail 8L3 (Reinforcement)
- Text as model and source 8T6 (Reinforcement)
- Questions/text as stimulus to talk 9L4 (Reinforcement)

Key language

¿Dónde vas de vacaciones?
Voy …
a Barcelona   a Mallorca
al campo   a la costa
a la sierra

¿Cómo vas?
Voy en …
autocar   ferry
avión   tren
coche

Descanso.   Hago surfing.
Me baño en el mar.   Monto en bicicleta.
Tomo el sol.   Saco fotos.
Voy de paseo.   Voy a discotecas.

Resources

Cassette B, side 2
CD2, tracks 18 and 19
Cuaderno B, page 34
Hojas de trabajo, Resource and Assessment File, pages 69 and 70 (*descansar, nadar, ir de paseo, montar en bici, ir de compras, tomar el sol, sacar fotos, hacer surfing*)
OHTs 21 and 22
Flashcards 31–38, 28 (*¡Listos! 1*)

Starter 1 [8S1]

Aim: thinking activity – matching verbs in the first person with an appropriate activity.

Write the following on the board in two columns (or prepare an OHT) and ask pupils to match them up.

First column: *me baño, tomo, voy de, voy a, monto en, saco, hago*

Second column: *el sol, paseo, bicicleta, fotos, surfing, en el mar, discotecas*

1a Escucha. Copia y rellena el cuadro. (AT1/4) [8L3]

✕ Listening for information/instructions, Level D

Listening. Pupils listen to different speakers saying where they normally go on holiday, how they get there and what they do there. In this first exercise, pupils must simply note down on a grid where each speaker goes and the means of transport they use. A support box on the page lists the different options they will hear and teachers should ensure pupils are familiar with this language before playing the recording.

Tapescript

1 – Carlota, ¿dónde vas de vacaciones normalmente?
  – Normalmente voy a la costa.
  – ¿Cómo vas?
  – Voy en coche.
  – ¿Qué haces?
  – Me baño en el mar, tomo el sol, hago surfing, voy a discotecas …
2 – ¿Dónde vas de vacaciones normalmente, Miguel?
  – Normalmente voy a un pueblo en la sierra.

  – ¿Cómo vas?
  – Voy en tren.
  – ¿Qué haces?
  – Descanso, saco fotos, monto en bici …
3 – Penélope, ¿dónde vas de vacaciones normalmente?
  – Normalmente voy a Barcelona a visitar a mis abuelos.
  – ¿Cómo vas?
  – Voy en avión.
  – ¿Qué haces?
  – Descanso, me baño en el mar, voy de paseo …
4 – ¿Dónde vas de vacaciones normalmente, José Luis?
  – Normalmente voy a Santander.
  – ¿Cómo vas?
  – Voy en autocar.
  – ¿Qué haces?
  – Me baño en el mar, tomo el sol, voy a discotecas, voy de paseo …
5 – ¿Dónde vas de vacaciones normalmente, Estrella?
  – Normalmente voy a Mallorca.
  – ¿Cómo vas?
  – Voy en ferry.
  – ¿Qué haces?
  – Me baño en el mar, tomo el sol, saco fotos, hago surfing …

Answers

	¿Dónde?	¿Cómo?
Carlota	a la costa	en coche
Miguel	a la sierra	en tren
Penélope	a Barcelona	en avión
José Luis	a Santander	en autocar
Estrella	a Mallorca	en ferry

1b Escucha otra vez. ¿Qué hacen las personas durante sus vacaciones? Escribe los números correctos. (AT1/4) [8L3]

✕ Listening for information/instructions, Level D

Listening. Pupils listen to the recording again, this time noting down the number of the pictures which show what each speaker does on holiday. Teachers may wish to give pupils aural practice of the phrases for the exercises – as individual phrases, then increasing this to pairs, threes and eventually fours – before playing the recording.

Tapescript

Tapescript as **1a**

Answers

Carlota: *2, 3,* 8, 5 **Miguel:** 1, 7, 6 **Penélope:** 1, 2, 4	
José Luis: 2, 3, 5, 4 **Estrella:** 2, 3, 7, 8	

2 Con tu compañero/a, mira los dibujos en **1a/1b**. Pregunta y contesta. (AT2/4) [8S4; 9L4]

✠ Speaking and interacting with others, Level D/E

Speaking. Pupils work in pairs to ask and answer questions about where their partner goes on holiday, how they travel and what they do when they get there, using the pictures and other information on page 62. They are supported by a model dialogue.

3a Lee el correo electrónico y empareja las dos partes de las frases. Utiliza un diccionario. (AT3/4) [8S1]

✠ Reading for information/instructions, Level E

Reading. Pupils read an email about what Isidro usually does on holiday and match up sentence halves. Encourage pupils to employ reading strategies before using dictionaries. Remind them that they do not need to understand every word. You could start by giving pupils two minutes to write down five words or phrases that are familiar. Pool this knowledge.

Answers

1 b	**2** d	**3** a	**4** g	**5** c	**6** h	**7** f	**8** e

Starter 2 [8W5; 9W5]

Aim: revising regular *-ar* verbs.

Ask pupils to choose two *-ar* verbs from the unit and conjugate them for: *yo, tú, él/ella.*

3b Escribe una respuesta al correo electrónico. (AT4/4) [8W2; 8S2; 8T6]

✠ Writing to establish personal contact, Level D/F

Writing. Pupils write a reply to Isidro's questions about how they spend their holiday. They should be encouraged to adapt Isidro's text, using a range of present-tense verbs in the first person singular and plural, as well as adverbs, such as *normalmente, generalmente* and *también,* and conjunctions such as *y* and *pero.*

R Teachers may wish to provide some pupils with a writing frame for support on an OHT or worksheet.

Plenary

Working with a partner, ask pupils to discuss strategies they used to help them read the email. Write two of them down and share with the class.

Cuaderno B, page 34

1a Lee las frases. ¿Quién habla? (AT3/2) [8S2]

✠ Reading for information/instructions, Level C

Reading. By looking at a picture grid and reading sentences, pupils work out and note down the name of the speaker in each case.

Answers

1 Juan	**2** Melania	**3** Marina	**4** Tamara	**5** Iván
6 Pablo				

1b Busca las palabras en las frases de **1a** para: *sometimes, in the summer, also, I love* and *usually* (AT3/2, AT4/1) [8W1]

✠ Reading for information/instructions, Level C

Reading and writing. Pupils must find and note down the Spanish for key expressions from **1a**.

Answers

1 a veces	**2** en verano	**3** también	**4** me encanta
5 normalmente			

1c Completa el cuadro para ti y escribe sobre tus vacaciones. Incluye las palabras subrayadas de **1b** si puedes. (AT4/3) [8S2]

✠ Exchange information/ideas, Level D/E

Writing. By adapting the sentences from **1a**, pupils write about their own holiday plans.

2 Emplea palabras del cuadro para escribir frases sobre los medios de transporte que usas. (AT4/2–3) [8S2]

✠ Exchange information/ideas, Level C

Writing. Using phrases from the support box, pupils write about what means of transport they use for different destinations.

Hojas de trabajo, Resource and Assessment File, pages 69 and 70

Cards for pairwork featuring weather and holiday activities: pupils match the pictures to the correct words.

3 ¿Dónde fuiste?

(Pupil's Book pages 64–65)

Main topics

- Saying where you went, what for and who with

Key Framework objectives

- Different tense modals 9S3 (Launch)
- Verb tenses (preterite) 8W5 (Part-Launch)
- Present tense, *past*, future 8S7 (Launch)
- Word, phrase and clause sequencing 8S1 (Reinforcement)
- Connectives 8S2 (Reinforcement)
- Expression in text 8T2 (Reinforcement)
- Dictionary use 8T4 (Reinforcement)
- Features for effect 9T2 (Reinforcement)

Grammar

- Preterite tense of *ir*

Key language

¿Dónde fuiste … ?
Fui …

a casa de mi amigo	al cine
a mi clase de piano	al estadio
a la piscina	al mercado
a la biblioteca	al parque
al centro comercial	
al centro de la ciudad	

¿A qué fuiste?
Fui a la tienda a comprar un CD.
Fui al polideportivo a jugar al voleibol.

Resources

Cassette B, side 2
CD2, tracks 20 and 21
Cuaderno B, page 35
Starter 1, Resource and Assessment File, page 68
Flashcards 52, 53, 54, 58, 65 (¡Listos! 1)

Starter 1 [8W1,4; 8L1]

Aim: vocabulary practice (places)/using the definite article.

Using *Resource and Assessment File*, page 68, ask pupils to solve the following anagrams and then write in the correct article (*el* or *la*). See who can finish first.

1 anciisp *(piscina)* **2** nceort mrccialoe *(centro comercial)* **3** cdoarme *(mercado)* **4** bboitelcai *(biblioteca)* **5** nice *(cine)* **6** asac de im igoma *(casa de mi amigo)* **7** entroc de al dadiuc *(centro de la ciudad)*

These words provide a good opportunity to focus on the pronunciation of '*c*'. Revise the rule for when '*c*' is hard or soft.

1 Escucha. Mira los dibujos y copia y rellena el cuadro. (AT1/5) [8S4; 8L3]

Listening for information/instructions, Level E

Listening. Pupils listen to someone answering questions about where they went on various days, at various times and complete a grid. This activity introduces the preterite of *ir*, which is explained in the *Gramática* box on page 64 and it is suggested that teachers refer pupils to this before playing the recording.

Tapescript

– ¿Adónde fuiste el viernes por la mañana?
– Fui al estadio a ver un partido de fútbol.
– ¿Adónde fuiste el sábado?
– Por la mañana fui a la tienda a comprar un CD.
– ¿Y por la tarde, dónde fuiste?
– El sábado por la tarde fui al polideportivo a jugar al voleibol.

– ¿Adónde fuiste el domingo?
– Por la mañana fui a casa de mi amigo.
– ¿Y dónde fuiste por la·tarde?
– Por la tarde fui al cine a ver una película.

Answers

viernes por la mañana	3
sábado por la mañana	1
sábado por la tarde	2
domingo por la mañana	4
domingo por la tarde	5

2 Con tu compañero/a, pregunta y contesta. (AT2/5) [8S1,6; 8L4]

Speaking about experiences/feelings/opinions, Level D

Speaking pairwork. Pupils take it in turns to ask and answer questions about what they did the previous weekend. They are supported by a model dialogue and a key language box.

Starter 2 [8W5; 9W5]

Aim: to recap the preterite of *ir*.

Use a dice, where dots correspond to each subject pronoun, e.g. one dot = *yo*, two dots = *tú*, three dots = *él*, etc. or dice with subject pronouns on them. Pupils work with a partner or in small groups, throwing the dice and conjugating the verb *ir* according to the dot or subject pronoun it lands on.

3a Escucha y mira los dibujos. Copia y rellena el cuadro en inglés. (AT1/5) [8W5; 8L3; 9W5; 9S3]

Listening for information/instructions, Level E

Listening. Pupils follow a series of pictures while they listen to people answering questions about where they went, why they went there and with whom, then copy and complete a grid. The recording uses examples of the construction *ir* in the preterite + *a* + infinitive, which is explained in the *Gramática* box on page 65 and pupils should familiarise themselves with this before doing the listening exercise.

Tapescript

1 – ¿Dónde fuiste el fin de semana pasado?
  – Fui al cine.
  – ¿A qué fuiste?
  – Fui a ver Blade III.
  – ¿Con quién fuiste?
  – Fui con mi hermana.

2 – ¿Dónde fuiste el fin de semana pasado?
  – Fui al polideportivo.
  – ¿A qué fuiste?
  – Fui a bañarme en la piscina.
  – ¿Con quién fuiste?
  – Fui con mis primos.

3 – ¿Dónde fuiste el fin de semana pasado?
  – Fui al centro comercial.
  – ¿A qué fuiste?
  – Fui a comprar unos zapatos.
  – ¿Con quién fuiste?
  – Fui con mi madre.

4 – ¿Dónde fuiste el fin de semana pasado?
  – Fui al parque.
  – ¿A qué fuiste?
  – Fui a jugar al fútbol.
  – ¿Con quién fuiste?
  – Fui con mis amigos.

5 – ¿Dónde fuiste el fin de semana pasado?
  – Fui a un restaurante.
  – ¿A qué fuiste?
  – Fui a celebrar mi cumpleaños.
  – ¿Con quién fuiste?
  – Fui con mi familia.

Answers

	¿Dónde?	¿A qué?	¿Con quién?
1	cinema	to see Blade III	sister
2	sports centre	to go swimming	cousins
3	shopping centre	to buy shoes	mother
4	park	to play football	friends
5	restaurant	to celebrate her birthday	family

3b Con tu compañero/a, mira los dibujos. Pregunta y contesta. (AT2/5) [8S4; 9L4]

✖ Speaking about experiences/feelings/opinions, Level D

Speaking. In pairs, pupils ask and answer questions about where they went, why they went there and with whom, following the model dialogue.

4a Lee la postal. Copia y rellena el cuadro. Utiliza un diccionario. (AT3/5) [8T2,4; 9S3; 9T2,4]

✖ Reading for information/instructions, Level E

Reading. Pupils read a postcard about what Marta did in Madrid last week and complete a grid. They should be encouraged to use reading skills and strategies to work out or guess new items of language before checking or looking up any unknown vocabulary in a dictionary. Teachers might wish to use this item as a 'jigsaw' reading task, by dividing the class into six groups and asking each group to find out what Marta did on a specific day and at a specific time (e.g. Friday morning or Saturday afternoon). A competitive element could then be introduced to see which group completes the task accurately in the shortest time.

Answers

¿Cuándo?	¿Dónde?	¿A qué?	¿Con quién?
viernes por la mañana	al parque del Retiro	ir de paseo	tía
viernes por la tarde	a la Plaza Mayor	comer tapas	tíos
sábado por la mañana	al Museo del Prado	ver cuadros famosos	prima
sábado por la tarde	al Palacio Real	visitar la residencia oficial del Rey	prima
domingo por la mañana	al Rastro	comprar recuerdos	tío
domingo por la tarde	al Estadio Bernabéu	ver un partido de fútbol	tío

4b Escribe una postal para describir tu fin de semana pasado. (AT4/5) [8S2; 8T6; 9S3]

✖ Writing to establish personal contact, Level E/F

Writing. Pupils write a postcard describing what they did last weekend.

➕ Able pupils should be encouraged to 'borrow' extra phrases from Marta's text to enhance their writing, such as *Después de (cenar), lo mejor de todo*, etc.

Plenary [8W5; 9W5]

Ask a volunteer to explain to the rest of the class when you use the preterite tense.

Quick fire: Go round the class and ask pupils *¿Dónde fuiste el sábado?*

módulo 4 — 3 ¿Dónde fuiste?

Cuaderno B, page 35

1 Empareja las frases. (AT3/2) [8S1; 9S3]

✖ Reading for information/instructions, Level D

Reading. Pupils match sentence halves, using the preterite of *ir*.

Answers

1 e	**2** a	**3** f	**4** c	**5** b	**6** d

2 Lee los textos y completa el cuadro. (AT3/5, AT4/2) [8S2; 9S3]

✖ Reading for information/instructions, Level E

Reading and writing. After reading two texts about what people did at the weekend, pupils complete a grid in Spanish.

Answers

		¿Adónde?	¿A qué?	¿Con quién?
Vanessa	**el sábado**			
	am	a casa de la profesora	clase de piano	–
	pm	al centro comercial	comprar un regalo	amiga Clara
	el domingo			
	am	parque	pasear	perro
	pm	cine	ver la nueva película de Harry Potter	padres
Raúl	**el sábado**			
	am	polideportivo	jugar al baloncesto	Juan y Manolo
	pm	cine	–	Alicia
	el domingo			
	am	casa de abuelos	comer	padres
	pm	estadio	ver un partido de fútbol	hermano

3 Lee el diario de Alejandro. Escribe un párrafo sobre tu fin de semana. Mira el texto de Raúl en **2** y cambia las palabras subrayadas. (AT3/3, AT4/5) [8S1,2; 8T6; 9S3]

✖ Exchange information/ideas, Level E

Reading and writing. Pupils read Alejandro's diary for last weekend and adapt one of the texts in exercise **2**, to describe what Alejandro did.

Answer

El sábado por la mañana fui al polideportivo a jugar al **voleibol** con **Ana, Luis y Bea**. Por la tarde fui al cine con **Isabel**. El domingo por la mañana fui **al museo de arte** con **mi tía Teresa y mi abuela**. Por la tarde fui **al Estadio Bernabéu** con **mi padre**.

módulo 4 4 ¿Adónde fueron?

(Pupil's Book pages 66–67)

Main topics

- Talking about where other people went

Grammar

- Revision of places in town
- The preterite of *ir*: *fui, fuiste, fue, fuimos, fuisteis, fueron*

Key Framework objectives

- Word endings 8W4 (Reinforcement)
- Verb tenses 8W5 (Reinforcement)
- Question types 8S4 (Reinforcement)
- Main inflections 9W4 (Reinforcement)

Key language

¿Adónde fue (Cristóbal Colón)?
¿Adónde fueron (Lucía y Tomás)?

Resources

Cassette B, side 2
CD2, tracks 22 and 23
Cuaderno B, page 36
Grammar, Resource and Assessment File, page 72
Flashcards 67–78 (*¡Listos! 1*)

Starter 1 [8W5; 8S4; 9W5]

Aim: to become familiar with the different forms of *ir* in the preterite.

Ask pupils to give you the Spanish for 'I went' (*fui*) and 'we went' (*fuimos*). Using deductive skills, can pupils find the Spanish for 'he/she went' from the quiz on page 66?

1a Lee las preguntas y elige las frases correctas. (AT3/5)

✖ Reading for information/instructions, Level E

Reading. Pupils do a general-knowledge quiz in Spanish about where various famous people went, and how or why. All the questions use either the third person singular or plural of *ir* in the preterite. Pupils could work on the quiz in pairs, using a dictionary to look up or check unknown vocabulary. Teachers could award points or a prize for the pair that completes the quiz correctly in the shortest time.

Answers

| 1 c | 2 b | 3 c | 4 c | 5 b | 6 b | 7 c | 8 b |

1b Escucha y comprueba tus respuestas. (AT1/5) [8L3]

Listening. Pupils listen and check their answers to the quiz.

Tapescript

1 – ¿Adónde fue Cristóbal Colón en 1492?
  – Fue al Caribe.
2 – ¿Quién fue a Australia en 1770?
  – Capitán Cook fue a Australia en 1770.
3 – En 1964 Geraldine Mock fue la primera mujer que viajó sola alrededor del mundo. ¿Cómo fue?
  – Fue en avión.
4 – Ellen MacArthur fue sola alrededor del mundo en 2001. ¿Cómo fue?
  – Ellen McArthur fue en barco de vela.

5 – ¿Quién fue a la luna en 1969?
  – Neil Armstrong, estadounidense, fue a la luna en 1969.
6 – ¿Cuál fue el primer equipo a llegar al Polo Sur en 1911?
  – Roald Amundsen y su equipo.
7 – ¿Cuántas personas fueron de vacaciones a España el año pasado?
  – Más de 60 millones de personas fueron de vacaciones a España el año pasado.
8 – ¿Por qué fueron Raúl y Michael Owen a Japón en junio de 2002? ¿Fueron de vacaciones?
  – No, ¡qué va! Fueron al Mundial.

1c Escribe las respuestas correctas. (1–8) (AT4/5) [8W5; 9W5]

✖ Exchange information/ideas, Level C

Writing. Pupils write a sentence for each question of the quiz.

Answers

1 En 1492 Cristóbal Colón fue al Caribe.
2 En 1770 Capitán Cook fue a Australia.
3 En 1964 Geraldine Mock fue sola alrededor del mundo en avión.
4 En 2001 Ellen MacArthur fue sola alrededor del mundo en barco de vela.
5 En 1969 Neil Armstrong fue a la luna.
6 En 1911 Roald Amundsen y su equipo fue el primer equipo a llegar al Polo Sur.
7 El año pasado más de 60 millones de personas fueron de vacaciones a España.
8 En junio de 2002 Raúl y Michael Owen fueron a Japón al Mundial.

Starter 2 [8W1]

Aim: vocabulary practice.

Set a time limit (three minutes) and ask pupils to write down as many places in a town as they can.

módulo 4

4 ¿Adónde fueron?

2a ¿Adónde fueron? Mira los dibujos y escribe frases. (AT4/5) [8W4; 9W4]

✕ Knowing about language

Writing. Pupils use the 'spaghetti' diagram to work out where various people went and write a sentence about each one. They should pay particular attention to whether they need to use the third person singular or plural of *ir* in the preterite. Teachers should also remind pupils of the fact that *a + el* becomes *al*.

Answers

As transcript for *2b*

2b Escucha y comprueba tus respuestas. (AT1/5) [8W4; 9W4]

Listening. Pupils listen and check their answers to **2a**.

Tapescript

1 Sara fue al polideportivo.
2 Edu y Rafa fueron a la playa.
3 Lucía, Mateo y Tomás fueron a la casa de sus abuelos.
4 José fue a la piscina.
5 Ester y Juan fueron al centro comercial.
6 Tamara y Eli fueron a la discoteca.
7 Julio fue al cine.

Note: No. 4 has been deleted from the Pupil's Book but currently still features on the recording.

3 Con tu compañero/a, pregunta y contesta. (AT2/5) [8W4,5; 8S4; 9W4,5]

✕ Knowing about language

Speaking. Pupils work in pairs to complete a series of questions and answers from picture prompts. The exercise involves using all parts of the verb *ir* in the preterite.

Plenary [8W4; 9W5]

Ask pupils to stand (behind desks or in a circle). Throw a fluffy toy or ball to a pupil and call out a subject pronoun (in the correct order to start with): each pupil conjugates *ir* in the preterite accordingly and throws the ball back. Start slowly and increase pace as pupils gain confidence.

Cuaderno B, page 36

1 Empareja las frases con los dibujos. (AT3/5) [8W5; 9W5]

✕ Knowing about language

Reading. A matching exercise, in which pupils must link statements using the preterite of *ir* to the relevant pictures.

Answers

1 e 2 a 3 d 4 f 5 c 6 b

2a Empareja las palabras con su equivalente en inglés. (AT3/1) [8S4]

✕ Reading for information/instructions, Level A

Reading. Pupils match question words to their English equivalents.

Answers

1 d 2 e 3 f 4 b 5 c 6 a

2b Completa las preguntas con las palabras apropiadas de **2a**. (AT3/5, AT4/1) [8S4]

✕ Knowing about language

Reading and writing. A gap-filling exercise, using the question words from **2a**, with questions and answers in the preterite.

Answers

1 Adónde 2 Cómo 3 Cuántas 4 Quién
5 Por qué 6 Cuándo

Grammar, Resource and Assessment File, page 72 (The preterite tense)

1 Pupils conjugate the verb *ir* in the preterite tense.

Answers

I	*Fui*	We	Fuimos
You (informal)	Fuiste	You (informal/plural)	Fuisteis
He/She	Fue	They	Fueron

2 Pupils translate a number of sentences in the past tense into Spanish using various parts of the verb *ir*.

Answers

a *Fui al cine.*
b Fuimos al centro comercial.
c Fueron a la piscina.
d ¿Fuiste al polideportivo?
e Fueron a la playa.
f Fue de paseo.

3 Pupils now write longer sentences by combining two shorter sentences and changing the second verb to the infinitive.

Answers

> **a** *Fui al cine a ver una película cómica.*
> **b** Fuimos a las tiendas a comprar un CD.
> **c** Fueron a la piscina a nadar.
> **d** Fui al polideportivo a jugar al baloncesto.
> **e** Fueron a la playa a tomar el sol.
> **f** Fue al parque a jugar al fútbol.

4 Pupils change the verbs within each sentence from the singular (I, you, he/she) to the plural (we, you pl., they).

Answers

> **a** *Fuimos de vacaciones a Sevilla.*
> **b** Salieron de casa a las siete.
> **c** ¿Visitasteis a su amigo?
> **d** Nadamos todos los días en la piscina del hotel.
> **e** Se acostaron muy tarde – a las dos de la mañana.
> **f** Se alojaron en una pensión barata.

5 ¿Lo pasaste bien?

(Pupil's Book pages 68–69)

Main topics

- Saying what you did on holiday

Key Framework objectives

- Present, *past* and future 8S7 (Reinforcement)
- Verb tenses 8W5 (Reinforcement)
- Word, phrase and clause sequencing 8S1 (Reinforcement)
- Connectives 8S2 (Reinforcement)
- Expression in text 8T2 (Reinforcement)
- Verb tenses 9W5 (Reinforcement)

Grammar

- Preterite tense

Key language

Fui a …
España, Escocia, Francia, Londres
Fui en …
autocar   ferry
avión, tren, coche
Me alojé en …
un camping, un chalet, un hotel
Visité …
un castillo, una catedral, un museo
Compré …
una camiseta, unas gafas de sol, una gorra, unos zapatos
Nadé en …
el lago, el mar, la piscina
Lo pasé …
fenomenal, muy bien, muy mal

Resources

Cassette B, side 2
CD2, tracks 24 and 25
Cuaderno B, page 37
OHTs 23 and 24
Flashcards 33, 62, 68, 70, 74 (*¡Listos! 1*)

Starter 1 [8W5; 8S4; 9W5]

Aim: using the preterite *ir.*

Write on the board *¿Adónde fuiste el sábado? ¿Con quién fuiste? ¿Cómo fuiste?*

Ask pupils to write down where they went last Saturday, who they went with and how they got there (encourage them to incorporate *fuimos* in their answer).

1 Escucha y escribe los dibujos en el orden correcto. (AT1/5) [8W5; 8L3; 9W5]

✄ Listening for information/instructions, Level C

Listening. Pupils listen to what various people did on holiday and note down the letter of the correct picture. This exercise presents the first person singular and plural in the preterite of the regular *-ar* verbs *comprar, nadar, viajar* and *visitar,* plus the reflexive verbs *acostarse, alojarse* and *despertarse,* the formation of which is explained in the *Gramática* box on page 68. It is suggested that teachers work through the *Gramática* box with pupils before tackling the listening exercise.

Tapescript

1 Compré una camiseta y unos zapatos.
2 Nadé en el mar.
3 Nos alojamos en un hotel muy bueno.
4 Visité el estadio.
5 Nos despertamos temprano.
6 Nadamos en el río.
7 Viajamos en autobús.
8 Me acosté a las cinco de la mañana.

Answers

1 c	2 a	3 e	4 h	5 b	6 g	7 f	8 d

2 Escucha y elige los dibujos apropiados. (AT1/5) [8W5; 8S4; 8L3; 9W5]

✄ Listening for information/instructions, Level E

Listening. Pupils listen to questions and answers about where someone went on holiday, where they stayed, what they visited and how it went. They must choose the correct four pictures from eight. They may need some help in understanding the last question *¿Qué tal lo pasaste?* and the answer *Lo pasé muy bien.*

Tapescript

1 – ¿Adónde fuiste?
– Fui a España.
2 – ¿Dónde te alojaste?
– Me alojé en un camping.
3 – ¿Qué visitaste?
– Visité un castillo.
4 – ¿Qué tal lo pasaste?
– Lo pasé muy bien.

Answers

1 b	2 b	3 b	4 a

3 Con tu compañero/a, pregunta y contesta (AT2/5) [8W5; 8S4; 9W5; 9L4]

✄ Speaking about experiences/feelings/opinions, Level D/E

Speaking. Pupils take it in turns to ask and answer questions about a holiday, choosing answers from the support grid on page 69. As this exercise uses a range of different question types, teachers should ensure pupils are clear about the meaning of each, including the difference between *¿Dónde?* and *¿Adónde?*, as well as checking that they understand all the options in the support grid.

Starter 2 [8W5; 9W5]

Aim: to recap *-ar* verbs in the preterite.

Write the following on the board in two columns and ask pupils to match them up.

Column 1: *compré, compramos, nadé, nadaste, visitaste, visité, me desperté, te despertaste*

Column 2: I swam, you visited, I visited, you woke up, I bought, I woke up, we bought, you swam

4 Copia y completa las frases con las palabras apropiadas. (AT3/5) [8W5; 8S7; 8T2; 9W5; 9T2]

✖ Reading for information/instructions, Level E

Reading. A gap-filling exercise in which pupils have to choose the correct verb in the preterite from those listed to complete each sentence. The first part of the text requires the first person singular of each verb, the second part requires the first person plural.

R Less-able pupils could be given a version of the texts on a worksheet or OHT with some letters of the missing verbs already inserted, for support.

Answers

Pasé un fin de semana en Barcelona. **Fui** en avión. *Me alojé* en un hotel en el puerto. El sábado por la mañana **visité** el estadio y la catedral. Por la tarde fui de compras. **Compré** una gorra y una camisa. El domingo **me desperté** tarde. Luego fui a la playa y **nadé** en el mar. Lo pasé fenomenal.

Fui de excursión a Escocia con mis compañeros de clase. **Fuimos** en tren y en bicicleta. **Nos alojamos** en un camping. **Nos despertamos** temprano. **Nadamos** en el río y en el lago de Loch Ness. ¡Qué frío! Menos mal que no encontramos al Monstruo.

5 Escribe seis frases similares sobre tus vacaciones. (AT4/5) [8W5; 8S1,2,7; 9W5]

✖ Exchange information/ideas, Level E/F

Writing. Pupils write six sentences, like those in exercise **4**, about their own past holiday. They may need some extra vocabulary for this, but should be guided to stick to the verbs which have already been introduced, to avoid irregulars (other than *ir*). They should be encouraged to include a simple opinion, using *lo pasé* + adjective. Encourage able pupils to

join ideas using *y, luego,* etc. For others focusing on the verbs alone will be appropriate.

Plenary [8W5; 9W5]

Write the subject pronouns on the board: *yo, tú él/ella/usted.* Ask someone to explain what the endings are for regular *-ar* verbs in the preterite.

Quick-fire questions: give the infinitive, e.g. *nadar,* and go round the class calling out a subject pronoun, e.g. *yo.* Pupils give the preterite.

Ask for pupils' ideas about how to remember the endings.

Cuaderno B, page 37

1a Empareja las frases. (AT3/5) [8W5; 8S1; 8T2; 9W5]

✖ Reading for information/instructions, Level E

Reading. Pupils match sentence halves about past holidays.

Answers

1 c	2 h	3 a	4 e	5 d	6 g	7 f	8 b
9 l	10 m	11 i	12 k	13 n	14 j	15 o	

1b Elige los dibujos apropiados para Claudia y Alejandro. (AT3/5) [8W5; 8S7; 9W5]

✖ Reading for information/instructions, Level E

Reading. Pupils show comprehension of the texts in **1b** by ticking a picture grid.

Answers

Claudia	✓		✓		✓
Alejandro		✓		✓	✓

2 Escribe sobre unas vacaciones reales o imaginarias. (AT4/5) [8S2; 8T2]

✖ Writing imaginatively, Level E/F

Writing. Pupils write about a past holiday, real or imaginary.

módulo 4

6 Fueron de excursión

(Pupil's Book pages 70–71)

Main topics

● Saying what other people did on holiday

Key Framework objectives

● Verb tenses 8W5 (Reinforcement)
● Connectives 8S2 (Reinforcement)
● Present, *past*, future 8S7 (Reinforcement)
● Questions/text as stimulus to talk 9L4 (Reinforcement)

Grammar

Preterite tense: third person singular and plural

Key language

Despertarse	*Bañarse*
Visitar	*Cenar*
Llegar	*Tocar*
Cantar	*Ir*
Acostarse	

Resources

Cassette B, side 2
CD2, track 26
Cuaderno B, page 38
Grammar, Resource and Assessment File, page 71

Starter 1 [8W5; 9W5]

Aim: more practice of regular -*ar* verbs in the preterite.

Write on the board part of the paradigm for *cantar*: *yo cant...* , *tú cant...* , *él cant...* , *nosotros cant...* , *vosotros cant...* , *ellos cant...*

Ask pupils to work with a partner and fill out as much of the paradigm as they can. They should be able to fill in endings for *yo*, *tú* and *nosotros* as these have already been met. See if some pupils know the other endings.

1a Empareja las frases con los dibujos. (AT3/5) [8W5; 8S7; 9W5]

✕ Reading for information/instructions, Level D/E

Reading. Pupils match up sentences in the preterite with a series of pictures, this time focusing on the third person singular and plural. This activity extends the range of regular -*ar* verbs used, to include *cantar, cenar, descansar, llegar, sacar, tocar* and the reflexive verb *bañarse*. The *Gramática* box on page 70 presents the full paradigm of a regular -*ar* verb (*cantar*) in the preterite.

Answers

1 g	**2** e	**3** a	**4** h	**5** c	**6** f	**7** d	**8** b

1b Escucha y comprueba tus respuestas. (AT1/5)

Listening. Pupils listen and check their answers to **1a**.

Tapescript

1 *Se despertaron temprano.*
2 *Javi y Marisol se bañaron pero ...*
3 *Miguel descansó.*
4 *Visitaron un castillo.*
5 *El monitor sacó una foto.*
6 *Llegaron tarde al campamento.*
7 *Cenaron al aire libre y después ...*
8 *... Marisol tocó la guitarra y todos cantaron.*

1c Mira los dibujos en **1a** otra vez y contesta a las preguntas. (AT3/5) [8W5; 8S4; 9W5]

✕ Reading for information/instructions, Level D/E

Reading. Pupils answer questions in Spanish about the pictures in **1a**, using the third person singular and plural in the preterite. Pupils' attention should be drawn to the use of *¿Quién?* and *¿Quiénes?* in questions 5 and 2 respectively. Teachers should check pupils' understanding of these question forms and the difference in use between the two words.

Answers

1 Se despertaron temprano.
2 Javi y Marisol se bañaron.
3 Miguel descansó.
4 Visitaron un castillo.
5 El monitor sacó una foto.
6 Llegaron tarde al camping.
7 Después de cenar Marisol tocó la guitarra y todos cantaron.

Starter 2 [8W5; 9W5]

Aim: practising the preterite in the first person.

Write a list of regular -*ar* infinitives on the board. Ask pupils to write these down in the first person singular.

2 Mira los dibujos. Copia y completa las frases con las palabras apropiadas. (AT3/5) [8W5; 8S7; 9W5]

✕ Knowing about language

Reading. Pupils copy and complete sentences to describe a series of pictures, choosing between a third person singular and a third person plural verb in the preterite in each case.

Answers

> 1 **Se despertó** temprano.
> 2 **Se baño** en el río.
> 3 Por la tarde **visitaron** el castillo.
> 4 **Cenaron** al aire libre.
> 5 **Llegó** tarde al camping.
> 6 **Tocó** la guitarra.
> 7 Todos **cantaron**.

3 Describe las excursiones. Tu compañero/a dice 'verdad' o 'mentira'. (AT2/5) [8W5; 8T3; 9W5; 9L4]

✖ Speaking to convey information, Level E

Speaking. Pupils look at information about two excursions in which all the verbs are in the infinitive. They then make statements in the third person singular or plural of the preterite about people who took those excursions, and their partner must decide whether each statement is true or false. As the task involves quick manipulation of the verbs, teachers may wish to give pupils whole-class oral practice of forming the third person singular and plural in the preterite, from the infinitive, before allowing them to work in pairs.

➕ This is a challenging activity and teachers may therefore wish to use it as extension work for more able pupils only.

4 Escribe frases sobre una de las excursiones. (AT4/5) [8W2; 8S2,7]

✖ Exchange information/ideas, Level E/F

Writing. Pupils write sentences in the third person singular and plural about people who took the excursions in exercise **3**. Encourage them to use phrases such as *por la mañana, por la tarde* and *luego*.

🆁 In order to make this exercise more accessible to less able pupils, teachers could provide a worksheet on which the verbs have already been put into the third person singular or plural in the preterite – *se despertó/se despertaron; fui/fueron,* etc. – pupils have to select the right form of each verb and use it to create a sentence.

Plenary [8W5; 9W5]
Now practise everything you have learned about regular *-ar* verbs in the preterite. Use a dice and allocate dots to each subject pronoun, e.g. one dot = *yo*, two dots = *tú*, three dots = *él*, etc., or dice with subject pronouns on them. Pupils work with a partner or in a small group, rolling the dice and conjugating the verbs according to the dot or subject pronoun it lands on.

Cuaderno B, page 38

1a Escribe la frase apropiada del cuadro para cada dibujo. (AT3/5, AT4/2) [8W5; 8S2,7; 9W5]

✖ Reading for information/instructions, Level E

Reading and writing. Pupils write captions for a picture story, using the phrases in the preterite that are provided.

Answers

> a Cenaron a las ocho y media.
> b Elsa sacó muchas fotos.
> c Por la tarde se bañaron en el río.
> d Se acostaron a las nueve y media.
> e Elsa y Maite se despertaron temprano.
> f Para la comida, compraron pan, queso y fruta.
> g Por la mañana visitaron un pueblo de montaña.

1b Pon los dibujos en **1a** en el orden correcto. (AT3/5)

✖ Reading for information/instructions, Level E

Reading. Pupils use the times in the phrases from **1a** to put the pictures into the correct sequence.

Answers

> e, g, b, f, c, a, d

2 ¿Verdad (✓) o mentira (✗)? (AT3/5) [8W5; 8S2,7; 9W5]

✖ Reading for information/instructions, Level E

Reading. A true/false exercise, based on the picture story in **1a**.

Answers

> 1 ✗   2 ✗   3 ✓   4 ✓   5 ✗   6 ✓   7 ✗   8 ✗   9 ✓

6 Fueron de excursión

Grammar, Resource and Assessment File, page 71 (The preterite tense)

1 Pupils fill in the blanks in a grid to give various –ar verbs in their infinitive and preterite forms (first person singular) together with their meanings.

Answers

Infinitive	Meaning	Preterite	Meaning
Alojarse	To stay	Me alojé	I stayed
Bañarse	To swim	Me bañé	I swam
Comprar	To buy	Compré	I bought
Nadar en el mar	To swim in the sea	Nadé en el mar	I swam in the sea
Pasarlo bomba	To have a great time	Lo pasé bomba	I had a great time
Visitar	To visit	Visité	I visited

2 Pupils rearrange the words to make complete sentences.

Answers

> **a** Visité un castillo con mis amigos.
> **b** El sábado por la mañana fui a la piscina.
> **c** Me alojé en un hotel maravilloso el año pasado.
> **d** Me bañé en la playa el jueves.
> **e** Me lo pasé bomba en la fiesta.
> **f** Antes de volver a casa compré unos regalos.

3 Pupils read a number of sentences and tick those which are in the past tense.

Answers

> b, c and e

Resumen y Prepárate
(Pupil's Book pages 72–73)

Resumen

This is a checklist of language covered in Module 4. There is a comprehensive **Resumen** list for Module 4 in the Pupil's Book (page 72) and a **Resumen** test sheet in Cuaderno B (page 42).

Prepárate

A revision test to give practice for the test itself at the end of the module.

Resources

Cassette B, side 2
CD2, track 27
Cuaderno B, pages 39–41
Skills, Resource and Assessment File, page 73
Skills, Resource and Assessment File, page 74

1 Escucha las respuestas de Isabel y Martín. Elige los dibujos apropiados. (AT1/4) [8S4; 8L3]

✖ Listening for information/instructions, Level D/E

Listening. Pupils listen to two people describing their holidays and write down the letter of the correct pictures that show where they go, how they travel, what there is there and what they do.

Tapescript

Interviewer:	¿Adónde vas de vacaciones normalmente, Isabel?
Isabel:	Voy a Benicasim. Es un pueblo en la costa.
Interviewer:	¿Cómo vas?
Isabel:	Voy en tren.
Interviewer:	¿Qué hay de interés en Benicasim?
Isabel:	Hay una playa muy buena y en agosto hay una fiesta. Es muy divertida.
Interviewer:	¿Qué haces cuando estás de vacaciones?
Isabel:	Voy a la playa y me baño en el mar. Por la tarde salgo con mis amigos por ahí y a veces vamos a una discoteca a bailar.
Interviewer:	¿Adónde vas de vacaciones normalmente, Martín?
Martín:	Voy al campo, al pueblo de mis abuelos.
Interviewer:	¿Cómo vas?
Martín:	Voy en coche.
Interviewer:	¿Qué hay de interés en el pueblo?
Martín:	Bueno, el pueblo es muy pequeño pero se puede ir de paseo. El campo es muy bonito.
Interviewer:	¿Qué haces cuando estás de vacaciones?
Martín:	Me baño en la piscina y monto en bicicleta.

Answers

1 Isabel b, Martín d
2 Isabel c, Martín b
3 Isabel b, c, Martín a
4 Isabel a, d Martín b, c

2 Habla de tus vacaciones. Contesta a las preguntas de **1** (1–4). (AT2/4) [8S4; 8L4]

✖ Speaking about experiences/feelings/opinions, Level D/E

Speaking. Pupils answer the four questions from exercise **1** and adapt them to talk about their own holidays.

3a Lee el texto. Copia y completa las frases con las palabras apropiadas. (AT3/6) [8W5; 8S7,8; 9W5; 9S3]

✖ Reading for information/instructions, Level E

Reading. A gap-filling task, based on verbs in the present tense and in the preterite.

Answers

Normalmente **voy** de vacaciones con mis padres a un pueblo en la sierra. **Vamos** a visitar a mis abuelos. Pero el verano pasado **fui** con mis compañeros del instituto a Jerez de la Frontera. **Fuimos** en tren. **Nos alojamos** en un hotel. En Jerez **visité** un museo y también fui a la escuela ecuestre. **Compré** un póster de los caballos. Todos los chicos **fuimos** a una discoteca y los profesores **fueron** a una bodega a ver un espectáculo de flamenco. ¡Lo **pasé** muy bien! Noelia

3b Contesta a las preguntas. (AT3/6)

✖ Reading for information/instructions, Level E

Reading. Pupils answer questions in English about the completed text in **3a**.

Answers

1 a village in the mountains
2 her parents
3 to Jerez de la Frontera, with her schoolfriends
4 by train
5 in a hotel
6 a museum and the equestrian school
7 a horse poster
8 she had a great time.

4 Escribe una carta similar sobre ti. (AT4/6) [8W5; 8S2; 8T2,6; 9W5; 9S3]

✖ Exchange information/ideas, Level E/F

Writing. Pupils adapt the text in **3a** to create a similar piece about their own holidays.

R Less able pupils could be given a writing frame in the form of a sentence-building grid for support.

Cuaderno B, page 39

Repaso

1 Lee la entrevista. ¿Verdad (✓) o mentira (✗)?
(AT3/5) [8W5; 8S2; 9W5; 9S3]

✖ Reading for information/instructions, Level E

Reading. A true/false exercise, based on a dialogue about holidays, which mixes the present and preterite tenses.

Answers

1 ✓	2 ✗	3 ✗	4 ✓	5 ✓	6 ✗	7 ✓	8 ✓

2 ¿Qué hace Susa normalmente cuando va de vacaciones? Elige los dibujos apropiados. (AT3/5) [8W5; 8S2,7; 9S3]

✖ Reading for information/instructions, Level E

Reading. Pupils show comprehension of present tense activities mentioned in the dialogue in exercise 1, by ticking the relevant pictures.

Answers

a ✓	b ✓	f ✓	g ✓

3 Emplea los verbos de la lista para escribir cinco cosas que se pueden hacer en Sevilla. (AT4/4) [8S3; 9S3]

✖ Exchange information/ideas, Level C

Writing. Pupils use the verbs listed to write about what you can do in Seville.

Answers

Se puede visitar la catedral.
Se puede nadar en la piscina.
Se puede comer en un restaurante.
Se puede ir al parque tématico.
Se puede ver una corrida de toros.

Cuaderno B, page 40

Gramática 1

1 Complete the sentences using the verbs in the box. (AT3/2, AT4/1) [8S3; 9S3]

✖ Knowing about language

Reading and writing. A gap-filling exercise, using infinitives to follow *se puede(n)*.

Answers

1 ir	2 ver	3 visitar	4 comprar	5 practicar

2a Complete the sentences with the first person singular form of the verbs in the box. (AT3/2, AT4/4) [8W5; 9W5]

✖ Knowing about language

Reading and writing. A sentence-completion exercise, using the first person singular of the present tense.

Answers

1 Me baño 2 Voy 3 Monto 4 Hago 5 Saco
6 Descanso

2b Write sentences about what you do and don't do on holiday. (AT4/3) [8W5; 8S5; 9W5]

✖ Knowing about language

Writing. Writing about holidays, using the first person singular of the present tense, including negatives.

3 Match the questions and answers. (AT3/5) [8W5; 8S4; 9W5]

✖ Knowing about language

Reading. Matching questions and answers in the preterite (first and second person singular).

Answers

1 b	2 d	3 c	4 a

Cuaderno B, page 41

Gramática 2

1 Write a sentence for each picture. (AT4/3) [8W4; 9W4]

✖ Knowing about language

Writing. Using *fui + al/a la +* noun to label pictures.

Answers

1 *Fui al estadio*
2 Fui al mercado
3 Fui al cine
4 Fui a la estación de trenes

2 Complete the sentences with *fue* or *fueron*. (AT3/5, AT4/1) [8W5; 9W5]

✖ Knowing about language

Reading and writing. Sentence-completion exercise, using the third person singular and plural of *ir* in the preterite.

Answers

| 1 fue | 2 fue | 3 fueron | 4 fue | 5 fueron | 6 fue |

3 Complete the text with the verbs in the box. (AT3/5, AT4/1) [8W5; 8S8; 9W5]

✕ Knowing about language

Reading and writing. Text-completion exercise, using verbs in the preterite (first person singular and plural).

Answers

*En Semana Santa **fui** de vacaciones a Italia.* **Fui** en avión. **Me alojé** en un hotel. **Me bañé** en el mar y en la piscina. **Visité** Roma. **Compré** una camiseta y gafas de sol. **Lo pasé** muy bien. Juan

*En el verano **fuimos** de vacaciones a Inglaterra.* **Fuimos** en coche. **Nos alojamos** en un camping cerca de la playa. **Nos bañamos** en el mar. **Visitamos** un zoo y un parque de atracciones. **Lo pasamos** fenomenal. Jaime y Roberto

4 Complete the sentences with the appropriate form of the verb. (AT3/5, AT4/1) [8W5; 9W5]

✕ Knowing about language

Reading and writing. Using the third person singular and plural of verbs in the preterite.

Answers

cantó, tocó, bailaron, sacó

Skills, Resource and Assessment File, page 73 (Word associations and analogies)

1

Answers

a *Como en un restaurante.*
b Juego al fútbol/al tenis.
c Nado en la piscina/en el mar.
d Viajo en avión/en coche.
e Visito a mis amigos/mis abuelos.
f Compro una bicicleta/un sombrero.

2

Answers

a *derecha*
b Inglaterra
c tarde
d fui
e nieva
f pequeño – moderno

3

Answers

a *viento*
b fútbol
c avión
d hermana
e fatal

Skills, Resource and Assessment File, page 74 (Writing paragraphs)

1

Answers

	Meaning	What the word/phrase conveys
por la mañana	*in the morning*	*when*
fui a la playa	I went to the beach	*where I went*
con mis amigos	with my friends	
nos quedamos	we arranged to meet	
un par de horas	a couple of hours	
en el mar	in the sea	
azul	blue	
tomamos el sol	we sunbathed	
nos divertimos mucho	we had a good time	

2

Answers

	Meaning	What the word/phrase conveys
por la mañana	*in the morning*	*when*
fui a la playa	I went to the beach	*where I went*
con mis amigos	with my friends	who with
nos quedamos	we arranged to meet	what we did
un par de horas	a couple of hours	how long
en el mar	in the sea	where
azul	blue	what something was like
tomamos el sol	we sunbathed	what we did
nos divertimos mucho	we had a good time	what something was like

3

Answers

Tells you when something happened:	
primero	*first of all*
luego	*then*
por la mañana	*in the morning*
ayer	*yesterday*
entonces	*then*
después	*afterwards, later*
a las dos	*at two o'clock*
Tells you who you were with:	
con mis padres	*with my parents*
con mi amigo	*with my friend (m)*
con mi hermana	*with my sister*
Tells you what happened:	
jugué	*I played*
visitamos	*we visited*
Tells you what something was like:	
era fenomenal	*It was great*
me aburrí	*I was bored*
hacía sol	*It was sunny*

4 Pupils add two phrases of their own to each of the groups in **3**.

5 Pupils make a list of five pieces of information that could be given to write a meaty paragraph.

7 ¡Extra! ¡Cuba!

(Pupil's Book pages 74–75)

Main topics

This is an optional extension unit which reviews some of the key language of the module: the main focus here is on Cuba.

Key Framework objectives

- Inflections as aid to comprehension 9S8 (Launch)
- Reporting and paraphrasing 9L3 (Launch)
- Dictionary detail 8W7 (Reinforcement)
- Dictionary use 8T4 (Reinforcement)
- Using grammar to understand words 9W8 (Reinforcement)
- Different tense modals 9S3 (Reinforcement)

Resources

Cassette B, side 2
CD2, tracks 28 and 29
Starter 2, Resource and Assessment File, page 68

Starter 1 [8W7; 8T4]

Aim: using knowledge of high-frequency words to aid comprehension and glossary work.

Ask pupils to scan the text on page 74 for words or phrases that they are familiar with. Give them two minutes to find as many items as they can. Pool the group's findings.

Now write down a list of words for pupils to look up in the glossary. Ask them to (1) write down the meaning, (2) say whether it is a noun, a verb or an adjective and (3) if a noun, say whether it is masculine or feminine. For example: *bordear, estrecho, la vida, el buceo, una caja de puros, ron*

1a Lee el texto de Diego y contesta a las preguntas. Utiliza un diccionario. (AT3/6) [8T4; 9W8; 9S3,8]

Reading for information/instructions, Level F

Reading. Pupils read a text about Diego's holiday in Cuba and answer questions in English. They should be given access to a dictionary, but encouraged to use it only as a last resort. Before looking up new vocabulary, they should first look for cognates/near-cognates and use context or logic to work out some of the unknown vocabulary.

Answers

1 last year 2 8 hours 3 a few days 4 the 1950s American cars 5 there is music everywhere
6 very hot 7 He sunbathed and relaxed; he did water sports (water skiing, snorkelling) and learned how to sail.
8 He went hiking, looked at the tropical surroundings, went horseriding and visited a tobacco plantation.
9 father – a box of cigars; grandmother – coffee
10 He watched a baseball game.

1b Escucha. ¿Qué diferencias hay entre lo que dice Diego y lo que escribe en **1a**? (1–15) (AT1/6) [8S7; 8L3,4; 9S3; 9L3]

Listening for information/instructions, Level F

Listening. Pupils listen to Diego describing his Cuban holiday and spot the differences between what he wrote and what he says, noting down the words or expressions which vary. Before undertaking this task, for an added challenge, teachers could give pupils time to reread the text, then have them close their books while the recording is played. As soon as a pupil spots a discrepancy, s/he puts up her/his hand and has to explain what the discrepancy is.

Tapescript

1 – El año pasado fui de vacaciones a Cuba. Cuba es la isla más grande del Caribe y en mi opinión es la más interesante.
– Fui en avión. El viaje duró nueve horas.
– Pasé tres días en La Habana, la capital.
– Me alojé en un hotel en el centro de la ciudad.

2 – La Habana es una ciudad fantástica con mucha vida callejera. Hay edificios antiguos muy bonitos, plazas y calles estrechas, parques y museos.
– Lo que más me gustó fueron los coches antiguos de los años cincuenta.

3 – Hay música en todas partes. Músicos tocan salsa y están en todos los bares y restaurantes, en las plazas, en los hoteles y ¡hasta en la playa!
– La vida nocturna es fenomenal. Bailé en bares casi todas las noches.

4 – Hay muchas playas bonitas en Cuba. Pasé unos días en la playa en Varadero.
– Hizo buen tiempo, tomé el sol, descansé y practiqué deportes acuáticos como el water ski y la pesca. Aprendí a hacer vela. Me encantó.

5 – También pasé unos días en el campo en Pinar del Río. Hice senderismo, observé la naturaleza tropical, monté a caballo y visité una plantación de tabaco.

6 – Volví a La Habana y fui de compras. Compré un póster de Che Guevara para mi hermano … una caja de puros para mi padre, ron para mi abuelo, café para mi abuela y una bolsa para mi madre. La última noche vi un partido de voleibol.

Answers

	1a (text)	*1b (recording)*
1	*bonita*	*interesante*
2	ocho horas	nueve horas
3	unos días	tres días
4	Malecón	el centro de la ciudad
5	monumentos	museos
6	americanos	antiguos
7	el aeropuerto	la playa
8	discotecas	bares
9	estupendas	bonitas
10	mucho calor	buen tiempo
11	el buceo	la pesca
12	una camiseta	un póster
13	una hamaca	una bolsa
14	béisbol	voleibol

Starter 2 [8W2]

Aim: to revise some useful high frequency words.

Make an OHT using *Resource and Assessment File*, page 68. Put the OHT on your projector upside down and 'back to front' with the wrong side showing. Ask your pupils to work in pairs to decipher what the words are and also write down what they mean in English. Remind pupils to use a dictionary if they are unsure. These words all appear in the text on Cuba.

es, muy, la, hay, también, los, una, como, y, en, las, tiene, el

2a Lee el diario de Miguel. Copia y rellena el cuadro. (AT3/5) [8S2; 8T2]

✄ Reading for information/instructions, Level E

Reading. Pupils read Miguel's holiday diary and complete a grid, noting down who did what in the morning and in the afternoon on each of the three days.

✚ The diary text uses the first person singular and plural in the preterite. Pupils could fill in the grid using infinitives. Alternatively, more able pupils could be encouraged to fill it in using the third person singular or plural in the preterite.

Answers

	lunes	
	mañana	**tarde**
Miguel	ir a la playa, tomar el sol, bañarse	bañarse en la piscina montar en bicicleta
Claudia	ir a la playa, tomar el sol, bañarse	
padre	ir a la playa, tomar el sol, bañarse	dormir la siesta
madre	ir a la playa, tomar el sol, bañarse	dormir la siesta

	martes	
	mañana	**tarde**
Miguel	practicar la vela	jugar al tenis, ir a la discoteca, bailar (salsa)
Claudia	practicar la vela	jugar al tenis, ir a la discoteca, bailar (salsa)
padre	practicar la vela	
madre	practicar la vela	

	miércoles	
	mañana	**tarde**
Miguel	ir de excursión alquilar unos caballos ir al campo a observar aves	
Claudia	jugar al voleibol	
padre	ir de excursión alquilar unos caballos ir al campo a observar aves	
madre	jugar al golf	

2b Eres Miguel. Con tu compañero/a, pregunta y contesta. (AT2/5) [8S4,6; 9C4]

✄ Speaking and interacting with others, Level E

Speaking. Pupils work in pairs to ask and answer questions about what they did on different days of the week, in the morning and in the afternoon. Pupils should be encouraged to use the verbs they have already come across in the preterite, rather than looking up new verbs, some of which may be irregular.

Plenary [8W7]

Ask your class: what must you do if you look up an adjective in the dictionary (Make sure you look for its masculine, singular form.)?

What must you do if you look up a verb (Look for it in its infinitive form.)?

What must you do if you find several definitions for the word you have just looked up (Look at the context of the word, don't choose the first definition you see.)?

módulo 4 — *Te toca a ti*

(Pupil's Book pages 118–119)

- Self-access reading and writing at two levels.

A Reinforcement

1 ¿Qué hay de interés? Lee los textos y escribe las letras de los dibujos. (AT3/4) [8S2; 9C4]

Reading for information/instructions, Level D

Reading. Pupils read about places of interest in Alicante, Puerto Banus and Ronda and write down the letters of the relevant pictures for each one.

Answers

> **Alicante**: *g, a,* f, h, e, d, i
> **Ronda**: k, b, e
> **Puerto Banus**: c, j, a

2 Lee las entrevistas y elige el lugar ideal de vacaciones de 1 para cada persona. (AT3/4) [8S2,4]

Reading for information/instructions, Level D

Reading. Pupils read interviews about three people's holiday preferences and choose a suitable destination from exercise 1 for each person.

Answers

> **1** Ronda **2** Puerto Banus **3** Alicante

3 Contesta a las preguntas y describe tus vacaciones. (AT4/4) [8W5; 8S4; 9W5]

Exchange information/ideas, Level D/F

Writing. Pupils write answers to questions about their own holidays: where they go, how they travel there and what they do.

B Extension

1 Empareja los textos con los dibujos. (AT3/5) [8S2; 8T2]

Reading for information/instructions, Level E

Reading. Pupils read three texts about past holidays and match each one with the correct picture.

Answers

> **1** b **2** c **3** a

2 Escribe frases sobre el viaje de cada persona. (AT4/5) [8W5; 8S4; 9W5]

Exchange information/ideas, Level E

Writing. Pupils fill in a grid about each person's holiday, from exercise **1**, changing the verbs in the texts from first person singular or plural to third person singular or plural, in the preterite.

Answers

	¿Adónde fue?	¿Con quién fue?	¿Cómo fueron?	¿Dónde se alojaron?	¿Qué visitaron?	¿Qué tal lo pasó?
Guillermo	Fue a Cuba.	Fue con su madre y su hermana.	*Fueron en avión.*	Se alojaron en un hotel en la costa.	Visitaron La Habana.	Lo pasó fenomenal.
Susa	Fue al campo.	Fue con sus amigos.	Fueron en tren.	Se alojaron en un camping.	Visitaron un castillo muy antiguo.	Lo pasó muy bien.
Max	Fue a Paris.	Fue con sus padres.	Fueron en coche y en ferry.	Se alojaron en un hotel en el centro.	Visitaron los museos y los monumentos históricos.	Lo pasó bomba.

3 Escribe sobre tu viaje. (AT4/5) [8W5; 8S4; 8T6; 9W5]

Exchange information/ideas, Level E/F

Writing. Pupils write about a past holiday of their own, prompted by six questions in Spanish.

Unit	Key Framework objectives	PoS	Key language and Grammar
1 ¿Quieres ir al cine? (pp. 78–79) Making arrangements to go out	8L6 Expressions in speech [L] 9L1 Listening for inferences [R] 9L2 Recognising rhetorical devices [R]	2a listen for gist and detail 2b correct pronunciation/ intonation 2c ask and answer questions 2d initiate/develop conversations 2g dealing with the unpredictable 2i report main points 3c use knowledge of English	*¿Diga?* *¿Quieres salir/venir al cine/conmigo (esta tarde)?* *¿A qué hora? ¿A (las siete).* *¿Adónde quieres ir?* *¿Dónde quedamos?* *En la bolera.*
2 ¿Qué tipo de películas te gustan? (pp. 80–81) Saying what sort of films you like Justifying an opinion	8L5 Unscripted speech [L] 9W1 Word discrimination [L] 9L5 Extended/frequent contributions to talk [L] 8W1 Adding abstract words [R] 8W2 Connectives [R] 8S6 Substituting and adding [R] 8L4 Extending sentences [R] 9C3 Youth attitudes to sport/culture	2c ask and answer questions 2i report main points 3c use knowledge of English 4c compare cultures 5e range of resources	*¿Qué tipo de películas prefieres?* *(No) Me gustan las películas de acción.* *Prefiero las películas de dibujos animados.* *¿Por qué?* *Porque son graciosas.*
3 Dos entradas, por favor (pp. 82–83) Buying cinema tickets	9T5 Simple creative writing [L] 8S8 Using high-frequency words and punctuation as clues [R] 8L3 Relaying gist and detail [R]	2a listen for gist and detail 2e adapt language 2i report main points 3b use context to interpret meaning 4a working with authentic materials 4c compare cultures 5e range of resources 5f using TL creatively 5h listening/reading for enjoyment	*Dos entradas, por favor.* *Para Quiero ser como Beckham.* *Para la sesión de las siete y media.* *¿Cuánto es?* *¿Qué pantalla es?* *Apta para todos los públicos …*
4 ¡Es genial! (pp. 84–85) Describing an event in the present tense	9S4 Building answers from questions [L] 8S4 Question types [R] 8S7 Present, past, future [R] 8L6 Expression in speech [R] 8C5 Colloquialisms [R] 9L3 Reporting and paraphrasing [R] 9C5 Regions of the country [R]	2c ask and answer questions 2d initiate/develop conversations 2f adapt language for different contexts 2g dealing with the unpredictable 2i scanning texts 4b communicating with native speakers 4c compare cultures	Present tense *¿Dónde estás?* *Estamos (en España).* *¿Con quién estás?* *Estoy aquí (con mi amigo).* *¿Qué tiempo hace?* *Hace (mucho sol).* *¿Cómo es?* *¡Es (fenomenal)!*
5 ¿Qué hiciste el sábado? (pp. 86–87) Describing an event in the past	8W2 Connectives [R] 8W5 Verb tenses [R] 8S2 Connectives in extended sentences [R] 8S7 Present, past and future [R]	2c ask and answer questions 2d initiate/develop conversations 2f adapt language for different contexts	Preterite tense *Salí de casa a las once.* *Fui en coche.* *Vi un partido entre el Arsenal y el Manchester United.* *Llevé una bufanda.* *Comí un perrito caliente.* *Bebí una naranjada.* *Vi a Raúl.* *Hice una llamada con mi móvil.*

Unit	Key Framework objectives	PoS	Key language and Grammar
6 El estadio estaba lleno (pp. 88–89) Describing what events were like	8T5 Writing continuous text [L] 9W2 Connectives in complex sentences [L] 9S6 Multiple-clause sentences [L] 9S7 Different tenses [L] 8S7 Present, past and future [R] 8S8 Using high-frequency words and punctuation clues [R]		Imperfect tense *Fui a Madrid.* *Hacía buen tiempo.* *Había muchas tiendas.* *Primero, después, luego, …*
Resumen y Prepárate (pp. 90–91) Pupils' checklist and practice test			
7 ¡Extra! Ídolos del fútbol, pasado y presente (pp. 92–93) Optional unit: two famous footballers, Maradona and Raúl	8T3 Language and text types [R] 8T6 Text as model and source [R] 8C2 Famous people [R] 8C3 Daily life and young people [R] 9W2 Connectives in complex sentences [R] 9S6 Multiple-clause sentences [R]	**3c** use knowledge of English **5d** respond to different types of language **5e** range of resources **5h** using TL for real purposes	
Te toca a ti (pp. 120–121) Self-access reading and writing at two levels			

1 ¿Quieres ir al cine?
(Pupil's Book pages 78–79)

Main topics

● Making arrangements to go out

Key Framework objectives

● Expression in speech 8L6 (Launch)
● Listening for inferences 9L1 (Reinforcement)
● Recognising rhetorical devices 9L2 (Reinforcement)

Grammar

● *conmigo, contigo*

Key language

¿Diga?/¿Dígame?
¿Quieres salir/venir conmigo?
No, no quiero salir contigo.
¿Adónde quieres ir?

la bolera   *el parque de atracciones*
el cine   *la pista de hielo*
el club de jóvenes

¿A qué hora?
A (las siete).
¿Dónde quedamos?/¿Dónde nos encontramos?
En la plaza.
Vale.

Resources

Cassette C, side 1
CD3, tracks 2 and 3
Cuaderno B, page 43
Hojas de trabajo, Resource and Assessment File, pages 90 and 91
Flashcards 39–42, 53 (*¡Listos! 1*)

Starter 1 [8L3]

Aim: to revise telling the time.

Get pupils to use little clocks they have made previously, or mini-whiteboards or paper and pen. Say some times and ask pupils to hold up their clock/board with that time written in figures. Then ask them to work in groups, with a leader saying times and the others showing that time on their clock/board. Alternatively, ask pupils to draw six clock faces and then to draw in the hands of the clock as you say each time.

1 Empareja los lugares con los dibujos.
(AT3/1) [8W1]

✄ Reading for information/instructions, Level A

Reading. Pupils match up places of interest with the relevant picture. They should be able to work out the first four of the five places as cognates or near-cognates and then work out the fifth (*la pista de hielo*) by process of elimination. Once pupils have completed this task, teachers may wish to give them aural discrimination practice of the five new items of vocabulary, prior to the listening tasks **2a** and **2b**.

Answers

a 3	b 1	c 4	d 2	e 5

2a Escucha y lee. Contesta a las preguntas.
(AT1/3) [8S4; 8L6; 9L1,2]

✄ Reading for information/instructions, Level D

Listening and reading. Pupils listen to and read a telephone conversation in which Gerardo and Marisa arrange to go to the cinema, then answer questions in Spanish. The dialogue includes an example of

conmigo, which is explained in the *Gramática* box on page 78. Afterwards, teachers could check understanding of the new key language in a 'find the Spanish for …' exercise. Useful expressions might include: Hello (on the telephone); Would you like to go out with me on Saturday?; Where do you want to go?; Where shall we meet?; See you tomorrow.

Tapescript

– ¿Diga?
– Hola, Gerardo. Soy Marisa. ¿Quieres salir conmigo el sábado?
– ¿Adónde quieres ir?
– No sé, al cine o a la bolera.
– Pues, prefiero ir al cine.
– Bueno. ¿A qué hora?
– A las siete.
– ¿Dónde quedamos?
– En la plaza.
– Vale.
– Hasta mañana.
– Adiós.

Answers

1 el sábado	**2** al cine	**3** a las siete	**4** en la plaza

2b Escucha. Copia y rellena el cuadro. (AT1/4)
[8L3; 9L3]

✄ Listening for information/instructions, Level D/E

Listening. Pupils listen to a series of dialogues in which people arrange to meet, then complete a grid with details of where each pair are going, at what time and the meeting place.

Tapescript

1 – ¿Dígame?
– Hola, Javier. Soy Felipe.
– Hola Felipe.
– ¿Quieres venir conmigo al club de jóvenes?
– ¿Cuándo?
– Esta tarde.
– Buena idea. ¿A qué hora quedamos?
– A las cinco y media.
– Bueno. ¿Dónde quedamos?
– En el bar.
– Vale.
– Hasta luego.
– Adiós.

2 – ¿Diga?
– Hola, Santiago. Soy Elena. ¿Quieres salir conmigo el domingo?
– ¿Adónde quieres ir?
– A la pista de hielo.
– Bueno. ¿A qué hora quedamos?
– ¿A las nueve?
– Vale, a las nueve. ¿Dónde quedamos?
– ¿En tu casa?
– Bueno, aquí en mi casa.
– Hasta luego.
– Adiós.

3 – ¿Diga?
– Hola, Mónica. Soy Raúl.
– Hola Raúl.
– ¿Quieres venir al parque de atracciones conmigo esta noche?
– ¿Al parque de atracciones? Sí, buena idea. ¿A qué hora quedamos?
– ¿A las ocho?
– No, mejor a las siete y media.
– Vale. ¿Dónde quedamos?
– En la plaza de toros.
– Bueno.
– Hasta luego.
– Hasta luego.

4 – ¿Dígame?
– Hola, Alejandra. Soy Marta.
– Hola Marta. ¿Qué tal?
– Bien, bien. Mira. ¿Quieres ir al club de jóvenes conmigo esta tarde?
– No, prefiero ir a la bolera.
– Bueno, pues vamos a la bolera. ¿A qué hora quedamos?
– ¿A las seis?
– Vale. ¿Dónde quedamos?
– ¿En la estación?
– Muy bien.
– Adiós.
– Hasta luego.

Answers

	¿Dónde?	¿A qué hora?	¿Dónde quedan?
1 Javier y Felipe	al club de jóvenes	a las cinco y media	en el bar
2 Santiago y Elena	a la pista de hielo	a las nueve	en la casa de Santiago
3 Raúl y Mónica	al parque de atracciones	a las siete y media	en la plaza de toros
4 Alejandra y Marta	a la bolera	a la seis	en la estación

2c Con tu compañero/a, pregunta y contesta. (AT2/4) [8S6; 8L4,6; 9L1,2]

✕ Speaking and interacting with others, Level D

Speaking. Pupils work in pairs on a role-play exercise in which they make arrangements to go out. They are supported by a model dialogue. Before tackling the role-play, teachers may wish to give pupils oral practice of manipulating the new language, using a *¿Cómo se dice en español … ?* exercise, checking and correcting their pronunciation along the way. Pupils could be encouraged to record their role-play, once polished, as a record of achievement.

➕ Able pupils should also be encouraged to add as much detail to the role-play as possible, using expressions such as *¡Diga!/¡Dígame!, Hasta mañana/ Hasta luego.* They could express simple opinions and even suggest alternatives, using expressions such as *Pues, prefiero … ,* or *No, mejor a … .*

Starter 2 [8S1]

Aim: reading skills – unjumbling a telephone conversation.

Write a jumbled up telephone conversation on an OHT (or the board if you have time) similar to that in exercise **2c**. Ask pupils to put the statements in the correct order, then practise with a partner.

3a Lee los mensajes y completa las palabras con las letras que faltan. (AT4/3) [8S1,8; 8T3]

✕ Exchange information/ideas, Level D

Writing. Pupils read text messages in Spanish in which people make arrangements to go out, and write them out in full. As a follow-up, teachers could invite pupils to try writing their own text messages, in Spanish, imagining how other words might be abbreviated.

módulo 5 ■■ 1 ¿Quieres ir al cine?

Answers

> ¿Qué tal? ¿Quieres venir a la bolera conmigo?
> Hola: ¿Cuándo?
> ¿El sábado por la tarde?
> Buena idea. ¿A qué hora?
> ¿A las ocho?
> Vale. ¿Dónde nos encontramos? ¿En la plaza?
> No, en mi casa.
> Bueno. Hasta luego.

3b Lee la conversación en **2a** otra vez y escribe otra similar. (AT4/4) [8S2,4; 8T6]

✖ Exchange information/ideas, Level D/E

Writing. Pupils reread the dialogue in **2a** and write a different version of it.

> ### Plenary
>
> Quick-fire questions to reinforce useful colloquial phrases:
>
> Ask your class the following: *¿Cómo se dice en español?*: Do you want to go to the cinema tonight? What time? Where shall we meet? Okay. I don't know. Hello (answering the phone) Good idea. See you later.

Cuaderno B, page 43

1a ¿A qué hora nos encontramos? Empareja los dibujos con las frases. (AT3/2) [8S8]

✖ Reading for information/instructions, Level C

Reading. Pupils match statements about time to the relevant clock faces.

Answers

1 d	**2** a	**3** c	**4** e	**5** b					

1b Escribe las palabras de **1a** para:... (AT4/2) [8W1]

✖ Reading for information/instructions, Level C

Reading and writing. Pupils copy the correct time phrases from **1a** to match the English equivalents.

Answers

> **1** esta mañana
> **2** mañana por la tarde
> **3** esta noche
> **4** esta tarde

2a Lee el diálogo y contesta a las preguntas. (AT3/3, AT4/3) [8S4; 8T2]

✖ Reading for information/instructions, Level D

Reading and writing. A dialogue about arranging to go out, followed by questions in Spanish.

Answers

> **1** Diego
> **2** a la discoteca
> **3** mañana por la noche
> **4** a las ocho y media
> **5** en la casa de Graciela

2b Escribe un diálogo para invitar a un(a) amigo(a) a salir contigo. Elige lugares de la lista para ir y para encontrarse. (AT4/4) [8S2; 8T2,6]

✖ Exchange information/ideas, Level D

Writing. Pupils use the dialogue in **2a** as a model for writing a similar dialogue, based on the prompts given.

Hojas de trabajo, Resource and Assessment File, pages 90 and 91

Cards for pairwork featuring places to go and attractions: pupils match the pictures to the correct words.

2 ¿Qué tipo de películas te gustan?

(Pupil's Book pages 80–81)

Main topics

- Saying what sort of films you like

Key Framework objectives

- Unscripted speech 8L5 (Launch)
- Word discrimination 9W1 (Launch)
- Extended/frequent contributions to talk (Launch)
- Adding abstract words 8W1 (Reinforcement)
- Connectives 8W2 (Reinforcement)
- Substituting and adding 8S6 (Reinforcement)
- Extending sentences 8L4 (Reinforcement)
- Youth attitudes to sport/culture 9C3 (Reinforcement)

Grammar

- *¿por qué?/porque*
- Revision of comparatives

Key language

¿Qué tipo de películas prefieres?
¿Te gustan las películas …

cómicas
románticas
de ciencia-ficción
de guerra
de terror

policíacas
de acción
de dibujos animados
del oeste

(No) Me gustan las películas de acción.
Prefiero las películas de dibujos animados.

¿Por qué te gustan las películas cómicas?
Porque son …

aburrido/a(s)
animado/a(s)
divertido/a(s)
emocionante(s)
gracioso/a(s)

infantil(es)
inteligente(s)
interesante(s)
tonto/a(s)

más, menos

Resources

Cassette C, side 1
CD3, tracks 4 and 5
Cuaderno B, page 44
OHTs 25 and 26

Starter 1 [8W1]

Aim: vocabulary extension – thinking activity.

Prepare an OHT or write up on the board the different types of films at the top of page 80 in the Pupil's Book. Ask pupils to work out what these are in English without looking in their books (using the strategies they have learned so far to help them work out the meaning of words).

1 Mira las palabras y nombra una película para cada tipo. (AT3/2) [8W1]

Reading for information/instructions, Level B

Reading. Pupils read and identify nine types of films in Spanish, then suggest a film title for each category. Many of the film types are cognates or near-cognates with English and the pictures also support pupils' understanding. Following this exercise, teachers may wish to give pupils aural practice of the film types in preparation for the listening exercise **2a**.

2a Escucha a los jóvenes. ¿Qué tipo de películas prefieren? (1–4) (AT1/4) [8L3; 9L3]

Listening for information/instructions, Level D

Listening. Pupils listen to young people talking about the types of films they like and why. As a first task, pupils must simply note down in Spanish the type of film each person prefers.

Tapescript

1 – ¿Qué tipo de películas prefieres, Juan?
– Pues, a mí me gustan las películas policíacas porque son inteligentes, pero prefiero las películas de acción porque son más emocionantes.

2 – ¿Te gustan las películas de dibujos animados, Pepa?
– No me gustan las películas de dibujos animados porque son infantiles. Prefiero las películas de terror porque son divertidas.

3 – ¿Qué tipo de películas prefieres, Joaquín?
– No me gustan las películas románticas porque son tontas. Prefiero las películas de guerra porque son emocionantes.

4 – Me gustan mucho las películas cómicas porque son graciosas. No me gustan las películas románticas porque son menos interesantes.

Answers

1	película de acción	**3**	película de guerra
2	película de terror	**4**	película cómica

2b Escucha otra vez. ¿Por qué prefieren las películas? (AT1/4) [8W2; 9W1]

Listening for information/instructions, Level D

Listening. Pupils listen again to the recording and this time write down why the speakers prefer a particular type of film. It is suggested that before undertaking this exercise teachers use the support box on the page to familiarise pupils with the key adjectives. This box can also be used to point out the need to use the plural form when referring to what type of films you

módulo 5

2 ¿Qué tipo de películas te gustan?

like. The *¡Ojo!* box on page 80 reminds pupils of the difference between *porque* and *¿por qué?*.

Tapescript

As exercise *2a*

Answers

1 *Porque son más emocionantes.*
2 Porque son divertidas.
3 Porque son emocionantes.
4 Porque son graciosas.

2c Haz un sondeo. Pregunta a cinco de tus compañeros/as. (AT2/4) [8S4,5,6]

✖ Speaking about experiences/feelings/opinions, Level E

Speaking. Pupils conduct a class survey on the type of films people prefer and why, using the model provided.

✑ As a follow-up, pupils could enter the findings of their survey into an Excel spreadsheet and create a bar graph or pie chart, using the chart wizard.

2d Escribe unas frases sobre los tipos de películas que prefieres. (AT4/4) [8S2]

✖ Exchange information/ideas, Level D/E

Writing. Pupils write a few sentences about the types of films they prefer and why, using the support box on page 80 as necessary.

Starter 2 [8L4,5; 9L3,5]
Aim: to recap language to discuss different types of films; pronunciation and fluency practice.

Ask pupils to try to do this exercise from memory and without looking in books. Working with a partner they take it in turns to ask which type of film they prefer and why. Pupils write their partner's answer down and then report back to the class at the end of the speaking exercise. For example: *John prefiere películas de acción porque son emocionantes.*

3a Lee las opiniones. Escribe 'Estoy de acuerdo' o 'No estoy de acuerdo' para cada frase. (AT3/3) [8C3; 9C3]

✖ Reading for information/instructions, Level D

Reading. Pupils read a series of sentences using the comparative (introduced in Module 1, Unit 1) contrasting various forms of entertainment, and write down in Spanish whether they agree or disagree with each statement. The vocabulary box on page 80 supports them with some of the new language.

3b Escribe seis frases similares comparando diferentes diversiones. (AT4/4) [8S2; 9C4]

✖ Exchange information/ideas, Level D

Writing. Pupils write six sentences along similar lines to those in **3a** comparing different forms of entertainment. They should be encouraged to use both *más … que …* and *menos … que … .* The exercise also offers the opportunity to discuss aspects of Spanish culture, such as flamenco, *pelota* and bullfighting.

Plenary [8W1]
Ask pupils to work with a partner. Give them three minutes to write down as many adjectives as they can remember to describe films. No looking in books! Take feedback at the end and write responses on the board.

Cuaderno B, page 44

1 Mira la información en el cuadro y lee las frases. ¿Quién habla? (AT3/2) [8S2,5]

✖ Reading for information/instructions, Level C

Reading Pupils must read a series of statements about the types of film various people prefer and use the grid to work out who made each statement.

Answers

1 Clara	2 Rafaela	3 Clara	4 Valdo	5 Zulema
6 Esteban	7 Fabio			

2 Empareja las preguntas con las respuestas. (AT3/3) [8S4,5]

✖ Reading for information/instructions, Level D

Reading. A matching exercise in which pupils link questions and answers on film preferences.

Answers

1 b	2 a	3 d	4 c

3 Escribe tus propias opiniones sobre las categorías de películas que te gustan y no te gustan. (AT4/3) [8S2,5]

✖ Exchange information/ideas, Level D/E

Writing. Pupils write about their own film preferences.

3 Dos entradas, por favor

(Pupil's Book pages 82–83)

Main topics

● Buying cinema tickets

Key Framework objectives

● Simple creative writing 9T5 (Launch)
● Using high-frequency words and punctuation clues 8S8 (Reinforcement)
● Relaying gist and detail 8L3 (Reinforcement)
● Language and text types 8T3 (Reinforcement)
● Authentic texts as sources 9T3 (Reinforcement)

Key language

Dos entradas, por favor.
Para Quiero ser como Beckham.
Para la sesión de las siete y media.
¿Cuánto es?
¿Qué pantalla es?
Apta para todos los públicos/mayores de … años

Resources

Cassette C, side 1
CD3, track 6
Cuaderno B, page 45

Starter 1 [8W8]

Aim: vocabulary extension – thinking activity.

Write a list of popular children's book titles or up-to-date films on the board in Spanish. Ask pupils to work with a partner and try to deduce what these titles are in English: *Cenicienta, la Bella Durmiente, Blancanieves y los Siete Enanitos*, etc.

Ask pupils how they worked these out.

1a Lee la conversación en el cine y contesta a las preguntas. (AT3/3) [8S4,8]

✠ Reading for information/instructions, Level D

Reading. Pupils read a conversation at a cinema box office and answer questions in Spanish. Afterwards, teachers may wish to check their understanding of the key phrases and vocabulary, including *entradas, sesión* and *pantalla*.

Answers

1 dos **2** *Quiero ser como Beckham* **3** las siete y media **4** once euros **5** dos	

1b Escucha las conversaciones (1–5) y contesta a las preguntas en **1a**. (AT1/4) [8L3; 9L3; 9T3]

✠ Listening for information/instructions, Level D

Listening. Pupils listen to dialogues in which people buy cinema tickets and answer the same questions as in **1a**.

Tapescript

1 – Buenas tardes.
 – Buenas tardes. Una entrada, por favor.
 – ¿Para qué película?
 – Para Quiero ser como Beckham.
 – ¿Para qué sesión?
 – Para la sesión de las nueve.
 – Aquí tiene.
 – ¿Cuánto es?

 – Son 5,50 euros.
 – ¿Qué pantalla es?
 – Es la pantalla tres.
 – Gracias.
 – De nada.
2 – ¿Qué desea?
 – Tres entradas, por favor.
 – ¿Para qué película?
 – Para Las Dos Torres.
 – ¿Para qué sesión?
 – Para la sesión de las ocho y cuarto.
 – Aquí tiene.
 – ¿Cuánto es?
 – 16,50 euros.
 – ¿Qué pantalla es?
 – Es la pantalla una.
 – Muchas gracias.
 – De nada, adiós.
3 – Buenas tardes. Cinco entradas, por favor.
 – ¿Para qué película?
 – Para Camino a la Perdición.
 – ¿Para qué sesión?
 – Para la sesión de las seis.
 – Aquí tiene.
 – ¿Cuánto es?
 – Son 27,50 euros.
 – ¿Qué pantalla es?
 – Es la pantalla cuatro.
4 – Buenas tardes.
 – Buenas tardes. Dos entradas para Insomnio.
 – Dos para Insomnio. ¿Para qué sesión?
 – Para la sesión de las siete.
 – Tome usted.
 – ¿Cuánto es?
 – 11 euros.
 – ¿Qué pantalla es?
 – La dos.
 – Gracias.
 – De nada.
5 – Hola. Cuatro entradas, por favor.
 – ¿Para qué película?
 – Para Señales.
 – ¿Para qué sesión?
 – Para la sesión de las diez. ¿Cuánto es?

– *Son 22 euros.*
– *¿Qué pantalla es?*
– *La número cinco.*
– *Gracias.*
– *De nada.*

Answers

> 1 1, *Quiero ser como Beckham,* a las nueve, 5,50 €, la pantalla 3
> 2 3, *Las Dos Torres,* a las ocho y cuarto, 16,50 €, la pantalla 1
> 3 5, *Camino a la Perdición,* a las seis, 27,50 €, la pantalla 4
> 4 2, *Insomnio,* a las siete, 11 €, la pantalla 2
> 5 4, *Señales,* a las diez, 22 €, la pantalla 5

1c Con tu compañero/a, haz un diálogo similar a lo de **1a**. (AT2/4) [8L6]

✄ Speaking and interacting with others, Level D

Speaking. Pupils work in pairs to create a dialogue similar to the one in **1a**. As before, once they have polished the role-play, pupils could add it to their record of achievement.

> *Starter 2*
>
> *Aim:* reading skills exercise to recap language used at the cinema.
>
> Make a gapped dialogue to put up on the OHT, using the one on page 82 as a model. You could supply the missing words or not, depending on your group.

2 Lee las categorías y elige una película apropiada para estas personas. (AT3/2) [8S8]

✄ Reading for information/instructions, Level C

Reading. Pupils look at a series of Spanish cinema posters, paying particular attention to the age categories, then choose a suitable film for four groups of people.

Answers

> | 1 *El libro de la selva 2* | 2 *Evelyn* |
> | 3 *El Núcleo* | 4 *Chicago* |
> | **Key** | |
> | The Cell = PG13 | Evelyn = PG |
> | Chicago = 12A | The Jungle Book II = U |

3 Mira el póster y contesta a las preguntas. (AT3/4) [8T3]

✄ Reading for information/instructions, Level C

Reading and writing. Pupils look at the cinema poster and answer the questions in English.

Answers

> | **a** science fiction | **b** everyone | **c** two | **d** 16,50 euros |
> | **e** no, 2, 4 or 6 pm | | | |

4 En un ordenador diseña un póster para un cine. Incluye: (AT4/4) [8T2,6; 9T2,5]

✄ Writing imaginatively, Level C/E

✎ *Writing.* Pupils design a film poster covering the areas listed on the page. Ideally, they should use a graphics or desktop publishing programme to make the poster as effective and eye-catching as possible. When finished they could be used for display purposes.

> *Plenary* [8S8]
>
> Ask pupils to write down a couple of techniques they use to retrieve information from posters such as the one on page 83. Take into account that if they are out and about they may or may not have a dictionary. Take feedback and write notes on the board.
>
> What other sources of information could they apply these techniques to (any sort of leaflet, tourist brochure, hotels and restaurants, etc.)?

Cuaderno B, page 45

1 Completa los diálogos con la información en las entradas. (AT3/3, AT4/2) [8S1]

✄ Reading for information/instructions, Level D

Reading and writing. A gapped dialogue to complete, based on buying cinema tickets. Pupils use the cinema ticket shown to fill in the missing information.

Answers

> – **Dos** entradas, por favor.
> – ¿Para qué pelicula?
> – Para *El señor de los anillos.*
> – ¿Para qué sesión?
> – Para le sesión de las ocho **y cuarto**.
> – Aquí tiene.
> – ¿Cuánto es?
> – Son **diez** euros.
> – ¿Qué pantalla es?
> – Es la pantalla **cinco**.

2a Lee la información y empareja la película con la categoría apropiada. (AT3/4) [8S8]

✄ Reading for information/instructions, Level C

Reading. Pupils read publicity material about three films and match each title to the relevant film classification.

Answers

1 c **2** a **3** b

2b Contesta a las preguntas. (AT3/4)

✕ Reading for information/instructions, Level C

Reading. Follow-up questions in English on the text in **2a**. Pupils write down the names of the three films in English.

Answers

> **1** Saturday and Sunday
> **2** January
> **3** *The Lord of the Rings/Harry Potter and the Philosopher's Stone/13 Ghosts*

3 Escribe un diálogo como en **1** para la película que quieres ver en **2a**. (AT3/4) [8T6]

✕ Writing imaginatively, Level D

Writing. Pupils write a conversation similar to that in activity **1** enquiring about a film they want to see.

Main topics

● Describing an event in the present

Key Framework objectives

● Building answers from questions 9S4 (Reinforcement)
● Question types 8S4 (Reinforcement)
● *Present*, past, future 8S7 (Reinforcement)
● Expression in speech 8L6 (Reinforcement)
● Colloquialisms 8C5 (Reinforcement)
● Reporting and paraphrasing 9L3 (Reinforcement)
● Regions of the country 9C5 (Reinforcement)

Key language

¿Dónde estás?
Estoy en (el parque zoológico).
¿Con quién estás?
Estoy aquí (con mi amigo).
¿Qué tiempo hace?
Hace (mucho sol).
¿Cómo es?
¡Es (fenomenal)!
¿Por qué?

Resources

Cassette C, side 1
CD3, track 7
Cuaderno B, page 46

Starter 1 [8W5; 9W5]

Aim: to revise weather idioms that take *hacer* and to reinforce the transferability of a high-frequency word.

Ask pupils to write down as many weather idioms as they can that start with *hace* (*hace sol, hace calor, hace frío, hace viento, hace buen tiempo, hace mal tiempo*). Ask pupils if they can remember any other phrases with *hacer*, e.g. *hago mis deberes*.

1 Empareja las preguntas con las respuestas apropiadas en la foto. (AT3/4) [8S4; 9S4; 9C5]

✖ Reading for information/instructions, Level D

Reading. Pupils read sentences about a visit to *La Tomatina* festival, near Valencia, and then match the sentences with the appropriate questions. The text covers a number of present-tense verbs in the first person plural, including *estar*, as well as weather phrases.

Answers

1 *d* 2 b 3 a 4 c,f 5 e 6 g 7 i 8 h 9 j

2a Escucha y empareja los textos con los dibujos. (AT1/4) [8L6; 8C5; 9L3]

✖ Listening for information/instructions, Level E

Listening. Pupils listen to people describing an event in the present tense, then match up five sentences with the relevant pictures. Teachers should first ensure that pupils understand the five sentences on the page. As the recorded speeches are longer than the sentences, pupils should be encouraged to listen for the key phrase in the question rather than try to understand everything. However, as a follow-up, teachers could play the recording again and ask pupils what extra information they can understand.

More able pupils could be asked to paraphrase. As a final exercise you could provide pupils with a copy of the transcript with some gaps. Pupils listen and fill the gaps in. You could target, for example, words and phrases that they might use in written or oral work.

Tapescript

1 *¡Hola! Estoy en el parque zoológico, con mi hermano. Hace buen tiempo. ¡Es genial! Los animales son muy simpáticos.*

2 *Hoy llueve pero da igual porque estamos en el Museo del Prado, en Madrid. Estoy con mis compañeros del instituto. Es enorme y es muy interesante. Son las nueve y media. Es temprano. No hay mucha gente pero hay muchos cuadros.*

3 *Aquí hace mucho frío. Está nevando. Estoy con mis padres. Estamos en las montañas. Las pistas son estupendas y no hay mucha gente. Esquiamos desde las nueve de la mañana hasta las cinco de la tarde. ¡Es estupendo!*

4 *¡Hola! Estamos en Puerto Banús en el sur de España. Hay una playa bonita y unas tiendas elegantes. Hace mucho sol. Hace calor. Estoy aquí con mis amigos. Es fenomenal. Por la mañana jugamos al fútbol en la playa. Por la tarde descansamos. Por la noche salimos.*

5 *Estoy en casa. Es aburrido porque todos mis amigos están de vacaciones y no hay nada que hacer. Hace mal tiempo, está nublado y hace frío. Además no puedo ir al cine porque no tengo dinero.*

Answers

1 e 2 b 3 a 4 d 5 c

Starter 2 [8S4]

Aim: question words – use of accents.

Ask pupils to write down as many question words as they can think of and what they mean in English. (*¿Cómo? ¿Dónde? ¿Cuándo? ¿Cuál? ¿Cuáles? ¿Cuánto? ¿Por qué?*)

Focus on correct spelling, including accents.

2b Elige un lugar de los dibujos en **2a**. Con tu compañero/a, pregunta y contesta. Utiliza información de **2a** o inventa respuestas. (AT2/4) [8S6; 9S4; 9L4]

✉ Speaking about experiences/feelings/opinions, Level D/E

Speaking. Pupils work with a partner on a role-play in which they ask and answer questions about an event in the present tense. For added authenticity, they could be asked to sit back-to-back and imagine they are talking to their partner on a mobile telephone. Teachers may first wish to brainstorm possible answers to the five questions with pupils, in particular *¿Qué tiempo hace?* and *¿Cómo es?*.

2c Mira los dibujos y escribe una conversación similar a la de **2b**. (AT4/4) [8T6]

✉ Exchange information/ideas, Level D/E

Writing. Pupils use picture prompts to write a dialogue like the one in **2b**.

R Teachers may wish to offer pupils additional support by listing some of the key language on an OHT or worksheet.

> ## *Plenary* [8S4; 9S4]
> Ask pupils to choose three of the questions words from the *Starter 2* exercise and write down three useful questions in the present tense. They should then swap these with a partner and ask them to answer the questions in the present.

Cuaderno B, page 46

1 Completa las tarjetas con las palabras apropiadas. (AT3/3, AT4/1) [8W5; 9W5]

✉ Knowing about language

Reading and writing. A gap-filling exercise. Pupils complete two holiday postcards with *es, estoy, hace* and *hay*.

Answers

> Hola Lucía:
> **Estoy** en Sevilla para la feria de abril. Es una fiesta muy bonita. **Hay** mucha gente. **Hace** buen tiempo. Hace sol pero no hace mucho calor. **Es** estupendo. Hasta pronto, Naomi
>
> Estimado Carlos:
> **Estoy** de vacaciones en Inglaterra con mis padres. Estamos en un hotel en Devon. **Hace** mal tiempo. Hace frío y llueve todas los días. No **hay** gente de mi edad aquí. **Es** aburrido. Abrazos, Antonio.

2 Elige un destino de tus vacaciones y escribe una tarjeta postal, usando las palabras apropiadas del cuadro. (AT4/4) [8W2; 8S2]

✉ Exchange information/ideas, Level C

Writing. Pupils use the frame on the page to write a holiday postcard, similar to the ones in exercise **1**. The *¡Ojo!* feature reminds them to use simple connectives to enhance their writing.

módulo 5 — 5 ¿Qué hiciste el sábado?

(Pupil's Book pages 86–87)

Main topics

- Describing an event in the past

Key Framework objectives

- Connectives 8W2 (Reinforcement)
- Verb tenses 8W5 (Reinforcement)
- Connectives in extended sentences 8S2 (Reinforcement)
- Present, *past*, future 8S7 (Reinforcement)

Grammar

- Preterite tense: full forms of -*er* and -*ir* verbs
- First person singular of some irregular verbs (*ver, venir, hacer*)

Key language

Salí de casa a (las cinco y media).
Fui en (coche).
Vi un partido entre (el Arsenal y el Manchester United).
Llevé (una bufanda).
Comí (un perrito caliente).
Bebí (una Coca-Cola).
Fui a los servicios.
Hice una llamada con mi móvil.
Leí el programa.

Resources

Cassette C, side 1
CD3, track 8
Cuaderno B, page 47
Grammar, Resource and Assessment File, pages 92 and 93
OHTs 27 and 28

Starter 1 [8W5; 9W5]

Aim: to revise the paradigm of the preterite for regular -*ar* verbs and the irregular verb *ir*.

Write a few verbs on the board that pupils know: *comprar, visitar, ir.* Use a dice, with dots allocated to each subject pronoun, e.g. one dot = *yo*, two dots = *tú*, three dots = *él*, etc., or dice with subject pronouns on them. Pupils work with a partner or in a small group, throwing the dice and conjugating the verbs according to the dot or subject pronoun it lands on.

1a Escucha y escribe la letra apropiada. (AT1/5) [8L3; 9L3]

✖ Listening for information/instructions, Level E

Listening. Pupils listen to someone describing a football match they went to at the weekend. They use the chart on the page to write down the letter of the correct picture for each question the speaker answers. This exercise extends the range of verbs in the preterite (introduced in Module 4) to the regular -*er* and -*ir* verbs: *beber, comer, leer* and *salir*, plus the irregular verb *ver*. The preterite of -*er* and -*ir* verbs, as well as three key irregulars, is explained in the *Gramática* box on page 87.

Tapescript

¿Qué hiciste el sábado?
El sábado fui a un partido de fútbol.
1 *¿A qué hora saliste de casa?*
  Salí de casa a las once.
2 *¿Cómo fuiste?*
  Fui en coche.
3 *¿Qué partido viste?*
  Vi un partido entre Barcelona y Betis.

4 *¿Qué llevaste?*
  Llevé una bufanda.
5 *¿Qué comiste?*
  Comí un perrito caliente.
6 *¿Qué bebiste?*
  Bebí una Coca-Cola.
7 *¿A quién viste?*
  Vi a Saviola.
8 *¿Qué hiciste en el descanso?*
  En el descanso fui a los servicios.

Answers

1 b	**2** b	**3** b	**4** c	**5** c	**6** a	**7** b	**8** b

1b Lee las frases y escribe la letra apropiada. (AT3/5) [8S4; 9S4]

✖ Reading for information/ideas, Level E

Reading. Pupils read the questions and give the letter of the appropriate illustration from **1a**.

Answers

1 Salí de casa a las once.
2 Fui en coche.
3 Vi un partido entre el Barcelona y el Betis.
4 Llevé una bufanda.
5 Comí un perrito caliente.
6 Bebí una Coca-Cola.
7 Vi a Saviola.
8 Fui a los servicios.

1c Con tu compañero/a, contesta a las preguntas en **1b**, sobre el partido. Elige las respuestas que prefieres (a–c). (AT2/5) [8W5; 9W5; 9L4]

⚐ Speaking about experiences/feelings/opinions, Level E

Speaking. Pupils take it in turns to ask and answer questions about a football match, choosing their own answers from the grid on page 86. Before they embark upon this, teachers should ensure they are confident and accurate in their production of the key language. This can be done by asking *¿Cómo se dice en español?* for the following sentences; 'I left the house at 11 o'clock' 'I went by car' 'I saw a match between Arsenal and Manchester United', etc.

> ### Starter 2 [8W5; 9W5]
>
> *Aim:* further practice of *-er/-ir* verbs in the preterite.
>
> Quickfire. Go round the class. Call out a subject pronoun. Pupils must give the correct part of the verb in the preterite.

2 Completa las frases con los verbos apropiados. (AT3/5) [8S7]

⚐ Reading for information/instructions, Level E

Reading. A gap-filling exercise, describing a disastrous day out in the countryside, in the preterite. The menu of missing words includes the new preterites *empezó* and *hice* and teachers should check pupils understand them before tackling the gap-filling task.

Answers

> El sábado *(1)* **fui** de excursión al campo con mis amigos. **(2) Salí** de casa muy temprano por la mañana, a las seis y media. **(3) Llevé** una mochila, un anorak, bocadillos, fruta y agua. A mediodía **(4) comimos** los bocadillos y la fruta. Por la tarde **(5) bebimos** todo el agua. Luego **(6) empezó** a llover. Además no **(7) leí** bien el mapa. ¡Nos perdimos! Por fin **(8) vi** una cabina de teléfono. **(9) Hice** una llamada a casa. Mi padre vino a buscarnos en el coche.

3 Escribe ocho frases sobre un partido de fútbol/una excursión. (AT4/5) [8W2; 8S2]

⚐ Writing imaginatively, Level D/F

Writing. Pupils write eight phrases to describe a football match or excursion, in the preterite.

🅡➕ Less able pupils should be encouraged to work from the grid on page 86, while the more able should aim to use as wide a range of verbs as possible, add opinions, and use connectives such as *luego*, *por fin* and *además*.

> ### Plenary [8W5; 9W5]
>
> See if any volunteers will recite a verb in the preterite.
>
> Ask pupils to write down a strategy to help them learn an irregular verb such as *ir*. Share ideas.

Cuaderno B, page 47

1a Lee los textos y escribe R (Rosa), S (Selena), V (Verónica) o J (José) para cada dibujo. (AT3/5) [8T2]

⚐ Reading for information/instructions, Level E

Reading. Pupils read two e-mail messages about recent events and match the pictures to the relevant person.

Answers

1 J	2 S	3 R	4 J	5 R	6 V	7 R	8 J

1b Busca las palabras y frases en los textos. (AT3/5, AT4/2) [8W1; 8S1]

⚐ Reading for information/instructions, Level E

Reading and writing. Pupils must find the Spanish equivalent in the texts in **1a** to the English expressions listed.

Answers

> 1 por la tarde
> 2 después
> 3 el sábado
> 4 hice mis deberes
> 5 vi un vídeo
> 6 jugué con mi Playstation
> 7 vi un partido de fútbol en la tele

2 Escribe un e-mail sobre lo que hiciste el fin de semana pasado. (AT4/5) [8T6]

⚐ Writing to establish personal contact, Level D/F

Writing. Pupils write an e-mail message about what they did last weekend.

Grammar, Resource and Assessment File, page 92 (More about the preterite tense)

1 Pupils identify the verbs in the sentences.

Answers

a jugué	b salí
c compré	d fui/pasé
e vi	f comí/bebí

2 Pupils fill in the blanks in the grid to translate various verbs into English. They then put them into the preterite (first person singular) with their corresponding meanings.

Answers

Infinitive	Meaning	Preterite	Meaning
comer	to eat	*comí*	*I ate*
salir	*to go out*	salí	I went out
beber	to drink	bebí	I drank
visitar	to visit	visité	I visited
comprar	*to buy*	compré	I bought
ver	*to see*	*vi*	I saw
ir	to go	*fui*	I went

3 Pupils use what they know about the verbs to decide which is the odd one out and say why.

Answers

ir – the preterite form is different to the infinitive and is always followed by *a*

4 Pupils write their own rules to help them remember the preterite endings for –er, –ar and –ir verbs, as well as irregular verbs.

Grammar, Resource and Assessment File, page 93 (Present and preterite tenses)

1 Pupils fill in the blanks in the grid with the present and preterite forms of the verbs in the first person singular.

Answers

Infinitive	Present	Preterite
ir	*voy*	*fui*
hacer	hago	*hice*
jugar	juego	*jugué*
visitar	*visito*	visité
tomar	tomo	tomé
escuchar	escucho	escuché
comer	*como*	comí
salir	salgo	salí
ver	veo	vi
viajar	viajo	viajé
bañarse	me baño	me bañé

2 Pupils complete each sentence by choosing the appropriate form of each verb (present or preterite).

Answers

a fui	**b** jugué
c fui	**d** tomé
e como	**f** fui
g hice	**h** salgo

3 Pupils look again at the sentences in 2 and find the Spanish equivalents of the English phrases.

Answers

a Cuando estoy …
b El sábado pasado
c Anoche
d Si es possible
e Esta mañana

4 Pupils use comparatives to give their own opinions on the activities mentioned, using the bracketed adjectives.

6 El estadio estaba lleno

(Pupil's Book pages 88–89)

Main topics

- Describing what things were like

Key Framework objectives

- Writing continuous text 8T5 (Launch)
- Connectives in complex sentences 9W2 (Launch)
- Multiple-clause sentences 9S6 (Launch)
- Different tenses 9S7 (Launch)
- Present, past, future 8S7 (Reinforcement)
- Using high-frequency words and punctuation clues 8S8 (Reinforcement)

Grammar

- the imperfect

Key language

¿Adónde fuiste?
Fui a (Madrid).
Fui al …

campo	museo
centro comercial	parque
cine	

Fui a la …	piscina
pista de hielo	plaza

¿Qué tiempo hacía?
Hacía …

buen tiempo	mal tiempo
calor	sol
frío	viento

¿Qué había en (Madrid)?
Había
muchas tiendas, iglesias, …
muchos cafés y restaurantes, museos, parques, …
mucho tráfico
mucha gente

Resources

Cassette C, side 1
CD3, track 9
Cuaderno B, page 48
Flashcards 52, 53, 54, 70 (*¡Listos! 1*)

Starter 1 [8W5; 8L6; 9W5; 9S7]

Aim: introducing the concept of the imperfect tense.

Write a few sentences about a place you went to last year, e.g. *El año pasado fui a París con un amigo. Fuimos en avión. Fuimos a la Torre Eiffel y comí crepés con chocolate.* Elicit from pupils that something is missing (expressing an opinion or saying what it was like). Write up *¡Era fenomenal!,* explaining that this is in the imperfect tense.

1a Escucha y elige los dibujos apropiados. (AT1/5) [8L3; 9L3]

✖ Listening for information/instructions, Level E

Listening. Pupils listen to people describing what past events were like (weather and opinions) and choose the letter of the correct picture. This exercise introduces the imperfect tense and teachers may wish to begin by referring pupils to the *Gramática* box on page 88, which explains this new tense. When the recording is played, pupils should be encouraged to listen for key word clues (*museo, sol, tráfico,* etc.), rather than trying to understand everything. Once pupils have completed the matching task, teachers could play the recording again, focusing on the use of the imperfect and other details.

Tapescript

1 *Hacía sol. Hacía mucho calor.*
2 *Llegamos tarde porque había mucho tráfico.*
3 *Era medianoche. No había nadie en la plaza.*

4 *Fui de vacaciones al Canadá en diciembre. Hacía mucho frío.*
5 *El estadio estaba lleno. No había asientos libres.*

Answers

1 *b*	**2** *c*	**3** *a*	**4** *d*	**5** *e*

Starter 2 [8W5; 9W5]

Aim: to recap expressions in the imperfect tense.

Write on the board these 'squashed' sentences. Ask pupils to separate them out. *hacíabuentiempo, habíamuchotráfico, eralauna.* You could then ask pupils to produce another sentence containing one of the three verbs.

2 Lee el texto y en la página 88 y contesta a las preguntas. (AT3/5) [8S7,8; 9S7]

✖ Reading for information/instructions, Level E

Reading. Pupils read a text about Enrique's weekend in Madrid and answer questions in English.

R As the text is a fairly substantial one, teachers might wish to divide it and the questions up, giving different sections to different pairs or groups of pupils, to make a 'jigsaw' reading activity.

Answers

> **1** last April, for the weekend   **2** There were lots of paintings there.   **3** It was sunny. There were lots of cafés and restaurants.   **4** They went to the shopping centre, and found lots of good shops.   **5** Yes, because there weren't any empty seats.   **6** There wasn't much traffic.   **7** Because the weather was fine   **8** It was really delicious.

3 Elige las palabras apropiadas para describir un fin de semana real o imaginario. Contesta a las preguntas de tu compañero/a. (AT2/5) [8T5; 9W2; 9S6]

✖ Speaking and interacting with others, Level E/F

Speaking. Pupils ask and answer questions about a real or imaginary weekend using the grids for support.

4 Utiliza palabras del cuadro y de ejercicio 3 para describir sobre un fin de semana real o imaginario.

✖ Writing imaginatively, Level D/F

Writing. Pupils write about a real or imaginary past weekend. They are supported by a sentence-building grid on page 89.

➕ Able pupils should be encouraged to go beyond the language contained in the support grid, using a wider range of verbs and vocabulary.

> *Plenary* [8W5; 9W5]
> Ask a volunteer to explain to the rest of the class what they think the imperfect tense is, and when it is used. Encourage pupils to ask him/her questions.
>
> Alternatively, ask pupils to work in pairs and do the above. Share ideas.

Cuaderno B, page 48

1 Lee el texto y pon los dibujos en el orden correcto. (AT3/5) [8S7,8; 8T3; 9S7]

✖ Reading for information/instructions, Level E

Reading Pupils read advertisements for events/attractions and an account of a weekend in Barcelona. They must then put a series of pictures into the correct order.

Answers

> d, b, e, a, c

2a Contesta a las preguntas. (AT3/5, AT4/5) [8W5; 8S7,8; 9W5]

✖ Reading for information/instructions, Level E

Reading and writing. Pupils answer the questions in Spanish about the weather in Barcelona last weekend, according to the text in exercise 1.

Answers

> **1** Hacía calor.
> **2** Hacía mal tiempo. Hacía viento y hacía frío.
> **3** Hacía sol.

2b Contesta a las preguntas en inglés. (AT3/5) [8S7,8; 9S7]

✖ Reading for information/instructions, Level E

Reading. More detailed questions in English about the texts in exercise 1.

Answers

> **1** they ate tapas.
> **2** a girl, because she bought a skirt
> **3** a huge bowling alley
> **4** a concert by The Chemical Brothers
> **5** yes, because the place was packed, with no empty seats
> **6** the famous white gorilla

3 Escribe un texto similar para describir un fin de semana en Londres. (AT4/5) [8T6]

✖ Writing imaginatively, Level D/E

Writing. Pupils use the model text in exercise 1 to write about a past weekend in London.

Resumen

This is a checklist of language covered in Module 5. There is a comprehensive **Resumen** list for Module 5 in the Pupil's Book (page 90) and a **Resumen** test sheet in Cuaderno B (page 52).

Prepárate

A revision test to give practice for the test itself at the end of the module.

Resources

Cassette C, side 1
CD3, tracks 10 and 11
Cuaderno B, pages 49–51
Skills, Resource and Assessment File, page 94
Resumen, Resource and Assessment File, page 96

1 ¿Qué tipo de películas les gustan? Escucha y elige el dibujo apropiado para cada diálogo. (AT1/3) [8L3; 9L3]

✖ Listening for information/instructions, Level D

Listening. Pupils listen to what sort of films the speakers prefer and note down the letter of the correct picture in each case.

Tapescript

1 ¿Qué tipo de películas prefieres, Lara?
Me gustan las películas de acción porque son emocionantes.

2 ¿Qué tipo de películas te gustan, Alejandro?
A mí me encanta ir al cine. Me gustan, sobre todo las películas de ciencia-ficción. Son muy interesantes.

3 ¿Te gustan las películas románticas, Miriam?
No, no me gustan las películas románticas ni las películas cómicas. Son aburridas. Me gustan las películas de terror.

4 ¿Te gustan las películas de terror, Miguel?
No, no me gustan. ¡Prefiero los dibujos animados!

Answers

1 b	2 c	3 d	4 a

2 Escucha los diálogos y completa la información. (AT1/4) [8L3; 9L3]

✖ Listening for information/instructions, Level D

Listening. Pupils listen to people arranging to go out and note down the key information in a grid.

Tapescript

1 – ¡Hola, Pablo! ¿Quieres salir conmigo el domingo?
   – ¿Adónde quieres ir?
   – Al club de jóvenes.
   – ¡Buena idea! ¿A qué hora?
   – A las cinco y media.
   – Vale. ¿Dónde quedamos?
   – En la plaza.
   – Vale.
   – Adiós.

2 – ¿Dígame?
   – Hola, Sergio. Oye, ¿quieres salir conmigo el sábado?
   – ¿Adónde quieres ir?

   – Al parque de atracciones.
   – Vale. ¿A qué hora?
   – A las once.
   – Bueno. ¿Dónde quedamos?
   – En la estación.
   – Vale.
   – Hasta mañana.
   – Adiós

3 – ¡Hola, Edu! ¿Quieres salir conmigo el viernes?
   – ¿Adónde quieres ir?
   – Al cine. A ver Las Dos Torres.
   – ¡Que buena idea! ¿A qué hora?
   – A las seis y media.
   – Vale. ¿Dónde quedamos?
   – En mi casa.
   – Vale. Hasta mañana.
   – Hasta mañana.

Answers

	¿Cuándo?	¿Adónde?	¿Dónde?	¿A qué hora?
1	el domingo	al club de jóvenes	en la plaza	a las cinco y media
2	el sábado	al parque de atracciones	en la estación	a las once
3	el viernes	al cine a ver *Las Dos Torres*	en la casa del amigo de Edu	a las seis y media

3 Con tu compañero/a, haz un diálogo similar usando la información del cuadro. (AT2/4) [8S6; 8L6]

✖ Speaking and interacting with others, Level D/E

Speaking. Pupils take part in a role-play in which they arrange to go out with their partner, using the model dialogue on the page as support.

4a Completa el correo electrónico con las palabras apropiadas. (AT3/5) [8W5; 8S7,8; 9W5; 9S7]

✖ Knowing about language

Reading. A grammar gap-filling exercise, using the preterite and the imperfect.

Answers

¡Hola, Elsa! ¿Qué tal?
El fin de semana **fui** a Sevilla con mis padres y mi hermano. **Fuimos** en tren. El sábado por la mañana **visitamos** la catedral. Hacía sol y **hacía** mucho calor. Por la tarde **fui** con mi hermano al parque temático, Isla Mágica. El domingo por la mañana fuimos de paseo. Después fuimos a un partido de fútbol. **Vimos** un partido entre el Betis y el Real Mallorca. ¡Lo pasé fenomenal!
Hasta pronto
Mario

4b Lee el correo electrónico otra vez y contesta a las preguntas. (AT3/5) [8S7,8; 9S7]

✗ Reading for information/instructions, Level E

Reading. Pupils read the completed text in **4a** and answer questions in English.

Answers

1 His parents and his brother.
2 By train.
3 They visited the cathedral.
4 It was sunny and very hot.
5 He went for a walk and then to a football match.
6 He thought it was fantastic.

4c Escribe un correo electrónico similar sobre lo que hiciste el fin de semana pasado. (AT4/5) [8T6]

✗ Exchange information/ideas, Level D/F

Writing. Pupils write a similar piece to the text in **4a** to describe a past weekend.

Cuaderno B, page 49

Repaso

1 Completa el crucigrama. (AT3/2, AT4/3) [8W5; 8S7,8; 9W5]

✗ Knowing about language

Reading and writing. A crossword puzzle to complete, using gapped clues in Spanish.

Answers

(crossword grid answers: E, L, N, CALOR, R; SÁBADO, AE, Í, IC; O, O, S, A; PELÍCULA, LA, A; E, E, L; HORA, A, E, H, H; AY, A, VERANO, C; BAÑÉ, L; ERA)

Cuaderno B, page 50

Gramática 1

1 Complete the grid with the correct forms of the adjectives. (AT3/1, AT4/2) [8W4; 9W4]

✗ Knowing about language

Reading and writing. A grid-completion exercise, based on adjective endings.

Answers

masculine singular	feminine singular	masculine plural	feminine plural	
aburrido	aburrida	aburridos	aburridas	boring
divertido	divertida	divertidos	divertidas	fun
romántico	romántica	románticos	románticas	romantic
tonto	tonta	tontos	tontas	silly
emocionante	emocionante	emocionantes	emocionantes	exciting
inteligente	inteligente	inteligentes	inteligentes	intelligent
interesante	interesante	interesantes	interesantes	interesting
infantil	infantil	infantiles	infantiles	childish

2a Complete the sentences with the correct forms of the adjectives. (AT3/2, AT4/3–4) [8W4; 8T7; 9W4]

✗ Knowing about language

Reading and writing. A gap-filling exercise, using adjectives. As well as completing the text, pupils must put the correct ending on to the adjectives.

Answers

1 divertida 2 infantiles 3 aburridas
4 emocionantes 5 interesante

2b Complete the sentences with your own adjectives. Delete the words as appropriate. (AT3/3, AT4/3–4) [8W4; 8S4; 9W4; 9S4]

Exchange information/ideas, Level D/F

Reading and writing. An open-ended activity, in which pupils must answer questions in Spanish, giving their opinion and using adjectives correctly.

Cuaderno B, page 51

Gramática 2

1 Write opinions on these types of films. (AT4/2) [8S2]

Knowing about language

Writing. Pupils use a writing frame to give their opinions of different types of films. The frame requires them to use the comparative.

2 Complete the postcard with the words from the box. (AT3/3, AT4/1) [8W5; 8S8; 9W5]

Knowing about language

Reading and writing. A gapped postcard to complete, using *es, son, estoy, hace* and *hay*.

Answers

> ¡Hola, Rocío!
> **Estoy** de vacaciones en Chile en Sudamérica para Navidad. **Es** verano aquí. **Hace** sol y hace calor.
> Imagínate: aquí se puede ir a la playa en diciembre.
> **Hay** muchos lugares bonitos para visitar y los chilenos **son** muy simpáticos.
> Un fuerte abrazo
> Francisco

3 Complete the sentences with the words shown. (AT3/5, AT4/1) [8W5; 9W5]

Knowing about language

Reading and writing. Pupils complete a series of sentences with verbs in the preterite, choosing from a list on the page.

Answers

> **1** Fui **2** Leí **3** Bebí **4** Comí **5** Vi **6** Hice

Skills, Resource and Assessment File, page 94

1

Answers

¿Cuándo?	When?
¿Dónde?	Where?
¿Qué tal?	What/like?
¿Qué?	*What?*
¿Cómo?	How?
¿Con quién?	Who with?

2

Answers

> **a** ¿Cuándo?
> **b** ¿Qué tal?
> **c** ¿Qué?
> **d** ¿Con quién?
> **e** ¿Dónde?

3

Answers

Cuándo?	¿Dónde?	¿Qué tal?	¿Qué?	¿Cómo?	¿Con quién?
el lunes	*en el salón*	era genial	comí	en coche	mis amigos
por la tarde	a la playa	me diverti	nadé	en autobús	mi hermanoé
por la mañana	al parque temático	era estupendo	jugué	en bici	mis padres
esta noche	al cine	era aburrido	salí	a pie	mis abuelos

4 Pupils add two more examples to each of the columns in **3**.

5 Pupils add to the sentences using phrases from the grid in **3**.

6 Pupils now write sentences of their own, trying to answer as many sentences from the grid headings in **3** as they can.

Skills, Resource and Assessment File, page 95 (Deduction skills)

Answers (example)

> **Ana** f (dancing at disco)
> **Nacho** a (various showings)
> **Margarita** d (food before swimming)
> **Josué** b/f (cheap/free)
> **Laura** a/f (cinema/dancing – i.e. not eating)
> **Samuel** c (outside)

Resumen y Prepárate

2

Answers

abiertas	open
dorada	golden
toda la noche	all night
precios competitivos	competitive prices
las dos Torres	The Two Towers
los anillos	rings

7 ¡Extra! Ídolos del fútbol, pasado y presente

(Pupil's Book pages 92–93)

Main topics

- This is an optional extension unit which reviews some of the key language of the module.

Key Framework objectives

- Language and text types 8T3 (Reinforcement)
- Text as model and source 8T6 (Reinforcement)
- Famous people 8C2 (Reinforcement)

- Daily life and young people 8C3 (Reinforcement)
- Connectives in complex sentences 9W2 (Reinforcement)
- Multiple-clause sentences 9S6 (Reinforcement)

Resources

Cassette C, side 1
CD3, track 12

Starter 1

Aim: working out meaning using cognates.

Put up a list of cognates/near-cognates from the text e.g. *fútbol, primera división, la Copa Mundial, marcar un gol, la selección española.* Tell pupils that all these words are from a text about a footballer. Give pupils a time limit in which to work them out.

1 Lee el texto y contesta a las preguntas. (AT3/6) [8T3; 8C2; 9W2; 9S6]

✖ Reading for information/instructions, Level F

Reading. Pupils read a magazine-style article about the footballers Maradona and Raúl and answer questions in English. They should be encouraged to use reading skills and strategies – looking for cognates/near-cognates, using context, etc. – to answer as many questions as possible before using a dictionary to check or look up new language.

Answers

a Buenos Aires, 30 October 1960.
b His family didn't have much money.
c The youth team for the Argentinos Juniors Football Club, in December, 1970.
d 17 years old.
e He played in the World Cup which Argentina went on to win.
f A Spanish football idol.
g Real Madrid
h 26
i In 1994, when he was 17.
j Like Maradona, he was 17 when he first played in the first division; he plays for his national team; he is also a forward.

2 Escucha y escribe M para Maradona o R para Raúl. (AT1/6) [8L3; 9L3]

✖ Listening for information/instructions, Level E/F

Listening. Pupils listen to a series of statements and decide whether each one refers to Maradona or Raúl.

Tapescript

1 *Vive en Madrid.*
2 *Durante 7 años vivió en Italia.*
3 *A los 15 años empezó a jugar en primera división, para los Argentinos Juniors.*
4 *Juega para el Real Madrid y para el equipo nacional de España.*
5 *Es delantero y marca muchos goles.*
6 *Jugó en 91 partidos para el equipo argentino y marcó 34 goles.*

Answers

1 R	2 M	3 M	4 R	5 M/R	6 M

3a Copia y completa la ficha para Maradona y Raúl. (AT4/4) [8T6]

✖ Exchange information/ideas, Level C/D

Writing. Pupils copy out and complete a profile form for the two footballers.

Nombre:	Diego Armando Maradona	Raúl González Blanco
Fecha de nacimiento:	30 de octubre 1960	27 de junio 1977
Ciudad:	Buenos Aires	Madrid
País:	Argentina	España
Nacionalidad:	argentino	español
Equipos:	Argentinos Juniors; Nápoli; Argentina	Atlético de Madrid; Real Madrid; España
Posición:	delantero	delantero

3b Busca información sobre un futbolista y escribe sobre su vida. (AT4/5–6) [8T6; 8C3; 9T5]

✖ Exchange information/ideas, Level D/F

🖰 Pupils look up information about another footballer and write a piece about him. They could research the project on the Internet, then use a graphics or desktop publishing programme to make

7 ¡Extra! Ídolos del fútbol, pasado y presente

their text look like a magazine article. The finished pieces of writing could be used for display or, if the school has a partner school in Spain, information about UK footballers could sent in exchange for information about Spanish players.

Pupils should be encouraged to use the reading text as a source of language. If you wanted you could do a 'find the Spanish for … ' activity to help highlight useful phrases.

You could model a text on the board with your class first.

Plenary [8T7]

Talk about how pupils approached their written work. Include discussion about checking work for accuracy.

● Self-access reading and writing at two levels.

A Reinforcement

1 Elige una frase para cada dibujo. (AT3/2)

✖ Reading for information/instructions, Level C

Reading. Pupils read a series of questions inviting someone to go out and complete a sentence for each picture.

Answers

a 5	b 1	c 4	d 2	e 3

2 Pon la conversación en el orden correcto. (AT3/3) [8S1,8]

✖ Reading for information/instructions, Level D

Reading. Pupils read a jumbled dialogue at a cinema box office and rewrite it in the correct order.

Answers

a, j, b, l, c, k, d, g, e, i, f, h

3 Elige una frase para cada dibujo. (AT3/2) [8S5,8]

✖ Reading for information/instructions, Level C

Reading. Pupils read a series of opinions about different types of films and match each one to the correct picture.

Answers

a 4	b 1	c 6	d 5	e 3	f 2

4 Emplea las palabras del cuadro para escribir tus opiniones sobre las películas. (AT4/4) [8S2,6]

✖ Exchange information/ideas, Level D/E

Writing. Pupils use adjectives in a support box to write their opinions of different types of films.

B Extension

1 Escribe cinco frases del cuadro para describir cada dibujo. (AT4/4) [8S1,6]

✖ Exchange information/ideas, Level B

Writing. Pupils use a sentence-building grid on the page to describe two pictures, in the present tense, referring to the seasons, weather and opinions.

Answers

a	b
Es verano.	Es invierno.
Hace buen tiempo.	Hace mal tiempo.
Hace calor.	Hace frío.
Hay mucha gente.	No hay mucha gente.
Es genial.	Es aburrido.

2 Lee el diario de Juan y contesta a las preguntas. (AT3/5) [8S7,8]

✖ Reading for information/instructions, Level E

Reading. Pupils read part of a boy's diary, written in the preterite and imperfect, and answer questions in English.

Answers

a He went to the cinema.
b Yes – he likes action films.
c It wasn't good – the weather was bad; it was cold.
d Yes – they had lunch in a restaurant and he had steak and chips and a Coca-Cola.
e He stayed at home – he got up late and had breakfast at midday, then he read the newspaper and a magazine, watched a comedy programme on the television and ate some chocolate.
f It was the holidays.

3 Escribe tu diario para el fin de semana pasado. (AT4/5) [8T6; 9T5]

✖ Exchange information/ideas, Level D/F

Writing. Pupils write their own diary for last weekend, using the verb prompts on the page, in the preterite and the imperfect.

La salud

(Pupil's Book pages 96–111)

Unit	Key Framework objectives	PoS	Key language and Grammar
1 ¿Qué te duele? (pp. 96–97) Saying what's wrong	8C4 Poems, jokes, songs and stories [L] 9L6 Formality of language [L] 8W4 Word endings [R] 8T4 Dictionary use [R] 9W4 Main inflections [R] 9T4 Using support materials [R]	**5g** listening/reading for enjoyment	*doler* Pronouns: *me, te, le, nos, os, les* *¿Qué te/le duele?* *Me duele la cabeza.* *Me duelen los pies.*
2 Me siento mal (pp. 98–99) Saying you're not feeling well	8L3 Relaying gist and detail [R] 8S6 Substituting and adding [R] 8T5 Writing continuous text [R] 9T5 Simple creative writing [R] 9L3 Reporting and paraphrasing [R]	**2a** listen for gist and detail **2f** adapt language for different contexts	*tener* and *estar* *Tengo tos.* *Tengo fiebre …* *Estoy enfermo/a, …*
3 En la farmacia (pp. 100–101) At the chemist	8S3 Modal verbs [R] 9S3 Different tense modals [R] 9L6 Formality of language [R]	**1a** sounds and writing **2a** listen for gist and detail **2b** pronunciation/intonation **2c** ask and answer questions **2i** report main points	*deber* in the present tense *¿Tiene algo para la diarrea?* *Deme una caja.* *este jarabe* *esta pomada* *estas pastillas* *¿Grande o pequeno/a?*
4 Hay que practicar mucho (pp. 102–103) Talking about how long you've been doing something Saying what you should or shouldn't do	8L2 Media listening skills [L] 8W5 Verbs [R] 8L3 Relaying gist and detail [R] 8T5 Writing continuous text [R] 9S6 Multiple-clause sentences [R] 9L3 Reporting and paraphrasing [R]	**4d** consider experiences in other countries **5d** respond to different types of language	*Hace dos años que estudio español.* *Hay que practicar mucho.* *Tienes que llevar ropa cómoda.* *Debes entrenar muchas horas.* *¿Cuánto tiempo hace que juegas al fútbol?* *Hace un año que juego al fútbol.*
5 Hay que comer fruta todos los días (pp. 104–105) Talking about a healthy lifestyle	9T6 Adapting for audience [L] 8S3 Modal verbs [R] 8S5 Negative forms and words [R] 8S7 Present, past and *future* [R] 8S8 Using high-frequency words and punctuation clues [R]	**2f** adapt language for different contexts	Revising the immediate future *Debes desayunar.* *Hay que beber dos litros de agua al día.* *Estoy de acuerdo.* *No estoy de acuerdo.*
Resumen y Prepárate (pp. 106–107) Pupils' checklist and practice test			

Unit	Key Framework objectives	PoS	Key language and Grammar
6 ¡Extra! Entrevista con una deportista (pp. 108–109) Optional unit: interview with a professional cyclist	8S4 Question types [R] 8L2 Media listening skills [R] 9S4 Building answers from questions [R] 9S7 Different tenses in sentences [R] 9T5 Simple creative writing [R] 9L2 Recognising rhetorical devices [R] 9L4 Questions/text as stimulus to talk [R]	**2g** dealing with the unpredictable **4a** working with authentic materials	Review of structures including examples of the preterite. *Tuve una caída.* *Me ayudó un chico.*
Te toca a ti (pp. 122–123) Self-access reading and writing at two levels			

1 ¿Qué te duele?

(Pupil's Book pages 96–97)

Main topics

- Saying what's wrong

Key Framework objectives

- Poems, jokes, songs, stories 8C4 (Launch)
- Formality of language 9L6 (Launch)
- Word endings 8W4 (Reinforcement)
- Dictionary use 8T4 (Reinforcement)
- Main inflections 9W4 (Reinforcement)
- Using support materials 9T4 (Reinforcement)

Grammar

- *doler*
  ¿Qué te/le duele?
  Nos duelen los pies.

Key language

¿Qué te/le duele?
Me duele/n …

el brazo	*la mano*
la cabeza	*las muelas*
el dedo	*los oídos*
la espalda	*el pie*
el estómago	*la pierna*
la garganta	*la rodilla*

Resources

Cassette C, side 1
CD3, tracks 13, 14, 15 and 16
Cuaderno B, pages 53
Hojas de trabajo, Resource and Assessment File, pages 114 and 115 (*el brazo, las muelas, la mano, el oído, el pie, la cabeza, la garganta, la pierna, la espalda, el estómago*)
OHTs 29 and 30

Starter 1 [8W4; 9W4]

Aim: practising the definite article/vocabulary practice.

Use colour OHTs 31–32. Blank out the definite article and ask pupils to fill in the gaps.

Alternatively, write down the parts of the body on the board and ask pupils to fill in the correct form of 'the'. Encourage them to use knowledge of patterns to do this task. ('*o*' endings tend to be masculine [exception *la mano*] and '*a*' endings feminine.)

1a Empareja las partes del cuerpo con los nombres. (AT3/1) [8W1; 8T4]

✠ Reading for information/instructions, Level A

Reading. Pupils match up the parts of the body with the picture. As most of the words are not cognates with English, teachers may wish to make this a 'dictionary race' exercise. Pupils work in pairs with a dictionary to look up all the words and complete the exercise. The first pair to complete the task correctly wins points or a small prize.

Answers

1 c	2 l	3 f	4 j	5 k	6 i	7 e	8 g	9 h	10 b
11 d	12 a								

1b Escucha y comprueba tus respuestas. (AT1/1) [8L1]

✠ Listening for information/instructions, Level A

Listening. Pupils check their answers to **1a** against the recorded version. If teachers wish, the recording could also be used for oral drilling of the new vocabulary, with pupils repeating each item as it is heard.

Tapescript

1 *las muelas*
2 *el dedo*
3 *la espalda*
4 *la rodilla*
5 *el pie*
6 *la pierna*
7 *el estómago*
8 *el brazo*
9 *la mano*
10 *la garganta*
11 *los oídos*
12 *la cabeza*

Answers

as tapescript

2a Lee y escucha la canción. ¿Qué partes del cuerpo no se mencionan? (AT1/4) [8L1; 8C4]

✠ Listening for enjoyment

Listening. Pupils listen to the song and identify which parts of the body shown in the picture in **1a** are not mentioned in the song. Following this, teachers may want pupils to learn and join in with the song.

Tapescript

Mueve tu cuerpo
Muévete, muévete.
Mueve tu cuerpo
Muévete, muévete.
(refrán)

Mueve la cabeza

Arriba, abajo.
Mueve la espalda
A la derecha, a la izquierda.
Mueve las piernas
Para adelante, para atrás.
Mueve los pies.

Mueve las manos
Arriba, abajo.
Mueve las rodillas
Para adelante, para atrás.
Mueve los brazos
El derecho, el izquierdo.
Mueve los pies.

Answers

la garganta, las muelas, los oídos, el estómago, el dedo

2b Escucha otra vez y mueve las partes del cuerpo como indica la canción. (AT1/4) [8C4]

✕ Listening for enjoyment

Listening. Pupils listen again and follow the instructions of the song, moving the parts of their body as they are mentioned.

Tapescript

As exercise **2a**

2c Dile a tu compañero/a que mueva varias partes del cuerpo. (AT2/3) [8W4; 9W4]

✕ Speaking and interacting with others, Level C

Speaking. In pairs, pupils take it in turns to instruct each other to move a part of the body.

Starter 2 [8W1]

Aim: vocabulary practice.

Write up a list of parts of the body on the board and number them (or put on OHT 32 and number them using a water-soluble pen). Point to parts of your body (silently). Pupils write down the part of the body or number. NB. Remember to keep a note of the order so you can go over the answers with the class at the end of the activity.

3a ¿Qué les duele(n) a estas personas? Escucha y elige el dibujo apropiado. (AT1/3) [8L3; 9L3,6]

✕ Listening for information/instructions, Level C

Listening. Pupils listen to people describing ailments and choose the correct picture for each speaker. This introduces the verb *doler* (*¿Qué te duele?/Me duele(n) …*), which is explained in the *Gramática* box on page 97. It is suggested that teachers refer pupils to this before playing the recording.

Tapescript

1 – *¿Qué te duele?*
    – *Me duelen los brazos.*
2 – *¡Ay!*
    – *¿Qué te duele?*
    – *He comido demasiado. Me duele el estómago.*
3 – *¡Uff! ¡Qué dolor!*
    – *¿Qué te duele?*
    – *Me duelen los pies.*
4 – *¿Qué le duele?*
    – *Me duele la muela.*
    – *¿Esta muela?*
    – *¡Ay, sí!*
5 – *¿Qué le duele, señor?*
    – *Me duele mucho la cabeza.*
6 – *No puedo cantar.*
    – *¿Qué te duele?*
    – *Me duele la garganta.*

Answers

| 1 *f* | 2 d | 3 c | 4 e | 5 b | 6 a |

3b Con tu compañero/a, haz conversaciones con tres de las personas en **3a**. (AT2/3) [8W4; 8S6; 9W4]

✕ Speaking and interacting with others, Level C

Speaking. Pupils work with a partner to create dialogues about ailments based on three of the pictures in **3a**. They should pay particular attention to the correct use of *duele* or *duelen*.

3c Escribe las respuestas de **3b**. (AT4/2) [8S1; 8T7]

✕ Exchange information/ideas, Level C

Writing. Pupils write down what their three chosen people from **3b** would say about their ailments.

4 Lee el diario de Héctor y contesta a las preguntas. Utiliza un diccionario. (AT3/6) [8S7; 8T4; 9S7; 9T4]

✕ Reading for information/instructions, Level E

Reading. Pupils read a diary account of Héctor's disastrous trip to the countryside and answer questions in English. This combines ailments with verbs in the preterite and the imperfect. The text contains several new items of vocabulary and pupils should be encouraged to use their reading skills and strategies before looking up words in a dictionary.

➕ As the text is fairly demanding, teachers might prefer to use it for extension work for more able pupils only.

Answers

> 1 He went hiking.
> 2 He has a sore throat and his arms hurt.
> 3 He hurt his knee.
> 4 He has sore legs and a sore bottom.

Plenary [8W4; 9W4]

Ask someone to explain why there are two ways of saying that something is hurting: *me duele, me duelen* (*doler* agrees with the noun that is being described, so if the noun is singular, e.g. *la cabeza*, you use *me duele* and if it is plural, e.g. *los pies*, you use *me duelen*).

Cuaderno B, page 53

1 Lee los globos y rellena el cuadro. (AT3/5) [8S8]

✖ Reading for information/instructions, Level D

Reading. Pupils read accounts of ailments and injuries and complete a grid.

Answers

	1 Marián	2 Ramón	3 Laura	4 Martín
1	✓		✓	
2			✓	
3	✓			
4			✓	
5		✓		
6		✓		
7			✓	
8		✓		✓
9		✓		✓
10		✓		
11		✓		✓

2 Mira los dibujos y completa las explicaciones. (AT3/4, AT4/2) [8W4; 9W4]

✖ Exchange information/ideas, Level C

Reading and writing. A sentence-completion exercise, based on two accounts of injuries or ailments.

Answers

> espalda, brazos, cabeza
> duele el brazo/tengo el brazo roto
>
> Ayer fui a la playa. Lo pasé muy bien pero hoy me duele **la espalda**. Me duelen los **brazos** y la **cabeza**.
>
> Fui al campo a visitar a mis tíos y mis primos. Monté a caballo pero me caí. Ahora me **duele el brazo/tengo el brazo roto**.

Hojas de trabajo, Resource and Assessment File, pages 114 and 115

Cards for pairwork featuring parts of the body and ailments: pupils match the pictures to the correct words.

2 Me siento mal

(Pupil's Book pages 98-99)

Main topics

● Saying you're not feeling well

Key Framework objectives

● Relaying gist and detail 8L3 (Reinforcement)
● Substituting and adding 8S6 (Reinforcement)
● Writing continuous text 8T5 (Reinforcement)
● Simple creative writing 9T5 (Reinforcement)
● Reporting and paraphrasing 9L3 (Reinforcement)

Grammar

● *tener* for ailments
● *estar* for ailments

Key language

¿Qué te pasa?/¿Qué tal?
Estoy constipado. Estoy enfermo/a.

Estoy mareado/a.
No me siento bien/Me siento mal.
Tengo catarro.   *Tengo una insolación.*
Tengo fiebre.   *Tengo una picadura.*
Tengo gripe.   *Tengo la pierna rota.*
Tengo tos.   *Tengo dolor de cabeza.*

Resources

Cassette C, side 1
CD3, tracks 17 and 18
Cuaderno B, page 54
Hojas de trabajo, Resource and Assessment File, pages 114 and 115 (*tengo fiebre, tengo una picadura, tengo tos, tengo una insolación, tengo catarro*)
OHTs 31 and 32
Flashcards 43–48

Starter 1 [8W5; 9W5]

Aim: using *tener* in a different context; saying what you have at home.

Ask pupils to write down four things they have at home. Start each with *tengo.* Encourage able pupils to expand their description, e.g. *Tengo un perro (que se llama Ben), Tengo una litera (amarilla), Tengo dos hermanos (se llaman Toby y William)*, etc.

1a Escucha y escribe los dibujos en el orden correcto. (1–8) (AT1/2) [8L3; 9L3]

✖ Listening for information/instructions, Level B

Listening. Pupils listen to people describing a new series of ailments and note down the letters of the relevant pictures in the order in which they are heard. All the expressions use the verb *tener*, which is explained in the *Gramática* box on page 98. Pupils' attention should also be drawn to the question *¿Qué te pasa?*, used in the recording.

Tapescript

1 – *¿Qué te pasa?*
– *Tengo tos.*
2 – *¿Qué te pasa?*
– *Tengo gripe.*
3 – *¿Qué te pasa?*
– *Tengo fiebre.*
4 – *¿Qué te pasa?*
– *Tengo catarro.*
5 – *¿Qué te pasa?*
– *Tengo una picadura.*
6 – *¿Qué te pasa?*
– *Tengo una insolación.*
7 – *¿Qué te pasa?*
– *Tengo la pierna rota.*

8 – *¿Qué te pasa?*
– *Tengo dolor de cabeza.*

Answers

1 c	2 g	3 d	4 f	5 e	6 a	7 b	8 h

1b Con tu compañero/a, pregunta y contesta. (AT2/3) [8S6]

✖ Speaking and interacting with others, Level C

Speaking. Pupils work in pairs, taking turns to ask each other what is wrong and to answer using an expression with *tener*. Teachers should ensure that pupils are confident in their pronunciation of the new key expressions before embarking upon the pairwork task.

2 Empareja las frases (a–d) con los dibujos apropiados. (AT3/2) [8W8; 8T4; 9T4]

✖ Reading for information/instructions, Level B

Reading. Pupils match up further new phrases for describing ailments (this time using *estar*) with the relevant pictures. Pupils should be warned that *constipado/a* is a 'false friend'. As most of the new words are not cognates with English, pupils may need to use a dictionary to complete this task.

Answers

a 4	b 1	c 2	d 3

3 Escucha. Copia y rellena el cuadro. (AT1/4–5) [8L3; 9L3]

✖ Listening for information/instructions, Level D/E

2 Me siento mal

Listening. Pupils listen to people describing their ailments and complete a grid in English. This combines expressions with *tener* and *estar* as well as some of the ailments introduced on page 97. Teachers should encourage pupils to spot the alternative way in which 'headache' and 'sore throat' are expressed here – *Tengo dolor de …* , in contrast to *Me duele …* , which they met previously.

✚ Able pupils could also try to spot how speakers 2 and 3 came by their injuries.

Tapescript

1 *Me siento mal.*
¿Qué te pasa?
Fui a la playa y ahora tengo una insolación.
¡Vaya!
Tengo fiebre y dolor de cabeza.
2 *(on telephone)*
¿Diga?
Hola Víctor. Soy Gerardo. ¿Quieres jugar al fútbol esta tarde?
No puedo.
¿Por qué?
Tengo la pierna rota.
¡La pierna rota! ¿Cómo es eso?
Pues, jugando al fútbol.
3 *¡Ay!*
¿Qué te pasa?
Tengo una picadura.
¿Una picadura? ¿Dónde?
En el brazo. Me ha picado una avispa.
4 *No me siento bien.*
¿Qué te pasa?
Estoy mareada.
5 *¿Qué tal?*
Mal, muy mal. Estoy enferma.
¿Qué te pasa?
Estoy constipada. Tengo tos y dolor de garganta.

Answers

	Problem	Symptoms (if any)
1	*sunburn*	*fever and headache*
2	broken leg	–
3	sting	–
4	–	dizzy
5	cold	cough and sore throat

Starter 2 [8W4,5; 9W4,5]

Aim: to recap the use of *tengo* and *estoy* with illnesses.

Write the following words in two columns and ask pupils to match them.

Column 1: *tengo tos, tengo fiebre, tengo la pierna rota, estoy enfermo, estoy mareado, estoy mareada*

Column 2: *I feel sick (girl), I've got a fever, I've got a broken leg, I'm ill, I feel sick (boy), I've got a cold*

4a Con tu compañero/a, haz conversaciones con las personas en **2**. (AT2/3) [8S6]

✖ Speaking and interacting with others, Level D

Speaking. Pupils work with a partner to create dialogues about ailments based on the pictures in activity **2**.

4b Escribe diálogos para los dibujos de **2**. (AT4/3–4) [8T6]

✖ Exchange information/ideas, Level C

Writing. Pupils write dialogues based on the pictures from exercise **2**.

5a Lee las notas. ¿Verdad (✓) o mentira (✗)? (AT3/5–6) [8S1; 8T2]

✖ Reading for information/instructions, Level D

Reading. Pupils read three school absence notes in Spanish and do a true/false exercise.

Answers

a ✗	b ✓	c ✗	d ✗	e ✗	f ✓	g ✗	h ✗

5b Corrige las frases falsas. (AT4/2) [8S6]

✖ Knowing about language

Writing. Pupils correct the false statements from **5a**.

Answers

a Margarita García está enferma.
c Tiene gripe.
d Sufrió un accidente de tráfico.
e Tiene un brazo roto.
g Tiene dolor de estómago.

5c Escribe una nota similar a tu profesor/a de parte de tu padre/madre. (AT4/4–6) [8T6]

✖ Exchange information/ideas, Level D

Writing. Pupils write a similar absence note to those in **5a**.

R Teachers may wish to provide some pupils with a sentence-building writing frame on a worksheet or OHT for this task.

Plenary [8W5; 9W5]

Ask a volunteer to tell you another way of saying *me duele …* (*tengo dolor de …*). Then ask other pupils to come up with the Spanish for 'I have' (*tengo*) and 'I am' (*estoy*).

Cuaderno B, page 54

1 Escribe las frases apropiadas para cada dibujo. (AT3/2, AT4/2) [8S7; 9S7]

✖ Reading for information/instructions, Level D

Reading and writing. Pupils must select phrases about illness and injuries from a list and label the pictures.

Answers

Melanie:	*Tengo gripe. Estoy constipada.* Tengo tos. Estoy enferma. Me siento mal. Tengo fiebre.
Juan:	Me caí de la moto. Me duele mucho la pierna. Tengo la pierna rota. No puedo moverla.
Contanza:	¡Ay! Me duele la mano. Tengo una picadura.
Itxaso:	Tengo una insolación. Me duele la espalda. Tengo dolor de cabeza.

2 Estás enfermo/a. Escribe una carta a un(a) amigo/a para decir que no puedes ir a su fiesta. (AT4/4–5) [8T5; 9T5]

✖ Writing to establish personal contact, Level D/E

Writing. A letter-writing task, in which pupils must explain why they cannot go to a friend's party.

Hojas de trabajo, Resource and Assessment File, pages 114 and 115

Cards for pairwork featuring parts of the body and ailments: pupils match the pictures to the correct words.

3 En la farmacia

(Pupil's Book pages 100–101)

Main topics

- At the chemist

Key Framework objectives

- Modal verbs 8S3 (Reinforcement)
- Different tense modals 9S3 (Reinforcement)
- Formality of language 9L6 (Reinforcement)

Grammar

- Present tense of *deber*

Key language

¿Tiene algo para la diarrea/el dolor de estómago?
Deme …

una caja de aspirinas/de pastillas
un tubo de crema antiséptica/de pomada
una botella de jarabe para la tos
un paquete de tiritas

¿Qué debo hacer?
Debe(s) …
tomar este jarabe, esta pomada, estas pastillas, …
ir al médico, al dentista, a la cama, …
ponerte una tirita

Resources

Cassette C, side 1
CD3, tracks 19, 20 and 21
Cuaderno B, page 55

Starter 1 [8W4,5; 9W4,5]

Aim: revision of illnesses using *tengo, estoy, tengo dolor de, me duele, me duelen.*

Write or say the above. Ask pupils to give an example for each. For example: *tengo fiebre, estoy enfermo(a), tengo dolor de cabeza, me duele el estómago, me duelen los oídos.* Go round the class and take feedback.

1a Escucha y repite. Pon atención a la pronunciación. (AT1/1) [8L1]

✕ Listening for information/instructions, Level B

Listening. Pupils listen to the new vocabulary for medicines and repeat each one, paying careful attention to pronunciation and following the labelled photographs on page 100 to support their understanding. This is a good opportunity to revise the '*j*' sound.

Tapescript

1 una caja de aspirinas
2 una caja de pastillas
3 una botella de jarabe para la tos
4 un paquete de tiritas
5 un tubo de pomada
6 un tubo de crema antiséptica

1b Escucha las conversaciones. Copia y rellena el cuadro. (1–5) (AT1/4) [8L3; 9L3,6]

✕ Listening for information/instructions, Level D

Listening. Pupils listen to a series of dialogues in a chemist's shop and fill in a grid, noting the ailment, the medicine bought, what container it comes in and the size. Pupils should also be encouraged to take note of the expression *¿Tiene algo para … ?* and the use of *este/esta/estos/estas* (introduced in Module 3, Unit 2).

Tapescript

1 – ¿Tiene algo para la tos?
  – Este jarabe es muy bueno.
  – Deme una botella.
  – ¿Grande o pequeña?
  – Pequeña, por favor.
2 – ¿Tiene algo para el dolor de cabeza?
  – Estas aspirinas son bastante fuertes.
  – Deme una caja.
  – ¿Grande o pequeña?
  – Grande, por favor.
3 – ¿Tiene algo para las picaduras?
  – Esta crema es muy buena.
  – Deme un tubo.
  – ¿Grande o pequeño?
  – Pequeño, por favor.
4 – ¿Tiene algo para la diarrea?
  – Estas pastillas son muy buenas.
  – Deme una caja.
  – ¿Grande o pequeña?
  – Grande, por favor.
5 – ¿Tiene algo para la insolación?
  – Esta pomada es muy buena.
  – Deme un tubo.
  – ¿Grande o pequeño?
  – Pequeño, por favor.

Answers

	Ailment	Medicine	Container	Size
1	tos	jarabe	botella	pequeña
2	dolor de cabeza	aspirinas	caja	grande
3	picaduras	crema	tubo	pequeño
4	diarrea	pastillas	caja	grande
5	insolación	pomada	tubo	pequeño

2a Mira los dibujos. Con tu compañero/a, haz una conversación entre el/la farmacéutico/a y el/la cliente. (AT2/4) [8S6]

✕ Speaking and interacting with others, Level D

Speaking. Pupils work in pairs to carry out a chemist shop role-play, adapting the model dialogue and choosing from a set of four picture prompts. The support box on page 100 lists the key phrases they need.

2b Escribe un diálogo para dos de los dibujos. (AT4/4) [8T6]

✕ Exchange information/ideas, Level D

Writing. Pupils write a dialogue based on two of the pictures in **2a**.

> **Starter 2** [8W4; 9W4]
>
> *Aim:* revision of demonstrative adjectives (*este, esta, estos, estas*).
>
> Write a list of medicines on the board (*jarabe, pomada, aspirinas, tiritas, pastillas, tubo de crema*) and ask pupils to put in the correct form of 'this' or 'these'.

3a Empareja las quejas con los consejos. (AT3/3) [8S3; 9S3]

✕ Reading for information/instructions, Level C

Reading. Pupils match a series of complaints with the correct advice. This introduces *deber* + infinitive, which is explained in the *Gramática* box on page 101 and it is suggested that teachers direct pupils to this before tackling the activity. Teachers should also ensure that pupils understand the infinitive *tomar*, which is used in **3a**. They may remember *ponerse*, from Module 3, Unit 4.

Answers

1 e	**2** d	**3** a	**4** f	**5** c	**6** b

3b Escucha y comprueba tus respuestas. (AT1/2)

Listening. Pupils listen and check their answers to **3a**.

Tapescript

1 – Me duelen las muelas.
  – Debes ir al dentista.
2 – Tengo tos.
  – Debes tomar este jarabe.
3 – Tengo dolor de cabeza.
  – Debes tomar unas aspirinas.
4 – Tengo una insolación.
  – Debes ir a la cama.
5 – Tengo una picadura.
  – Debes ponerte una tirita.
6 – Estoy enfermo.
  – Debes ir al médico.

3c Mira los dibujos y elige unas quejas. Di qué te pasa. Tu compañero/a da consejos. (AT2/3) [8S3,6; 9S3]

✕ Speaking and interacting with others, Level D

Speaking. Pupils work in pairs using the picture prompts. One explains his/her ailment and the other gives advice, using *debes*.

3d Escribe consejos para cada queja en **3c**. (AT4/3)

✕ Exchange information/ideas, Level D

Writing. Pupils write mini-dialogues for each picture in **3c**.

> **Plenary** [8S3]
>
> Use a dice, with dots allocated to each subject pronoun, e.g. one dot = *yo*, two dots = *tú*, three dots = *él*, etc. or dice with subject pronouns on them. Pupils work with a partner or in a small group, throwing the dice and conjugating the verb *deber* according to the dot or subject pronoun it lands on: *debo, debes, debe, debemos, debéis, deben*.

Cuaderno B, page 55

1 Escribe una frase para cada dibujo. (AT4/1) [8W1]

✕ Exchange information/ideas, Level B

Writing. Pupils label pictures of medicines, using vocabulary from the support box.

Answers

> *Example: una caja de aspirinas*
> **1** una botella de jarabe
> **2** un paquete de tiritas
> **3** un tubo de pomada
> **4** un tubo de crema antiséptica
> **5** un paquete de pastillas

2 Pon las palabras en el orden correcto. (AT3/2, AT4/2) [8S1]

✕ Knowing about language

Reading and writing. Pupils must put words into the correct order to form sentences giving advice about how to deal with various ailments.

Answers

1 Debes ir al dentista.
2 Debes tomar este jarabe.
3 Debes ir a la cama.
4 Debes ponerte esta crema antiséptica.
5 Debes ir al hospital.
6 Debes tomar unas aspirinas.

3a Empareja las frases. (AT3/3) [8S4; 9S4]

✉ Knowing about language

Reading. A matching exercise, linking questions to answers in a dialogue about illness and injuries.

Answers

1 c 2 b 3 f 4 e 5 d 6 a

3b Escribe un diálogo similar con el médico. (AT4/4) [8T6]

✉ Writing imaginatively, Level D/E

Writing. Pupils adapt the dialogue in **3a** to write a similar conversation between a doctor and a patient.

4 Hay que practicar mucho

(Pupil's Book pages 102–103)

Main topics

- Talking about how long you've been doing something
- Saying what you should or shouldn't do

Key Framework objectives

- Media listening skills 8L2 (Launch)
- Verb tenses 8W5 (Reinforcement)
- Relaying gist and detail 8L3 (Reinforcement)
- Writing continuous text 8T5 (Reinforcement)
- Multiple-clause sentences 9S6 (Reinforcement)
- Reporting and paraphrasing 9L3 (Reinforcement)

Grammar

- *Hace … que* + verb (present tense)
- *Hay que …Tienes que … Debes …*

Key language

¿Cuánto tiempo hace que …?
juegas al fútbol, baloncesto, tenis
estudias español, francés
vives en Londres
llevas el pelo corto/largo

Hace un año/dos años que …
Hay que practicar mucho.
Tienes que llevar ropa cómoda.
Debes entrenar muchas horas.

Resources

Cassette C, side 1
CD3, tracks 22 and 23
Cuaderno B, page 56

Starter 1 [8W5; 9W5]

Aim: revising verbs in the present tense.

Write on the board an infinitive to represent each of the three groups of verbs. For example: *estudiar, vivir, cantar.* Write up the subject pronouns and ask pupils to fill in as much of the paradigm as they can for each.

1 Empareja los dibujos con las frases. (AT3/3) [8S1]

✂ Reading for information/instructions, Level C

Reading. Pupils read a series of sentences, which all use the expression *hace … que …* and match each one to the correct picture. The new construction is explained in the *Gramática* on page 102 and it should be pointed out to pupils that this expression uses the present tense in Spanish, in contrast to the use of the perfect continuous in English.

Answers

1 *d*	2 a	3 e	4 b	5 c

2 Escucha. ¿Cuánto tiempo hace que cada persona practica su deporte? (1–5) (AT1/3) [8L3; 9L3]

✂ Listening for information/instructions, Level D

Listening. Pupils listen and write down how long each speaker has been practising the sport they mention. They should also be encouraged to spot the two different question forms used: *¿Cuánto tiempo hace que …?* and *¿Hace mucho tiempo que …?*, as well as how you say 'only' (*sólo*).

Tapescript

1 – ¿Cuánto tiempo hace que juegas al fútbol?
  – Hace diez años.
2 – ¿Cuánto tiempo hace que practicas el atletismo?
  – Hace tres años.
3 – ¿Hace mucho tiempo que juegas al golf?
  – No, hace sólo un año que juego.
4 – ¿Cuánto tiempo hace que practicas el surfing?
  – Hace dos años … y me encanta.
5 – ¿Cuánto tiempo hace que practicas el ciclismo?
  – Hace mucho … a ver, hace quince años.

Answers

1 *10 años*	2 3 años	3 1 año	4 2 años	5 15 años

3 Con tu compañero/a, pregunta y contesta. (AT2/4) [8S1,6; 9S6]

✂ Speaking and interacting with others, Level D

Speaking. Pupils take it in turns to ask and answer questions about how long their partner has been doing something, using the support grid to construct their questions and answers. Teachers should first ensure pupils understand all of the verbs used in the support box and give them oral practice of saying these key phrases.

Starter 2 [8W5; 9W5]

Aim: revision of the radical changing verb *jugar.*

Write the following paradigm for *jugar* on the board. Ask pupils to fill in the gaps.

Yo jueg… , Tú jueg… , Él jueg… , Ella jueg… , Nosotros jug… , Vosotros jug… , Ellos jueg… , Ellas jueg…

4 Hay que practicar mucho

4a Escucha y lee. (AT3/4) [8L2]

✕ Reading for information/instructions, Level D

Reading and listening. Pupils read and listen to an interview with a teenage skateboarder. As well as *deber*, the interview includes the use of *hay que …* and *tienes que …* + infinitive, which are explained in the *Gramática* on page 103. Teachers may wish pupils to first listen and read for gist, asking them to spot familiar language (such as the clothing vocabulary), and then getting them to work out the fine detail by using a range of strategies, such as looking/listening for cognates or near-cognates (*la técnica, practicar mucho, cómodo/a*), applying logic and using context to work out other meanings (such as *aprender, patinar, entrenar, 'los trucos'*). They could then be asked to guess the sense of the new expressions *hay que …* and *tienes que …* before referring to the *Gramática* box for a full explanation.

Tapescript

¡Listos!:	¡Hola! ¿Cómo te llamas?
Sergio:	Me llamo Sergio.
¡Listos!:	¿Cuánto tiempo hace que patinas?
Sergio:	Hace tres años.
¡Listos!:	¿Cómo aprendes la técnica?
Sergio:	Aprendes en la calle, con los amigos. Luego hay que practicar mucho.
¡Listos!:	¿Qué tienes que llevar?
Sergio:	Tienes que llevar ropa cómoda: pantalones anchos, una camiseta y zapatillas.
¡Listos!:	¿Cuántas horas a la semana debes entrenar para patinar bien?
Sergio:	¡Muchas! Para aprender 'los trucos' tienes que practicar mucho.

4b Contesta a las preguntas sobre la entrevista en **4a**. (AT3/4) [8L3; 9L3]

✕ Reading for information/instructions, Level D

Reading. Pupils answer questions in English about the interview in **4a**.

Answers

1 3 years
2 in the street
3 comfortable clothes: loose trousers, a T-shirt and trainers
4 practise a lot

4c Copia y completa las frases con las palabras apropiadas. (AT4/4) [8S1]

✕ Knowing about language

Writing. A gap-filling exercise, in which pupils must use *(no) hay que …* and *(no) tienes que …* correctly.

Answers

a Aprendes la técnica en la calle y luego **tienes que** practicar mucho.
b **Tienes que** llevar ropa cómoda y práctica.
c **No tienes que** llevar ropa ajustada.
d **Tienes que** llevar zapatillas.
e **Tienes que** entrenar muchas horas a la semana para patinar bien.

✚ As an extension, pupils could be encouraged to write a piece about their favourite sport: how long they have been practising it, how/where you learn it, what you have to wear and how long you have to practise to do it well. Once their writing has been checked, they could memorise it and give a short oral presentation to the class, perhaps bringing in specialist clothing or equipment as props. [8T5; 9T5]

Plenary [8S4; 9S4]

Go round the class asking the following questions: *¿Cuánto tiempo hace que estudias español? (Hace … que estudio español.) ¿Cuánto tiempo hace que vives en … ? (Hace … años que vivo en …)* (Plus any other questions you care to add).

Cuaderno B, page 56

1 Elige una respuesta para cada pregunta. (AT3/4) [8S8]

✕ Reading for enjoyment

Reading. Pupils read and complete a questionnaire about whether they are football fanatics.

2 ¿Qué debes y no debes hacer si eres un verdadero aficionado al fútbol? Escribe seis frases. (AT4/4) [8S3; 9S3]

✕ Exchange information/ideas, Level C/E

Writing. Pupils write six phrases about what you must or must not do to be a true football fanatic.

5 Hay que comer fruta todos los días

(Pupil's Book pages 104–105)

Main topics

- Talking about a healthy lifestyle

Key Framework objectives

- Adapting for audience 9T6 (Launch)
- Modal verbs 8S3 (Reinforcement)
- Negative forms and words 8S5 (Reinforcement)
- Present, past, *future* 8S7 (Reinforcement)
- Using high-frequency words and punctuation 8S8 (Reinforcement)

Grammar

- Revising the immediate future

Key language

(No) Debes …
(No) Hay que …
(No) Tienes que …
… beber dos litros de agua al día.
… comer cinco raciones de fruta o verdura al día.
… desayunar todos los días.
… dormir ocho horas al día.
… hacer deporte tres veces a la semana.
… organizar bien los estudios.
… comer chocolate todos los días.
… cenar muy tarde.
Estoy de acuerdo.
No estoy de acuerdo.

Resources

Cuaderno B, page 57
Starter 1, Resource and Assessment File, page 112
Grammar, Resource and Assessment File, pages 116 and 117

Starter 1 [8W5; 8T4; 9W5]

Aim: revising and categorising infinitives/glossary work.

Use *Resource and Assessment File*, page 112, or write the following infinitives on the board and ask pupils to group them under these headings: *-ar, -er, -ir* and irregular verbs.

comer, beber, hacer, practicar, dormir, descansar, jugar, ir, salir, nadar, correr.

If there is time, get pupils to write down the meanings of the infinitives. Ask them to try and remember what these are and to look them up in the dictionary or glossary if they get stuck.

1 Lee las frases. ¿Estás de acuerdo o no? (AT3/4) [8S3,8; 8T4; 9T4]

✄ Reading for information/instructions, Level D

Reading. Pupils read a series of phrases about healthy living, using the pictures to help with meaning, and write down in Spanish whether they agree or disagree with each one. They should look up any unknown vocabulary in a dictionary, having first used their reading skills and strategies to work out the unfamiliar language.

2 Elige cinco frases de **1**. Tu compañero/a dice si está de acuerdo o no. (AT2/4) [8L6]

✄ Speaking about experiences/feelings/opinions, Level C

Speaking. Pupils work in pairs, taking it in turns to read out one of the sentences from activity **1** and say whether they agree or not. Teachers should first ensure pupils are confident about using the phrases and the expression *(No) Estoy de acuerdo.*

3 Escribe ocho frases para dar tus opiniones sobre cómo vivir sano. (AT4/4) [8S3,5; 9S3]

✄ Exchange information/ideas, Level C/D

Writing. Pupils write eight sentences, giving their opinions about how to live healthily.

R + While less-able pupils could simply copy phrases from activity **1**, more-able learners should be encouraged to adapt the phrases, for example by swapping around *(No) Debes, (No) Hay que …* and *(No) Tienes que …* and also using these constructions to create completely new sentences.

Starter 2 [8W5; 8S8; 9W5]

Aim: to revise the structures *hay que* and *tienes que.*

Write on the board or prepare an OHT for the following four sentences.

1 *Hay que … 2 litros de … al día.*
2 *Hay que … 5 raciones de … .*
3 *Tienes que … todos los días.*
4 *Hay que … … todos los días.*

Ask pupils to fill in the gaps to make a sensible sentence describing how to live a healthy lifestyle.

4 Lee el texto y contesta a las preguntas. (AT3/4) [8S8; 8T3]

✕ Reading for information/instructions, Level E

Reading. Pupils read a magazine-style article about sports training in summer and answer questions in English.

Answers

a early in the morning or late at night (7–9 a.m./8–10 p.m.)
b a lot of water before, during and after training and isotonic drinks as well
c enough fruit, salad and fish
d few clothes (breathable and light coloured) and use a baseball cap if it's very sunny
e do fewer kilometres in summer than in winter

5a Completa las frases con las palabras apropiadas. (AT3/5) [8W5; 8S7; 9W5]

✕ Knowing about language

Reading. A gap-filling exercise, based on what summer sports and activities two people are going to practise. Most of the vocabulary should be familiar to pupils.

Answers

Durante el verano voy a hacer deporte todos los días. Voy a **(1) nadar** y voy a jugar al **(2) tenis** y al bádminton. También voy a montar en **(3) bicicleta**. Mi hermano y yo vamos a **(4) correr** tres veces a la semana. Voy a **(5) beber** mucha agua y **(6) comer** frutas, ensaladas y pescados. Laura
Durante las vacaciones voy a descansar mucho. No voy a levantarme temprano. Voy a **(1) levantarme** tarde todos los días. Voy a jugar con videojuegos, **(2) escuchar** música, leer y ver la tele. Voy a **(3) salir** con mis amigos. No voy a hacer **(4) deporte** pero voy a ir a la **(5) playa**. Manuel

5b Escribe sobre lo que vas a hacer durante el verano. (AT4/5) [8W2; 8S2,7; 9T6]

✕ Exchange information/ideas, Level D/F

Writing. Pupils write a similar piece to the texts in **5a** about what they are going to do during the summer. Teachers should remind pupils of how to use the key construction *ir a* + infinitive to express future plans. Encourage pupils to use words and phrases to link and extend their sentences, e.g. *y, también, tres veces a la semana.*

✚ Pupils can imagine that it's the end of their holiday and write an account in the past tense.

Plenary [8S1]

Brainstorm. Ask your class what you need to do to lead a healthy lifestyle: *Para vivir una vida sana hay que … .* Write responses down on the board and number them. Ask your pupils to write them down in order of importance. Compare notes. Go on to ask pupils if they can produce a sentence using *hay que* or *tienes que* to say what you have to do at school.

Cuaderno B, page 57

1a Escribe las palabras apropiadas en los espacios para dar tus opiniones sobre la vida sana. (AT3/2, AT4/1) [8S5,8]

✕ Reading for information/instructions, Level D

Reading and writing. A gap-filling exercise. Pupils give their own opinions, using *(no) debes, (no) hay que* and *(no) tienes que*. The sentences all relate to healthy living.

1b Completa las frases con las ideas de **1a** para expresar tus propias opiniones. (AT3/2, AT4/3)

✕ Reading for information/instructions, Level D/E

Reading and writing. Pupils take ideas from **1a** to complete three sentences, giving their own advice and opinions. [8S2; 9S3]

2 Escribe frases para decir lo que vas o no vas a hacer para estar en forma. (AT4/5) [8S7]

✕ Exchange information/ideas, Level D/F

Writing. Pupils must write about how they are going to keep fit, using *ir a* + infinitive.

Grammar, Resource and Assessment File, page 116

Saying what hurts

1 Pupils use the correct form of the verb *doler* (*duele/duelen*) to make a sentence with the ailments given.

Answers

a *Me duele la cabeza.*
b Me duelen los pies.
c Me duelen las muelas.
d Me duele la garganta.
e Me duele el estómago.
f Me duelen los oídos.

Some key verbs

2 Pupils choose the correct verbs from the box to complete the sentences.

Answers

> **a** Tus notas del cole son malas. Tienes que **estudiar** más.
> **b** No me gusta mi nuevo colegio porque hay que **llevar** uniforme.
> **c** Para coger el autobús debes **salir** de casa a las ocho.
> **d** Si tienes dolor de cabeza hay que **tomar** una aspirina.
> **e** Para seguir una dieta equilibrada tienes que **comer** mucha fruta y verduras.
> **f** Si quieres estar en forma debes **hacer** ejercicio.

3 Pupils translate the instructions left by Ricardo's mother into English.

Answers

> **a** Wash the dishes
> **b** Call his grandmother
> **c** Do his homework
> **d** Tidy his room

Grammar, Resource and Assessment File, page 117

The near future

1 Pupils change the verbs within each sentence from the present to the immediate future.

Answers

> **a** Juego al tenis. *Voy a jugar al tenis.*
> **b** Hago mis deberes. Voy a hacer mis deberes.
> **c** Salgo con amigos. Voy a salir con amigos.
> **d** Voy a la playa. Voy a ir a la playa.
> **e** Hago surfing. Voy a hacer surfing.
> **f** Voy al instituto. Voy a ir al instituto.

What verb? What tense?

2 Pupils identify the verbs within the paragraph and place them in the appropriate column of the grid according to tense.

Answers

Meaning	Preterite	Imperfect	Near future
I went	*fui*		voy a ir
I travelled	Viajé	viajaba	
I stayed	Me alojé	Me alojaba	
I had a great time	me lo pasé fenomenal	pasaba	
(The weather) was		*Hacía*	
It was		Era	
There was		Había	
I sunbathed	tomé el sol		
We went out	salimos		
We're going to go			*Vamos a ir*
I'm going to visit			voy a visitar

Resumen y Prepárate

(Pupil's Book pages 106–107)

Resumen

- This is a checklist of language covered in Module 6. There is a comprehensive **Resumen** list for Module 6 in the Pupil's Book (page 106) and a **Resumen** test sheet in Cuaderno B (page 62).

Prepárate

- A revision test to give practice for the test itself at the end of the module.

Resources

Cassette C, side 2
CD3, tracks 24 and 25
Cuaderno B, pages 58–61
Skills, Resource and Assessment File, page 118 and 119
Resumen, Resource and Assessment File, page 120

1a ¿Qué les duele a estas personas? Escucha y elige el dibujo apropiado. (AT1/3) [8L3; 9L3]

✖ Listening for information/instructions, Level D

Listening. Pupils listen to a series of people explaining their ailments and match each speaker to the correct picture.

Tapescript

1 – *¿Tiene algo para la tos?*
 – *Para la tos, le recomiendo este jarabe.*
 – *Bueno, deme una botella grande, por favor.*
2 – *Me duele mucho la cabeza.*
 – *¿Tiene Ud fiebre?*
 – *Sí, tengo fiebre.*
 – *Bueno, puede tomar aspirinas – dos aspirinas, tres veces al día.*
 – *Vale. Deme una caja de aspirinas, una caja pequeña.*
3 – *Hola. ¿Cómo puedo ayudarle?*
 – *Tengo unas picaduras. ¿Qué recomienda Ud para las picaduras?*
 – *A ver … esta crema es buena.*
 – *Deme un tubo, por favor, un tubo pequeño.*
4 – *¿Tiene algo para la diarrea?*
 – *Para la diarrea recomiendo estas pastillas.*
 – *Deme una caja por favor, una caja grande.*

Answers

1 c	**2** b	**3** a	**4** d

1b Escucha otra vez y elige el dibujo de la medicina apropiada. (AT1/3)

✖ Listening for information/instructions, Level D

Listening. Pupils listen to the recording again and write down the letter of each correct medicine mentioned.

Tapescript

As exercise 1a

Answers

1 f	**2** e	**3** l	**4** g

2 Elige tres dibujos en **1a** (a–d) y di a tu compañero/a lo que te pasa. (AT2/3) [8S1]

✖ Speaking to convey information, Level C

Speaking. Pupils choose three pictures from **1a** and tell their partner what their ailments are.

3 Empareja los textos (1–5) con los consejos (a–e). (AT3/3) [8S3; 9S3]

✖ Reading for information/instructions, Level D

Reading. Pupils match up sentences about ailments with the correct advice.

Answers

1 c	**2** e	**3** b	**4** d	**5** a

4 Tus amigos te mandan estos mensajes. Escribe tus consejos. (AT4/2) [8S3; 9S3]

✖ Exchange information/ideas, Level C/D

Writing. Pupils read two messages about ailments and write down their advice for each one.

Sample answers

a Tienes el brazo roto. No debes moverte. Tienes que ir al médico o al hospital.
b Debes ir a la cama. Puedes tomar un jarabe para la tos y pastillas para la garganta.

Cuaderno B, page 58

Repaso

1a Completa el diálogo en la farmacia. (AT3/3, AT4/1) [8S8]

✖ Knowing about language

Reading and writing. A dialogue-completion task, based on a conversation in a chemist's.

Answers

> ● ¡Buenos días! ¿Qué quiere?
> ○ Hace dos días que me duele mucho la **garganta**.
> ● Bueno, estas **pastillas** son muy buenas para el dolor de garganta.
> ○ ¿Tiene algo para la **tos**?
> ● Este jarabe es muy bueno.
> ○ Deme una **botella**, por favor.
> ● ¿Algo más?
> ○ Tengo dolor de **cabeza**.
> ● ¿Tiene fiebre también?
> ○ Sí, tengo **fiebre**.
> ● Debe tomar **aspirinas** cuatro veces al día.
> ○ ¿Le duelen la **espalda** y las **piernas**?
> ● Sí, sí. Me duele todo el cuerpo. Me siento **mal**.
> ○ Usted tiene gripe. Debe ir a la **cama**.

1b Marca los síntomas que tiene el chico que va a la farmacia. (AT3/3)

✖ Reading for information/instructions, Level D

Reading. Pupils tick a list to show comprehension of the ailments mentioned in **1a**.

Answers

The following should have ticks by them:

> Está enferma.
> Tiene dolor de cabeza.
> Tiene dolor de garganta.
> Tiene fiebre.
> Tiene tos.

1c Marca la medicina y los consejos del farmacéutico. (AT3/3)

✖ Reading for information/instructions, Level D

Reading. Pupils tick a list to indicate what medicines and advice the chemist gives in **1a**.

Answers

The following should have ticks by them:

> aspirinas (4 veces al día)
> jarabe para la tos
> Debe ir a la cama.
> pastillas para el dolor de garganta

2 Escribe diálogos en la farmacia. (AT4/4) [8T6]

✖ Exchange information/ideas, Level D/E

Writing. Using the model dialogue in **1a**, pupils write other conversations in a chemist's, based on the picture prompts and phrases given.

Answers (*example*)

> **1** Tengo dolor de estómago y diarrea.
> *Estas pastillas son buenas.*
> **2** ¿Tiene algo para las picaduras?
> *Esta pomada es muy buena.*
> **3** ¿Tiene algo para la insolación?
> *Esta crema es muy buena.*

Cuaderno B, page 60

Gramática 1

1 Complete the sentences with *el, la, los* or *las*. (AT3/2, AT4/1) [8W4; 9W4]

✖ Knowing about language

Reading and writing. A gap-filling exercise, using the definite article with parts of the body and ailments.

Answers

> **1** la **2** el **3** la **4** la **5** las **6** los **7** el **8** las
> **9** el **10** la

2 Complete the sentences with the correct form of the verb *deber*. (AT3/2, AT4/1) [8S3; 9S3]

✖ Knowing about language

Reading and writing. Pupils complete sentences using the correct part of *deber*.

Answers

> **1** debe **2** deben **3** debemos **4** debo **5** debéis
> **6** debes

3 Choose words from the grid to write sentences about yourself. (AT4/2) [8S6]

✖ Knowing about language

Writing. Pupils use the support box to write about how frequently they do various things.

Cuaderno B, page 61

Gramática 2

1 Write five sentences using the correct words from the grid. (AT4/2) [8S2]

✖ Knowing about language

Writing. Pupils use the support box to give advice about how to do various things.

2 Write sentences using the information in the grid. (AT4/2) [8S1]

Knowing about language

Writing. Pupils write sentences using *hace* + a length of time, based on prompts taken from the grid.

Skills, Resource and Assessment File, page 118 (Word games)

1

Answers

> **a** 27 (all parts of the body except *train*)
> **b** 23 (all illnesses except *year*)
> **c** 25 (all containers except *water*)
> **d** 18 (all parts of the body except to *eat*)
> **e** 22 (all dates/lengths of time except *breakfast*)
> **f** 28 (all nationalities except *leg*)
> **g** 3 (all illnesses except *aspirin*)
> **h** 26 (all types of transport except *packet*)

2

Answers

> **a** *pequeño*
> **b** una lechuga
> **c** los dedos
> **d** una famacia
> **e** el jarabe
> **f** España
> **g** el desayuno
> **h** un plátano
> **i** el agua
> **j** el ciclismo

3

Answers

> **a** cabeza
> **b** jarabe
> **c** aspirinas
> **d** oídos
> **e** tos
> **f** estómago
>
> Sentence a, c and e.
> c, d, f
> Pupils add sentences of their own to give another winning line.

Skills, Resource and Assessment File, page 119 (Connectives)

1

Answers

para terminar	finally
también	also
y	and
pero	but
porque	because
siempre	always
por eso	so

2

Answers

> Doctor Muñoz
> No sé que me pasa. Estoy cansado **porque** no puedo dormir. **Siempre** estoy sin energía y **por eso** es difícil hacer mis deberes. **También** tengo dolor de cabeza. Tengo hambre pero no puedo comer. **Para terminar** estoy nervioso **y** trabajo demasiado. ¿Qué me aconsejas?
> Ana

3

así que	so
cuando	when
o	or
si	if

4 Pupils make use of the connectives they have practised to write their own letter about how to keep healthy using the prompts given.

6 ¡Extra! Entrevista con una deportista

(Pupil's Book pages 108–109)

Main topics

- Understanding and conducting an interview

Key Framework objectives

- Question types 8S4 (Reinforcement)
- Media listening skills 8L2 (Reinforcement)
- Building answers fom questions 9S4 (Reinforcement)
- Different tenses in sentences 9S7 (Reinforcement)
- Simple creative writing 9T5 (Reinforcement)
- Recognising rhetorical devices 9L2 (Reinforcement)
- Questions/text as stimulus to talk 9L4 (Reinforcement)

Grammar

- Review of structures with some further examples of the preterite and imperfect tenses.
- Questions

Key language

Tuve una caída.
Me ayudó un chico.
Me casé.

Resources

Cassette C, side 2
CD3, tracks 26 and 27

Starter 1 [8W5; 9W5,8; 9S2; 9T1,3]

Aim: To learn to recognise various –*er* and –*ar* verbs in their present, preterite and perfect tense forms. Write up the selection of verbs from the text (see below). Ask pupils to categorise them under present tense, preterite tense, imperfect tense and 'not sure' headings. Pupils could work in pairs. Not all the verbs have been met in these forms so pupils will have to use deductive skills and really focus on endings in some cases. Take feedback. How did pupils work out the tense? Establish the meaning of the verbs and ask pupils to supply the infinitives.

empecé, me encanta, pensé, tienes, pasó, estoy, se llamaba, volví, es, hago, era

1a Lee y escucha la entrevista. (AT1/6, AT3/6) [8S7; 8T4; 8L6; 9S7; 9L2; 9T4]

✄ Reading for information/instructions, Level F

Reading. Pupils read and listen to an interview with the cyclist Joane Somarriba. Some of the new vocabulary is given at the bottom of page 108. However, as always, pupils should be encouraged to use the full range of their reading and listening skills to work out any unknown language before checking or looking words up in a dictionary. The interview provides a good opportunity to revise and extend pupils' range of verbs in the preterite tense.

Tapescript

¡Listos!: *¡Hola, Joane! ¿Cuánto tiempo hace que practicas el ciclismo?*

Joane: *¡Hace veinte años! Empecé cuando tenía ocho años.*

¡Listos!: *Tuviste un accidente en la bicicleta, ¿verdad?*

Joane: *Sí, en 1991 tuve una caída. Tuve una lesión en la espalda. Pensé en dejar el ciclismo.*

¡Listos!: *¿Cómo volviste al deporte?*

Joane: *Me ayudó un chico que conocía que también era ciclista profesional. Se llamaba Ramón González Arrieta.*

¡Listos!: *¿Te recuperaste del accidente?*

Joane: *Sí.*

¡Listos!: *¿Y luego qué pasó?*

Joane: *¡Me casé con Ramón! Y también volví a entrenar y a competir.*

¡Listos!: *Una historia feliz.*

Joane: *Eso es.*

¡Listos!: *¿Cómo es la vida de una ciclista profesional?*

Joane: *Es una vida dura porque tienes que entrenar muchas horas y todos los días, pero en fin estoy contenta porque hago un deporte que me encanta.*

1b Contesta a las preguntas. (AT3/6) [8S4,7; 9S4,7]

✄ Reading for information/instructions, Level F

Reading. Pupils answer questions in Spanish about the interview. As the text and questions are quite challenging, teachers might wish to turn it into a 'jigsaw reading' exercise, by dividing the questions up between pairs or groups of pupils.

Answers

1 *Joane Somarriba es campeona de ciclismo.*
2 Es española.
3 Tiene 29 años.
4 Su deporte es el ciclismo.
5 Ganó el Tour de Francia Femenino y el Giro de Italia.
6 Hace veinte años.
7 Empezó a los ocho años.
8 (Tuvo) un accidente/una caída.
9 Ramón González Arrieta, un ciclista profesional, la ayudó.
10 Es una vida dura.
11 Tiene que entrenar muchas horas y todos los días.
12 Hace un deporte que le encanta.

2 Escucha la entrevista con otro ciclista profesional y contesta a las preguntas. (AT1/6) [8L2,3; 9L3]

✕ Listening for information/instructions, Level F

Listening. Pupils listen to an interview with another professional cyclist and answer questions in English. Get them to study the questions before listening. After completing the exercise ask them to talk about the strategies they used to deal with this interview.

Tapescript

¡Hola! ¿Cómo te llamas?
Me llamo Óscar Sevilla.
¿De dónde eres?
Soy de España. Soy español.
¿Cuánto tiempo hace que practicas el ciclismo?
Hace quince años.
¿En qué carreras competiste este año?
En el Tour de Francia, en el Giro de Italia y también en la Vuelta a España.
¿Qué tienes que hacer para ser un buen ciclista?
Tienes que entrenar mucho.
¿Cuál es tu ambición para el futuro?
Mi ambición es ganar el Tour de Francia.

Answers

1 Spain
2 15 years
3 France, Italy, Spain
4 train a lot
5 to win the Tour de France

Starter 2 [8S4]

Aim: to recap asking questions.

Ask pupils to think of four questions they would include in an interview and write them down. Compare notes.

3a Con tu compañero/a, contesta a las preguntas. (AT2/6–7) [8S4,6; 9S4; 9L4]

✕ Speaking and interacting with others
Speaking about experiences/feelings/opinions, Level E/F

Speaking. Pupils work with a partner to create an interview-style dialogue on the subject of sport. Using the prompts, draw pupils' attention to the fact that you can often use a question to help you with an answer, e.g. by repeating/adapting part of it to start off your answer. As some pupils might be less sporty than others, the class could be given the option of either taking the role of a famous sportsperson or being themselves. Once they have perfected their interview, pupils could record it as a marker of achievement. The interviews could also be used by the whole class for further listening comprehension work.

3b Escribe la entrevista de **3a**. (AT4/6–7) [8T5; 9T5]

✕ Writing imaginatively, Level E/F

Writing. Pupils write out their interview from **3a**.

⌨ Pupils could use a graphics or desktop publishing programme to make their interview look like a magazine article. The finished interviews could then be used for display or for other pupils to read for interest and enjoyment.

Plenary

Ask pupils what strategies they used to read the interview with Joane Somarriba on page 108. Take feedback.

Te toca a ti

(Pupil's Book pages 122–123)

● Self-access reading and writing at two levels

A Reinforcement

1 Marisa fue a la playa y ahora se siente mal. Lee el texto y contesta a las preguntas. (AT3/6) [8S7; 9S7]

✕ Reading for information/instructions, Level E

Reading. Pupils read a text about Marisa's weekend trip to the beach and subsequent ailments, then answer questions in English.

Answers

a She went to the beach.
b Good – it was sunny and very hot.
c She went windsurfing, went swimming in the sea and played volleyball. She ate a delicious paella.
d No – she feels terrible.
e She has a headache and diarrhoea and feels sick. She feels dizzy. Her legs and shoulder hurt.
f She thinks she has sunburn.
g Yes – she was outside in the hot sun for a long time. No – she might also have food poisoning, as she has diarrhoea and feels sick.

2 Escribe frases para ti, empleando verbos del cuadro. (AT4/4) [8S1]

✕ Exchange information/ideas, Level C/D

Writing. Pupils write six sentences with *hace … que*, using the verbs *toco, juego, vivo, estudio, me duele(n)* and *practico*.

B Extension

1 Empareja las frases con los dibujos. (AT3/2) [8W5; 9W5]

✕ Reading for information/instructions, Level B

Reading. Pupils match up sentences about ailments with the correct picture.

Answers

1 d	**2** c	**3** f	**4** a	**5** b	**6** g	**7** e

2 Empareja los textos (a–e) con los textos (1–5). (AT3/5–6) [8S7; 9S7]

✕ Reading for information/instructions, Level E

Reading. Pupils match up short texts about accidents and ailments with the correct advice.

Answers

a 5	b 2	c 1	d 4	e 3

3a Tus amigos están enfermos en España pero no hablan español. Escríbeles unas frases para decir al médico. (AT4/4) [8S1]

✕ Exchange information/ideas, Level C/D

Writing. Pupils use picture prompts to write sentences describing various ailments to a doctor to help non-Spanish speaking friends.

Answers

a Me siento mal. Me duele la garganta y tengo fiebre.
b Me siento mal. Tengo una insolación. Me duelen la espalda y la cabeza. Me duelen las piernas. Estoy mareada.
c Me duele el estómago. Tengo diarrea.

3b Escribe consejos para cada persona en **3a** (a–c). (AT4/4) [8S3; 9S3]

✕ Exchange information/ideas, Level D

Writing. Pupils write advice for each person's ailment in **3a**.

Answers

a Debes tomar aspirinas. Hay que beber agua y zumo de fruta. Debes quedarte en casa.
b Tienes que beber mucha agua. Tienes que quedarte en casa. No debes estar al sol. Debes tomar aspirinas.
c No debes comer. Debes beber agua.